TOWARDS A HISTORY OF IRISH SPIRITUALITY

Peter O'Dwyer O Carm

Towards a History of Irish Spirituality

the columba press

First published in 1995 by
the columba press
93 The Rise, Mount Merrion, Blackrock, Co Dublin

Cover by Bill Bolger
Origination by The Columba Press
Printed in Ireland by Colour Books Ltd, Dublin

ISBN 1 85607 124 3

The author and the publisher gratefully acknowledge the permission of the following to quote material in which they hold copyright: Thomas Kinsella for his translation of 'The Breastplate of St Patrick'; Brian Ó Cuív for various translations; Pádraig Ó Fiannachta for his own poems; Sáirséal Ó Marcaigh for poems by Seán Ó Ríordáin and Máire mhac an tSaoi; An Clóchomhar for poems by Seán Ó Leocháin and Mícheál Ó Huanacháin. If we have failed to identify correctly the copyright holders in any other quotations used, we offer our apologies and invite the copyright holders to contact us.

Contents

Preface

I feel a little like St Patrick in my reasons for compiling this contribution. While his expression, 'This is my confession before I
die', might seem melodramatic on my lips, I feel that I should
make available whatever I have been able to learn about Irish
spirituality over the years. This has entailed putting my notes
into chronological order and commenting on them. The lacuna
which I have felt in regard to this subject is the lack of quotations
or citations showing how this spirituality expressed itself in
word and deed through the centuries. This attempt is merely a
beginning which will be corrected and expanded. If that hap-
pens my purpose will have been achieved.

I was tempted to include a chapter on the contributions from the
Churches of the Reformation but felt that this should be done by
a member or members of these particular churches. In the meantime, I would like to pay tribute to the late Dr George Otto Simms,
who was a good friend of mine, who made an initial contribution to this subject in his article, 'Irish Spirituality: Some Insights
from the Churches of the Reformation'.[1]

I wish to thank the library staff of the Royal Irish Academy, of
Trinity College, of the National Library, and of Milltown Park
library for their assistance and courtesy. I also take the opportunity of thanking my confrères in Gort Muire for their assistance,
and Muireann Ní Bhrolcháin for her contribution to the final
preparation of the text.

My hope is that the work may give us an appreciation of our
great heritage and help us to understand our church in its ups
and downs. May this lead us to make our contribution.

Peter O'Dwyer O Carm
Lá 'le Pádraig 1995.

1. Michael Maher (ed.), *Irish Spirituality* (Dublin 1981) chap. 8.

Abbreviations

AA.SS.Hib.: Acta Sanctorum Hiberniae
A.C.L.: Archiv für Celtische Lexikographie
A.P.D.: Ár bPaidreacha Dúchais
AI: The Annals of Innisfallen
Aith.D.: Aithdioghluim Dána
A.L.C.: The Annals of Loch Cé
Anderson: Alan Orr Anderson and Marjorie Anderson
        (Adomnán's Life of Columba)
Ann. Conn.: Annála Connacht
Arch. Hib.: Archivium Hibernicum
AU: The Annals of Ulster (William H. Hennessy)
Bk. Lismore: Lives of the Saints from the Book of Lismore
Bradshaw: Brendan Bradshaw, *The Dissolution of the Religious*
        Orders in Ireland.
CD: Célí Dé
CIH: The Course of Irish History
Coll. Hib.: Collectanea Hibernica
Dán Dé: Lambert McKenna S.J.
DBM: Dán na mBráthar Mionúr
DDB: Duanaire Dháibhidh Uí Bhruadair
DDU: Dánta Diadha Uladh
Di.D Dioghluim Dána
ECI: Early Christian Ireland
EIL: Early Irish Lyrics
FM: The Annals of the Four Masters
FO[1]: Félire Oengusso (Dublin,1880)
FO[2]: Félire Oengusso (London,1905)
Hist. Eccl.: Historia Ecclesiastica (Bede)
IBP: Irish Bardic Poetry

ICE: Irish Catholic Experience
Ir. Coll.: Irish College (Archives, Rome)
IER: Irish Ecclesiastical Record
IHS: Irish Historical Studies
Ir. Mon.: Irish Monasticism
Ir. Pen.: Irish Penitentials
Ir. Spir.: Irish Spirituality
Ir. Trad.: Irish Tradition
ITS: Irish Texts Society
LH: The Irish Liber Hymnorum
LU: Lebor na h-Uidre
JRSAI: Journal of the Royal Society of Antiquaries of Ireland
Kenney: (J.F.) The Sources for the Early History of Ireland
McLysaght: Irish Life in the Seventeenth Century
Mart.Tall.: The Martyrology of Tallaght
Mary: Mary, A History of Devotion in Ireland
Med. Irel.: Medieval Ireland (J.Watt)
NÍ Bhrolcháin: Muireann Ní Bhrolcháin (Maolíosa Ó Brolcháin)
Pen. Columbani: Penitentiale Sancti Columbani
RIA: Royal Irish Academy
Sodality: The Sodality of the B.V. Mary in Ireland
Spic. Oss.: Spicilegium Ossoriense
Stud. Hib.: Studia Hibernica
TCD: Trinity College, Dublin
VSH: Vitae Sanctorum Hiberniae
ZCP: Zeitschrift für Celtische Philologie

CHAPTER I

The Fifth to the Seventh Centuries

'This is my confession before I die.' (*St Patrick*)

While we have no concrete information, it seems probable that laity were the first members of the Christian church in Ireland. The statement found in Prosper of Aquitaine's *Chronicon* in 431, 'Palladius, ordained by Pope Celestine, is sent to the Irish believing in Christ as their first bishop' shows that there were believers who probably had become Christians through contact with foreign traders, friends and British slaves captured by the Irish. This is evident from Patrick's lifestory and his evangelical work.

It was standard missionary policy to aim at evangelising the top ranks of society. The church was organised, as it was elsewhere, around bishops and their clergy. Probably every *túath* had both a king and a bishop. The bishop was equal in status to the king of a *túath*. The clergy were accepted as members of the *aes dána*, people of learning, side by side with the pagan sages, except that the clergy assumed the role of intermediaries with the other world. Up to c. 550 the annals record mainly the deaths of bishops, not of other ecclesiastics. By 550-600 the two cultures had reached an acommodation which in certain matters remained uneasy. A number of Christian terms found their way into archaic Old Irish in the fifth century. *Cáisc* (Easter), *cruimther* (priest), *caille* (veil), *fescor* (vespers) and *sléchtad* (prostration) are some examples. The claim that Ciaran of Saigir, Ailbe of Emly, Ibar of Wexford and Declan of Ardmore were pre-Patrician saints may well be true but cannot be proved conclusively. The annals indicate that Ibar and Ailbe died in the sixth century[1] but these are not always trustworthy.[2]

Patrick

The most celebrated missionary to come to Ireland in the fifth century was Patrick. It does not serve my purpose to discuss the question of the two Patricks so I limit my remarks to the Patrick who wrote the *Confession* and the *Letter to Coroticus*. Incidentally these are the oldest documents in existence relating to the Irish or British churches. The facts which Patrick recounts of his life are few. He was born in Britain, his father was a Roman official, not of high standing, and also a deacon. Patrick was captured during a raid by Irish soldiers when he was sixteen years of age and was used as a slave in Ireland where he spent six years at this difficult task. He escaped, caught a boat and rejoined his family in Britain, who had given up hope of ever seeing him again. Though the crew of the boat were pagans. Patrick, when appealed to, saved them from starvation through his prayers.

That same night he recounts an extraordinary experience: 'When I was asleep Satan assailed me violently ... falling on me like a rock, so that I could not stir a limb.' Patrick cried out and Christ freed him. 'I believe that Christ my Lord sustained me and His spirit cried out on my behalf.' (20)[3] This passage reminds one of St Anthony of Egypt and of other hermits who struggled with demons. The experience is often found in the lives of people destined to initiate some great spiritual movement. This was probably a dream of a supernatural character, perhaps such as St Joseph experienced when Mary's pregnancy was explained to him. God was indicating his future work to Patrick.

He tells us that 'the voice of the Irish' haunted him in his thoughts and dreams. He returned to them as a bishop after many years, he says, to preach the gospel. This entailed many difficulties and personal trials. On at least one occasion, he was imprisoned. He was also exposed to the severe criticism of his fellow British clergy. But these experiences were outweighed by the fruits with which God blessed his labours, which made numerous converts and took him to regions unvisited by any other missionary before him. He was whole-hearted in his dedication to his mission and overcame the desire to visit or return to his colleagues in Gaul. He decided to remain in Ireland till death claimed him.

He gives us many insights into his spiritual life which are of great value, as they reveal the real Patrick. He wrote the *Confession* to tell of God's work in him. 'I am Patrick, a sinner most unlearned, the least of all the faithful and utterly despised by many.' (1) 'Although I am imperfect in many things, I nevertheless wish that my brethren and kinsmen should know what sort of person I am.' (6) He speaks of himself as a youth not knowing God but living in death and unbelief. He is probably in mature old age when writing this account and in his later years he is touched deeply by God's goodness and his own unworthiness. He probably exaggerates the sins of his youth as he looks back on them. In his slavery he found support in prayer which led him to intimacy with God. 'After I came to Ireland the love of God and His fear came upon me more and more and my faith grew strong.' He prayed night and day in the woods and on the mountains, before dawn, in rain, frost and snow, and thought little of it because the spirit in him was fervent. God was preparing him by the way of the cross. Loneliness and hardship made him fall back on his faith. He was not abandoned by God. He tells us that he prayed hundreds of times during the day. This must mean repeated aspirations or the few prayers that a youth in his late teens would know from memory. His slavery lasted six years when, through God's direction and support, he escaped. (17)

During his life he had some mystical experiences. Patrick uses the Pauline description: 'Another night, whether within or beside me I know not, God knoweth, they called me unmistakeably with words I heard but could not understand, except that at the end of the prayer He spoke thus. He that laid down His life for thee, He it is that speaketh to thee and so I awoke full of joy.' (24) Here we find his conviction and experience of Christ praying in him. He did not understand them fully but realised that God was taking a strong hand in directing him. He relates a third experience which was unconnected with the other two. He was praying and became aware of another praying within him. (25) He could 'clearly hear him above me, that is over the inward man, praying mightily with groanings.' (25) He revealed himself as the Spirit of God. This experience seems to have been much loftier and clearer than the other two and was probably intended to confirm them, thereby impressing his future apostolate on him as being willed by God.

Gaul was probably the scene of his studies. He was very familiar with scripture and he quotes it spontaneously which would tend to show that he used it for his prayer and reading. There are 155 references from scripture in his *Confession*. Being convinced that God had chosen him to return as a missionary to Ireland, he met with a very severe setback, probably his greatest, when he was rejected for this post, due to a priest-friend's revelation. (26) 'My conscience does not blame me now or for the future ... but I am very sorry for my dearest friend that we had to hear what he said. Some of the brethren told me that he would stand up for me in my absence.' (In fact he revealed a fault which Patrick had committed thirty years previously.) 'He even said to me: You should be made a bishop. Why then did he leave me down before everyone in public?' (32) 'On that day I was so stricken that I might have fallen now and for eternity.' (26) His reaction is extraordinary. 'But this was for my good for thus was I purified by the Lord, and He made me fit that I might be now what was once far from me – that I should care and labour for the salvation of others.' (26) That very night God comforted him with a mystical favour the detail of which is not clear but it was an assurance of his call. (29) He heard God referring to him as the apple of his eye. Patrick was ordained bishop and the 'journey on which he had decided and the work he had learned from Christ the Lord were not frustrated.' (30)

His reaction to this is very revealing and may be summed up in permanent gratitude to and trust in God:

> I give unwearied thanks to God who kept me faithful in the day of my temptation, so that to-day I can confidently offer Him my soul as a living sacrifice, to Christ who saved me out of all my troubles. Thus I can say – Who am I, Lord, and to what hast Thou called me? Thou who didst assist me with such divine power and to-day I constantly exalt and magnify Thy name among the heathens, wherever I may be, and not only in good days, but also in tribulations. (34)

Patrick was grateful for having been allowed to come back to Ireland, 'a thing I never expected in my youth.' (15) He was 'Christ's letter of salvation' to the farthest part of the earth. He is grateful that he has persevered in so many temptations. 'The hostile flesh ever drags us towards death, that is the forbidden satisfaction of our desires. Even though I did not lead a perfect life ... the love and fear of God have grown in me and thanks to His grace I have kept the faith.' (44) He is confident that God will protect him in his labours. He desires no other glory than a holy people. (47) The virgins were the flower of his flock and the pride of his apostolic heart. One passaage of the *Confession* speaks of his desire for martyrdom which has similarities with the desire expressed by St Ignatius of Antioch:

> Greatly and exceedingly do I wish and am ready that God would give me His chalice to drink, as He gave it to others who loved Him. And if ever I have done any good for my God whom I love, I beg Him to grant me that I may shed my blood with these exiles and captives for His name, even though I should be denied a grave, and my body woefully torn to pieces limb by limb by hounds or wild beasts, or the birds of the air devour it. (57,59)

Other virtues and character traits are also found in Patrick's *Confession*. He felt his exile keenly. 'How I would have loved to go to my country and my parents (relatives?) and to visit the brethren in Gaul.' (43) He refused gifts even though he offended the willing donors. (49) He readily forgave those who spoke against him. (46) Yet his true greatness does not lie in his work but in his love. He considered his labours as God's gift to him. Very touchingly he concludes his *Confession*:

> I pray that those who read this writing that Patrick, a sinner, unlearned, has composed in Ireland, that they should never say it was mine if I showed forth anything however small according to God's good pleasure, but rather think, as is the truth, that it was the gift of God. This is my confession before I die. (62)

The *Letter to Coroticus* is probably earlier than the *Confession* and gives further insight into the man. Coroticus, a British prince, made a raid on Ireland, slew a number of Patrick's converts, plundered homes and took a number of young men and women to sell as slaves. Patrick had had the same experience. The victims had only recently been baptised. Patrick touchingly describes the scene. 'The day after the newly-baptised, still bearing their chrism, still in their white dress – it was giving out its scent on their foreheads while they were being ruthlessly massacred and slaughtered.'[4] He sent a delegation to Coroticus, headed by a priest whom he had taught from childhood, with a letter requesting the return of the captives and the booty. But the party was scoffed at. This angered Patrick so he publicly and severely denounced Coroticus in the *Letter* and threatened him with excommunication which he enforced. In mourning the newly-baptised who had been slaughtered, he finds consolation:

> Consequently I mourn for you, I mourn, my dearest. But again rejoice within myself: I have not laboured in vain nor has my pilgrimage been useless. And if this crime so horrible, so unutterable, had to happen, thanks be to God you baptised believers have departed from this world to paradise. I observe you: you are beginning the journey to where there will be no night nor mourning, nor death anymore, but you will rejoice like calves loosed from their tethers and you will tread down the wicked and they will be as ash under your feet. You therefore will reign with the apostles, prophets and martyrs.[5]

Patrick gives us a certain consolation from the faults in his character. His strident language against Coroticus and the Picts exceeds the bounds of moderation. He had an inferiority complex with regard to those who criticised him as he refers to the matter frequently in his *Confession*. Hanson remarks:

> We follow with interest, sympathy and pleasure his story from the helpless boy dragged ruthlessly away from his home and his parents to exile and slavery, through all the incidents of an adventurous life, until we leave him an old bishop, by his own wish separated from his native land, devoted entirely to his task of converting the Irish in spite of opposition and misunderstanding. His life ends, as far as we are concerned, in total darkness, lit only by the will-o'-the-

wisp of later legend. But he has left us an imperishable memorial his *Confession*.[6]

Finnian

Ludwig Bieler points out, in his treatment of Christianity in Ireland in the fifth and sixth centuries:

> The historian of early Irish Christianity must face a severe handicap – the scarcity of authentic sources and the abundance of later material of unequal and often of doubtful value. Contemporary evidence is almost entirely lacking for the more than 100 years between the *Confession* in the second half of the fifth century, and the letters of St Columbanus written within the last decade of the sixth century and the early years of the seventh. Of slightly earlier date is the *Penitential* of Vinnianus, on which the *Penitential* of Columbanus was modelled. These two documents are of considerable interest from several points of view. They testify, among other things, to the transition from the 'vindictive' to 'remedial' penance, to the growth of private penance among the laity, to the influence of John Cassian on Irish monasticism, to the absorbtion into the penitential practice of the Irish church of certain elements of traditional law.[7]

Finnian's *Penitential* cannot be dated with any degree of accuracy. Certainly it is older than that of Columbanus, which is probably later than 591. Finnian was an abbot and his work was intended primarily for his own monks. He is generally taken to be either Finnian of Clonard (+549) or of Moville (+579). He distinguishes between sins of thought and sins of deed. This is followed by a consideration of and appropriate penances for strife, wounding and homicide. Penances for clerics differ from those for the laity guilty of the same sin. He then deals specifically with clerical sinners in the matter of fornication and the killing of offspring of an unlawful union. He also prescribes penances for various forms of magic, homicide, theft, greed and anger. He recalls Cassian's principle, *contraria contrariis curantur*:

> Let us make haste to cure contraries and to cleanse away these faults from our hearts and introduce heavenly virtues in their places: Patience must arise for wrathfulness; kindli-

ness, or the love of God and one's neighbour, for envy; for detraction, restraint of heart and tongue; for dejection, spiritual joy; for greed, liberality.[8]

He also deals with the problem of deathbed repentance and with the duties of the married state. It is difficult to say how much this *Penitential*, which is obviously based on earlier ones, reflects the moral standards of sixth century Christianity in Ireland. Pierre Payer, in his article *Sex and the Penitentials*, says that between 24% and 45% of canons in *Penitentials* deal with sexual offences and argues that the sexual content in them is an accurate account of behaviour.[9] He may well be right when one considers that it is one of the commonest and most natural sins, especially in a people who are being converted to a much stricter Christian code. But one must also take into account that similar penances already existed in his sources, taken from scripture and from very learned men.[10] It should also be borne in mind that the early Irish church, due to a desire to legislate in the light of the Bible, gave the Old Testament an all too important part. While it is hard to tell the extent to which the penitential norms were applied, these works represent a remarkable attempt to clarify and apply Christian spirituality to daily living.

The emphasis throughout is on whole-hearted conversion from sin. Phrases like 'he shall seek help from God by prayer and fasting', 'he must pray with weeping and tears that he may obtain the mercy of God', 'it is better to do penance and not to despair – for great is the mercy of God'[11] show what lay behind the mind of the legislator. The confessor was required to take into account the good will of the penitent and also aggravating or mitigating circumstances in his or her case. Finnian ends his work with a short epilogue:

There are still some other authoritative decisions concerning either the remedies or the several kinds of things that are to be cured, which now a concern for brevity, or the situation of the place, or the poverty of my talent does not permit me to set down. But if any diligent searcher of divine reading should for himself find out more, or bring forth and write down better things, we, too, shall agree and follow him. Here

ends the little work which Finnian adapted for the sons of his
bowels, out of affection and in the interest of religion, overflowing with the waters of the scriptures, in order that by all
men evil deeds may be destroyed.[12]

The early Irish monks placed special emphasis on human effort,
on the performance of great works of prayer and penance.

Brigid

She was born (c. 454) to Dubhthach of the Uí Fotharta sept of the
Uí Failghe, and Broicsech his Christian slave. According to a
strong local tradition she was born near Uinmearas, which lies
between Rathangan and Monasterevin. She was an attractive
girl so her father naturally wished to fix a marriage for her. But
Brigid wished to consecrate herself to God's service. Her father
refused permission but, seeing her determination, he consented
to allow her to take the veil. She vowed her virginity either to
MacCaille or to Bishop Mel and stayed for a period under his direction in Ardagh. Then she returned to her native district and
settled in Kildare (the church of the oak).

Her life was that of an active nun, living with her community
but often travelling either for evangelical or charitable purposes.
Cattle were the main support of her monastery. Hospitality,
almsgiving and care of the sick were her main preoccupations.
Though her monastery was small in her lifetime, her reputation
for holiness earned her the title of Mary of the Gael. Cogitosus,
her biographer, mentions that it was a double monastery under
her direction and that of Bishop Conleth. By the eighth century
she is entitled 'leader of the virgins of Ireland'. Her influence
continued to grow so that churches were dedicated to her not
alone in Ireland, where Kilbride is a very common placename,
but also in Wales, Scotland, France, Switzerland and Italy. The
Office in her honour is found in more than two hundred manuscripts. Her feast, February 1, coincides with the coming of
spring, the old pre-Christian festival of *Imbolc*. 'She was abstin-
ent, innocent, prayerful, rejoiced in God's commandments, firm,
humble, loving, forgiving. She was a temple of God, a consecrated
casket of Christ's Body and Blood. Her heart and her mind were
a throne of rest for the Holy Spirit.' She died in 524.[13]

It is worth noting that the sixth century is one of great monastic development in Ireland. Aran was founded by Enda early in the century. Búithe of Monasterboice (Co Louth) was probably a little earlier since he died AD 521 and he would be a contemporary of Finnian of Clonard. Clonmacnoise was founded by Ciaran who died in 545. Colum Cille founded Derry in 546, Durrow about a decade later, Iona in 563 and possibly Kells later. Clonfert was founded by Brendan in 559, Terryglass by Colum son of Crimhthann in 549, Achadh Bó in Ossory by Canice (+600), Daimhinis by Molaisse (Laisren) (+564), Lothra by Ruadhán in the sixth century.[14]

More important was Bangor, founded by Comgall c. 555-59. Finnian (+579) founded the monastery of Mag Bhile (Moville). Cluain Eidnech (Clonenagh) in Laois was founded by Fintan, a disciple of Colum of Terryglass, Clonfertmulloe by Molua or Lugaid, on the border of Leinster and Munster, Dairinis by Maelanfaid (+608), Lann Elo (Lynally), near Tullamore, by Colman (+611) aged 56, while Kevin, founder of Glendalough, died in 618. Later in the sixth century belong Jarlath of Tuam, Colman or Mocholmóc of Dromore, Senan of Inis Cathaig (Scattery Island), Fachtna of Ross Ailithir (Rosscarbery), Nessan founder of Mungaret and Bairre founder of Cork. All these founders were bishops or priests except Nessan who remained a deacon.[15]

Colum Cille

Colum or, as he is frequently styled Columba, is dated 521-597. We owe most of our information regarding him to Adomnán who was born c. 624 and was abbot of Iona from 679 till 704. He wrote Columba's *Vita*. Scholars such as James Carney and others would hold that the *Amra Coluim Cille*, composed by Dallán Forgaill, may date from the end of the sixth century. It is a eulogy of extraordinary obscurity and consequently of little use in seeking to gain an insight into the man. To return to Adomnán, he composed two works, *De Locis Sanctis* (683-86) and the *Life of Columba*. He is considered to be a reliable writer using Bishop Arculf's account of the Holy Places[16] but question has been raised as to his accuracy in the *Vita*.[17] Miraculous occurrences loomed large in the *Vita*. These, however, are normally associated with particular people, many of whom were well-known. It would be foolish to exclude the possibility of miracles wrought by God at the behest of a saint, but one also must be cautious in admitting miracles easily. It was probably written between 692 and 697. Adomnán used both written and oral tradition and was in a particularly favourable position as he had contact with people who actually knew Columba and with others who knew his contemporaries.

Though he was the founder of Derry, Durrow, Iona and probably Kells, he went to Scotland as a missionary. He emerges from the *Life* as a person not circumspect in his youth (as was also Patrick's case), highly intelligent and powerful but also very sympathetic and kindly. A person's humanity and sanctity form a unity. He was a man of affairs who was involved in the political activities of his day, e.g. in the choice of rulers in Dál Riada. Obviously he was 'a man of great ability, learned, seeing the world as a whole in the light of eternity and of contemporary science, but also very much the capable island soldier ... as adept in handling a boat in a storm as a pen in his cell ... He genuinely liked people and went out of his way to help them. He did not throw a poor man a coin and then forget him but looked into the particular circumstances and found some way of giving him permanent help.'[18] Seeing a poor man's plight, Columba cut for him a stake that would trap wild animals and thereby keep him supplied with food.[19] He was annoyed when the robber Erc came to steal what Columba regarded as his seals on the coast of Iona. He prevented and rebuked him and then added kindly: 'When you want anything then come to us and we will give you what you ask.' Erc received a shipload of wethers instead of seals and, when he died, Columba sent meat and grain for the wake.

Quite unwittingly Adomnán shows the genuine interest of Columba in such things as a difficult birth for a woman (though it must be added that she was connected with him on his mother's side) but also his joy with ordinary folk such as the Irish smith, Colum Coilrigin, and his daily work which won him heaven and with the all too familiar 'good woman who fought for the soul of

her not so devout husband.'[20] He was very balanced in his judgment of people and their motives. He suspected the apparently
penitent man.[21] He denounced evildoers in no uncertain terms
but the genuine penitent was received with open arms. Parts of
the *Vita* suggest mystical contemplation through his union with
the Holy Spirit.[22] His adieu to his confrères is expressed very
beautifully in the words:

> I commend to you, my children, these last words, that you
> shall have among yourselves mutual and unfeigned charity
> with peace. If you follow this course after the example of the
> holy fathers, God, who gives strength to the good, will help
> you, and I, abiding in him, shall intercede for you. And not
> only will the necessaries of this life be provided by him, but
> also the rewards of eternal good things will be bestowed, that
> are prepared for those who follow the divine command-
> ments.[23]

Tradition associates Columba with poets and poetry, so much so
that many compositions later than his time were 'fathered' on
him. Two Latin poems may be his – the *Altus Prosator* and the
Noli Pater.[24] The first is a long and, to the present day mentality,
somewhat tedious poem. Each stanza begins with a successive
letter of the alphabet. It praises the Trinity, describes the creation of the world and of human beings, the fall, hell and its tor-
ments, and the details of the final judgment. The second stanza
is one of the best:

> *Bonos creavit angelos ordines et archangelos*
> *principatum ac sedium potestatum,virtutum*
> *uti non esset bonitas otiosa ac maiestas*
> *trinitatis in omnibus largitatis muneribus*
> *sed haberet caelestia in quibus privilegia*
> *ostenderet magnopere possibili fatamine.*[25]

> He created good angels and archangels, the orders of princi-
> palities and thrones, of authorities and powers that the
> goodness and majesty of the Trinity might not be inactive in
> all offices of bounty but have creatures in which it might
> richly display heavenly priviliges by a word of power.[26]

The tradition which connects him with the hymn *Noli Pater* is very strong. The hymn is short and mentions both fire and John the Baptist. The final couplet is a good instance of a constantly recurring desire among early Irish poets:

Manet in meo corde dei amoris flamma
ut in argenti vase auri ponitur gemma.[27]

The flame of God's love remains in my heart
like a golden gem placed in a silver vase.

The letter of Gregory the Great to Augustine of England, written a little later than 600, helps us to appreciate another aspect of these years of conversion. He advises the missionary that the people be left their harmless joys:

For if one does not begrudge the people these external enjoyments, it is easier for them to find the inner joy as well. It is, after all, not possible to take away everything at the same time from still unopened hearts. Whoever wants to climb a mountain does not do so in jumps but step by step and slowly.[28]

Columbanus

'My desire was to visit the heathens and that the gospel be preached to them by us.' (Columbanus)

In the centuries of the barbarian invasions and conquest, Ireland contributed two special gifts to Europe. One was high moral seriousness, the acceptance of God's law and of the gospel counsels, and the putting of these into effect without compromise. The other was the emphasis on the cultivation of the mind. Columbanus is the only sixth-century Irish saint who has left us a collection of writings which enable us to determine the character of saintliness of the Irish church in early medieval times.

He was born in Leinster c. 543. His mother was not happy with his decision to become a monk and she expressed her opposition by lying across the doorway of their house as he was leaving, but he stepped over the prostrate body and betook himself to Sinell, one of Finnian of Clonard's disciples, who had a monastery at Cleenish on Lough Erne. He made great progress and here or in Bangor, to which he later moved, compiled a learned commentary on the psalter, which has not survived. His biographer, Jonas, who entered Columbanus' monastery in Bobbio in 618, three years after Columbanus died, says that 'he composed many works that were profitable for instruction or suitable for song'. Possibly his work, *De mundi transitu*, dates also from this period.[29]

Hearing of the severity of the discipline in Bangor and of the devotion of its abbot Comgall, who had founded the monastery c. 558, Columbanus decided to embrace the life followed there. Later he became a priest. His talents led to his appointment to teach and in time he became the chief lecturer in the monastic school there. Michael Lapidge makes a very good case for the hymn, *Precamur Patrem*, being composed by him before he left Ireland.[30] After close on thirty years, 'he began to desire pilgrimage'. This must have presented Comgall with a replacement problem, but he was prevailed upon to let him go. He set out in 591 with the traditional twelve companions, one of whom was Gall and another was Bishop Aid.

He began his missionary work in Burgundy in France and succeeded in founding three monasteries, Annegray, Luxeuil and Fontaines. Fifty-three other monasteries were founded from these over a period of time. Columbanus composed a *Regula monachorum* and a *Regula coenobialis* for his followers. Living a strict life and demanding the same from his monks, he had no hesitation in attacking the degenerate local clergy, the immoral court and undesireable local customs. For this he was expelled by King Theuderic but he managed finally to wend his way into Switzerland where he founded monasteries at St Gallen and Bregenz (in Austria). Later he crossed the Alps and founded a monastery in Bobbio near Milan. He must have made a deep impression as quite a number of places and parishes are named after him. He left a considerable corpus of writings, consisting of letters, some of which were written to Popes, sermons, two *Rules*, a *Penitential* and a number of poems. Walker gives a broad picture of his character, part of which I reproduce:

> All his activities were subordinate to this one end, and with the self-sacrifice that can seem so close to self-assertion, he worked out his soul's salvation by the one sure pathway that

he knew. He was a missionary through circumstance, a monk by vocation, a contemplative too frequently driven to action by the vices of the world, a pilgrim on the road to paradise. And this detachment was the source of his great influence.[31]

His letter to Pope Gregory I, dated AD 600, is nicely abridged by the late Tomás Ó Fiaich:

Grace and peace to you from God our Father and from the Lord Jesus Christ. I wish, Holy Father, (do not think it excessive of me), to ask about Easter, in accordance with that verse in Scripture: 'Ask your Father and he will show you, your elders and they will tell you'… I have read your book containing the pastoral rule, brief in style, comprehensive in doctrine, crammed with sacred things. I acknowledge that the work is sweeter than honey to one in need. In my thirst, therefore, I beg you for Christ's sake to present me with your tracts on Ezechiel, which I have heard you composed with remarkable skill. I have read six books of Jerome on him, but he did not expound even half. But, if you please, send me something from your lectures delivered in the city. I mean the last things expounded in the book. Send me as well the Song of Songs from the passage in which it says 'I will go on the mountain of myrrh and to the hill of incense', as far as the end.[32]

An excerpt from his sermons reminds one of his deep spiritual life and has shades of the writings of St Teresa of Avila almost a thousand years later:

Inspire our hearts, I beg Thee, O our Jesus, with that breath of Thy Spirit, and wound our souls with Thy love, so that the soul of each one of us may be able to say in truth: 'Show me Him who my soul has loved, for by him I am wounded.' I desire that those wounds may be in me, O Lord. Blessed is such a soul which is thus wounded by love; such seeks the Fountain, such drinks, though it ever thirst in drinking, ever quaff in longing, and it ever drinks in thirsting; for thus in loving it ever seeks while it is healed in being wounded; and with this healing wound may our God Lord, Jesus Christ, the

Physician of righteousness and health, deign to wound the inward parts of our soul, who with the Father and the Holy Spirit, is one unto ages of ages. Amen.[33]

He expresses what is deepest in him in the prayer:

Inspire us with thy charity, O Lord, that our loving quest for thee may occupy our inmost thoughts: that thy love may take complete possession of our being, and divine charity so fashion our senses that we may not know how to love anything but in thee.[34]

His *Penitential* points out that 'true penance is not to commit things which need repentance but to lament what has been committed (in the past). But since the weakness of many, nay all, makes this practically impossible, the measures of penance must be known'.[35] He compares the healing labours of the confessor to that of the doctor[36] and concludes the *Penitential* with an interesting approach to the Eucharist:

For Christ's throne is the altar, and his body there with his blood judges those who approach unworthily ... we must refrain and cleanse ourselves from interior vices and the sicknesses of a drooping spirit before the covenant of true peace and the bond of eternal salvation.[37]

It also informs us that there was a sermon on Sundays:

Before the sermon on the Lord's Day, let all, except for fixed requirements, be gathered together, so that none is lacking to the number of those who hear the exhortation, except for the cook and the porter, who themselves also, if they can, are to try hard to be present when the gospel bell is heard.[38]

All Columbanus' writings are in Latin. His *Regula Monachorum*, like most of the extant Irish *Rules*, is a general treatise on the virtues which particularly characterise monastic life and seems to have been composed in fragments from time to time, after the manner of an *aide-memoire*. Obedience even 'unto death' is frequently mentioned. Poverty and chastity have separate chapters. He follows the spirit of Egyptian worship in his emphasis on nocturnal psalmody and the importance of solemn vigils on Saturday and Sunday. The vigils (probably the *iairmhéirghe* which is mentioned so frequently in later religious poetry) is for him the chief part of the Office, preceded by short services at nightfall and midnight and followed by Terce, Sext, None and Intercessions.[39] Compline and Prime are also mentioned in the *Antiphonary of Bangor*. Time was also to be given to private prayer and meditation on the scriptures. Bernard says that Columbanus established the *laus perennis*, a service of perpetual praise maintained by relays of successive choirs.[40] This *Regula* had considerable influence on later compositions.

His *Regula Coenobialis* provides a more detailed commentary on the daily life of the monk. It begins with the evangelical precept that he should love God totally and his neighbour as himself. His obedience is shown to God immediately. One who answers back is a destroyer. Silence and peace nurture righteousness; consequently one should speak only when it is proper and necessary. The standard fare was poor and one was to avoid repletion and intoxication. Food and drink were to maintain life. Vegetables, beans, flour mixed with water and a small loaf of bread was the normal food. This is true discretion, 'that the possibility of spiritual progress may be kept with a temperance that punishes the flesh'. Temperance must be a virtue – 'we must fast daily just as we must eat daily ... because we must go forward daily, pray, work and read daily'.[41]

He adds that nakedness and disdain of riches are the first perfection of monks. The second is the purging of vices; the third is the most perfect and constant love of God and things divine. A monk's chastity is judged in his thoughts. Lust lies in the heart. One must be a virgin both in body and mind.[42]

In treating of the choir Office, I omit the externals since they are treated in Michael Curran's *The Antiphonary of Bangor*. I am more interested in the spiritual approach to this prayer. They kept the night watch.[43] We shall see that the *Célí Dé* also did this. The monk should measure his period of watching in accordance with his strength. He refers occasionally to Cassian and to the monks to Egypt. Quarrels were to be avoided.[44]

Like Benedict, he allots considerable space to the gift of discretion. Since error besets those who proceed without a path, intemperance is at hand for those who live without discretion. God made all things good but the devil sowed evil over them. Everywhere we should seek true sufficiency. The man to whom true sufficiency is not enough has overstepped the measure of discretion and whatever oversteps the measure of discretion is clearly a vice. 'My God, enlighten my darkness, since in You I am rescued from temptation'. Temptation is part of the life of man on earth.

He passes on to self-denial. 'The chief part of the monk's rule is mortification … Do nothing without counsel.'[45] Monks must everywhere beware of a proud independence and learn true holiness. Lowliness of heart is the repose of the soul when wearied with vices and toils. This is the bliss of (white?) martyrdom. Columbanus has his three–fold scheme in martyrdom: (1) not to disagree in mind, (2) not to speak as one pleases with the tongue, (3) not to go anywhere with complete freedom. One should always say to a senior: 'Not as I will but as thou wilt.'

Perfection for the monk consisted in living under the discipline of a father in community. He should learn lowliness from one, patience, silence and meekness from others. He should obey injunctions, come weary to his bed, be made to rise before his sleep is finished. He should be silent when he suffers wrong. He should fear, love and obey his *propositus* as a father nor should he pass judgement on the opinion of an elder whom he is bound to obey.[46]

One short poem addressed to Hunaldus, possibly a pupil of his, will provide a taste of his poetry:

> In countless ways life's seasons disappear,
> They all pass by, the months complete the year,
> With every moment tottering age draws near.

> Into eternal life that you may go,
> Spurn now the sweet deceits of life below,
> Soft lust can upright virtue overthrow.

No breast to blind desire and greed is cold,
A mind rapt up in cares can't judge a deed,
To gold all silver yields, to virtue gold,
The highest peace is but to seek one's need.

This trifling poem I've sent you; read it oft,
Give entrance in your ears to these my words,
Let not some whim seduce you transient, soft,
See how power is brief of kings and lords.

Quickly the fame of mortal life is gone,
Pardon my words, perhaps they're overdone,
Excess of any kind, remember, always shun.[47]

By choosing solitude, Columbanus acquired public influence; teaching humility he found himself obliged to correct both popes and kings. 'While hot to enter a dispute whenever he believed that wrong had been committed, his pent-up energies, like a peal of thunder, quickly cleared the air, and he was at once able to return to the sober calm of common sense; his quick resentment harboured no lingering fires.'[48] The real man in all his simplicity and tenderness was jealously guarded by an aversion to any display of sentiment; but in rare unguarded moments, he was found playing with a little girl at her father's villa, or sending to one of his monks the kiss which, in the haste of exile, he had omitted to bestow. The poor, the sick and the unfortunate were drawn to him by his sharing in their common lot; even criminals released from their fetters, felt impelled to kneel beside him as he prayed; and rough soldiers asked his pardon when they came to take him from Luxeuil.[49]

The above is Walker's impression. Comparing Columbanus with Gregory I, Bouyer writes:

> He drew his inspiration for the penitentials from St Gregory's teaching though he lacks the latter's comprehension of human frailty, and during his lifetime writing to a synod in Gaul, holds Gregory up as a saint, putting him on a level with St Jerome … A stray sentence here and there betrays a sensitive heart, even occasionally a shade of tenderness, but the Irishman's gravity is always harshly austere. He spends little time on the psychological aspect of problems of con-

science; interior man's disposition must be one of complete renunciation ... Gregory's gentle influence lasted longer, but Columbanus' harshness was effective at the time; possibly his violence was fruitful for the men of that rough and brutal age.[50]

Other writings of the seventh century

I have suggested that the *Abgitir Crábaid* (Alphabet or Primer of Piety) may stem from the early days of the *Célí Dé* movement and that its author may have been Mocholmóc Úa Líatháin.[51] Pádraig Ó Néill puts forward a more convincing set of reasons for the authorship of Colmán of Lann Elo and that its date is c. 600. He sums up by stating that 'this author was a monk, who probably composed it in the very early period of Irish monasticism, as suggested by the various types of evidence in the text: the emphasis on Cassian and the Old Testament sapiential books, the non-Roman form of renunciation at baptism, the references to non-Christians in Irish society, and perhaps also to the *athlaech* (*monachus conversus*), the use of prosodic techniques borrowed from the oral tradition of the *filid*'.[52] It is almost completely in Irish with Latin titles and a very occasional Latin sentence within the text. It opens with a list of virtues and qualities that are combined in holiness such as: 'Faith with deeds, desire with perseverance, placidity with diligence, chastity with humility, fasting with moderation, poverty with generosity, silence with conversation'. The author stresses charity as the central point. Then he asks the question: 'What does the love of God do to man?' and replies that it purifies the heart, banishes vices, earns rewards and prolongs life. A balance between the positive and negative is seen in the four things which cure the soul, i.e. fear, penitence, love and hope.

The next heading asks: 'What should be learned by mankind?' The answer is 'perseverance with holiness' (*foss oc etlai*) which is identical with Fursa's reply found in the Tallaght documents.[53] The reply to the next question: 'What should be shunned by a holy person?' shows that the tract was written for a monastic community. A holy person should avoid amongst other things animosity or unruliness towards the *airchinnech* (superior). He lists the four things which obscure truth – false love, fear, partiality and necessity. Section III speaks of the virtues of the soul and the author lists fifteen: faith, meekness, humility, patience, mortification, obedience, charity, righteousness, mercy, generosity, clemency, calmness, moderation, holiness and almsgiving. The practice of these reduces our purgatory and increases our reward in heaven.

Paragraph 31 asks 'What is best for piety? Simplicity and simplemindedness.' 'What is best for the mind? Broadness and humility.' 'What is worst for the mind? Narrowness, hardness and constraint.' The reader is also put on his guard against sins of omission. The three principal commandments are listed as charity, humility and patience as the author holds that these embrace all others. The really prudent man is one who, before dying, has prepared for what he fears after it.[54] The use of alliteration would make a work such as this more easily memorised. It may easily have served as a manual or summary of the spiritual life, which served as an initiation text to be used by the director of the young. The Rawl. B.512 text indicates that it was meant for the young beginning *Cosc Mo-Cholmaócc m(a)cu Beonna dond óclaig* (Mocholmóc maccu Beonna's Admonishment to youth).[55] The fact that one of the versions is interpolated into the account of *The Monastery of Tallaght* is not without significance. The scribe had copies of both to hand at the same time. He 'placed the Alphabet among the rules not in ignorance but for fear of omitting it'.[56]

One is struck by the excellent exegetical tradition in Ireland. The text, *De Duodecim Abusivis saeculi*, (c.630-50) treats of the things which are hateful to God. Its gnomic aspect is well illustrated in the lines:

A wise man without good works,
An old man without religion,
A young man without obedience,
A rich man without alms,
A woman without modesty,
A master without virtue,
A grumbler of a Christian,

A poor man who is proud,
An evil king,
A negligent bishop,
A crowd without discipline,
A people without law.[57]

Bede, in his *Ecclesiastical History*, refers to great numbers of English people coming to Ireland in the second half of the seventh century and notes that they were not just interested in copies of the Bible but rather in studying scriptural exegesis. Hence Ireland must have developed a reputation in that field some years previously. He also refers to Aidan of Lindisfarne's preaching:

The king always listened humbly and readily to Aidan's advice, and diligently set himself to establish the church of Christ throughout his kingdom. And while the bishop, who was not yet fluent in the English language, preached the gospel, it was most delightful to see the king himself interpreting the word of God to his thanes and leaders; for he himself had obtained perfect command of the Scottish tongue during his long exile.[58]

In a *Life of St Mochua*, who died in 654 or 658, the final paragraph gives an image of the ideal of the Irish saint. It is impossible to date this paragraph precisely. I quote a short section:

Now this man, Mochua, from the beginning of his life, gave all his service to wisdom and devotion ... He stored up in his heart everything that God used to say to him. He never looked at anything which it was not right for him to see. He never took a step towards ignorance. He abated his sense from coveting things earthly. It is he that bound the meditation of his mind in the hallowed heavens. He never let an idle hour pass from him without fruit. He never let his heart go from God. He desired to endure everything for Christ's sake in order that he might attain to the heavenly fatherland. He prepared the eternal rest for himself by abating his flesh in fast and abstinence, *quia crucifixus est mundus illi et ipse mundo*.[59]

One notices the absence of miraculous doings and also the combination of the struggle against the flesh and worldly possessions, balanced by suffering and charity, especially to the poor and the slave.

A hymn to Colum Cille mentions Mo Chumma or To Chumma as abbot of Iona who returned to Ireland c. 661, so the poem is probably mid-seventh century. David Greene and Frank O'Connor hold that this poem contains some of the finest lines in Irish poetry:

> Let me while in Colum's care,
> Be guarded by the heavenly throng;
> When I tread the path of fear
> I have a leader, I am strong.[60]

We are deeply indebted to Fr Michael Curran MSC for his masterly study of *The Antiphonary of Bangor*.[61] It was composed between 680 and 691 and is a collection of prayers and hymns used in that monastery to celebrate the Divine Office. Most of the material in it was composed by Irish authors writing in the second half of the sixth or early seventh century. What surprises one is the fluency and depth displayed by the Irish in the composition of hymns and versified prayers in Latin, about a century after the initial conversion of the country.

The *Audite omnes*, later attributed to Secundinus, a bishop from abroad who helped Patrick, is without a doubt an Irish composition and dates probably from the end of the sixth century. It depends largely on the writings of Patrick and creates a glowing portrait of him as apostle and bishop of Ireland. While not fully historical, it expresses the esteem in which the saint was held by the author. The *Hymnum dicat*, attributed to St Hilary of Poitiers, but almost certainly an Irish composition, was the most popular of all the hymns of the early Irish church. It is a lyrical song to Christ, simple in language, based on the New Testament account of his life. Bede calls it 'that most beautiful hymn' and it appears to have been sung for morning prayer in Bangor and before long it was sung frequently during the day. Finally, the *Sancti venite*, a beautiful eucharistic hymn give a very good taste of Irish hymnology in the sixth and seventh centuries. It consists

of eleven short stanzas and I cite the first and final one, adding
D. F. McCarthy's free translation:

> *Sancti venite*
> *Christi corpus sumite,*
> *Sanctum bibentes*
> *Quo redempti sanguinem.*

> *Alpha et Omega*
> *Ipse Christus Dominus*
> *Venit venturus*
> *Judicare homines.*

> Draw nigh, ye holy ones, draw nigh
> And take the Body of the Lord,
> And drink the sacred blood outpoured.

> The source, the stream, the first, the last,
> Even Christ the Lord who died for men
> Now comes – but he will come again
> To judge the world when time hath passed.[62]

Curran draws special attention to the hymn *Sanctissimi Martyres*
which has a metrical form unknown in Latin hymnody. He also
adds that it is somewhat unusual to have a hymn on martyrs
composed in Ireland in view of the fact that the early Irish
church had no martyrs. But those who were slain by Coroticus
were probably martyrs even though they were not celebrated.
He points out that no particular martyrs are mentioned, but the
Irish concept of the red, white and green (blue) martyrdom lies
behind the wholehearted commitment of the Irish monk or virgin to Christ, who is the first martyr, by following him on the
way of the cross, thus triumphing over death.

> Before all others You suffered the Cross;
> With death o'ercome, You wonderfully enlightened the world;
> You ascended to heaven to the right hand of God;
> To You the saints proclaim Alleluia.

> You, Christ, are the powerful help of martyrs,
> Who entered into battle for Your holy glory.

> Worthy of praise is your wonderful power;
> Through the Holy Spirit You strengthened the martyrs

> To crush the devil and to conquer death;
> To You the saints sang Alleluia.

> Let us suppliantly implore the grace of Christ God,
> That we at death may share their glory,
> And in Jerusalem, the holy city of God
> We may say to the Trinity with the saints Alleluia.[63]

This hymn was sung in Bangor not alone on the feasts of martyrs but also on every Saturday.

Indications of devotion to Mary appear in the *Hymnum dicat*. The author refers to Christ's birth from Mary:

> *Virginis receptus membris*
> *Gabriele nuntio,*
> *Crescit alvus prole sancta,*
> *Nos monemur credere.*

> *Rem novam nec ante visam*
> *Virginem puerperam*
> *Tunc Magi stellam secuti*
> *Primi adorant parvulum.*

> Received in the organs of a virgin
> as Gabriel was announcing (it),
> The womb grows from the holy progeny
> we are admonished to believe.

> Something new, never before seen,
> a virgin giving birth to a child,
> then the Magi, having followed the star
> (were the) first to adore the little One.[64]

In the poem *Versiculi Familiae Benchuir*, we find the beautiful tribute:

> *Virgo valde fecunda*
> *Haec, et mater intacta,*
> *Laeta ac tremebunda*
> *Verbo Dei subacta.*

> Virgin most fruitful and yet
> inviolate mother, joyous and
> trembling, prepared for the
> Word of God.[65]

The *Lament for Cummíne Foto,* who died in 661 (AU) at the age of seventy–two, is dated to the second half of the seventh century. Though short it is remarkable for its personal feeling and great respect:

> A corpse towards me from the south, another from the north; unwelcome the returning hosts: replace, O King of bright heaven, the lack of friends whom You have sent home…

> Not only was he a bishop, he was a king: MoChuimme was an overking … The heart will never break although you may weep for a death hard to bear, whose fate soever it may be, now that west of Cliu the ears of the living have not burst after Cummine's death.[66]

We have noted Patrick's familiarity with scripture. Preparation for the priestly ministry in these early centuries, both in the east and in the west, was based largely on the knowledge and the love of the scriptures. This is very true of the situation in Ireland as Kenney states:

> The chief study in the monastic schools of early christian Ireland was the Bible … The predominance thereof is witnessed by the whole literary remains of the early Irish church. The monastic tradition as set down by a later age in almost innumerable lives of saints tell the same story; the important element in an ecclesiastical education was the reading of the Scriptures and – it may be remarked – in especial the reading of the psalms.[67]

Between 650 and 800 there are some forty works, written in Ireland or Europe but under Irish influence, commenting on the Bible, mainly on the New Testament.[68] The young aspirant, male or female, on entering a monastery, or studying under the guidance of a local priest, was introduced as soon as possible to the psalter as a prayer-book and also as a textbook for learning Latin. The psalms in particular were adapted to Christian prayer by taking them as messianic or by considering them as the words or the Holy Spirit. The Irish approach to the psalter was mainly a historical or literary one. They used a special series of psalm-headings to help their prayer by keeping the person of Christ before them. We find this series in Ireland in the early seventh century and the *Cathach* (c.630) has them. Indeed the practice may have originated in Ireland.[69] It certainly became very popular in Europe.

The idea and practice of pilgrimage is a very important aspect of Irish spirituality. Patrick left his native land. Colum Cille and Columbanus followed suit. Tradition ascribes to Colum Cille many phrases and poems expressing how hard he found it to part from his people and country. In passing, it is interesting to note that Colum Cille asked God for three things: virginity, wisdom and pilgrimage. Triads were very popular in Ireland and the belief that one may make three wishes on entering a church for the first time is still alive and popular.

Notes:

1. AU 499, 500, 503, 526. AI 531.

2. Bieler, L., 'Christianity in Ireland during the fifth and sixth centuries', *Irish Ecclesiastical Record* CI (1964) 164. Henceforth *IER*.

3. References are to the translation of the *Confessio* by L. Bieler in *Ancient Christian Writers* (London,1953). Fr N. Kinsella's article 'The Spirituality of St Patrick's Confession' *IER* (1959) 161-73 is, to my mind, the best on the subject.

4. Hanson, R .P. C., *The Life and Writings of St Patrick* (New York, 1983) 60.

5. Ibid. 72.

6. Ibid. 55.

7. *IER* CI (1964) 162.

8. Bieler, L., *The Irish Penitentials* (Dublin,1963) 85 n. 29. Henceforth *Ir. Pen.*

9. *The Journal of Ecclesiastical History*, Vol. 38 (April, 1987) 276-77.

10. *Ir. Pen.* 93-95.

11. Ibid. 77 n. 2; 77 n. 8; 81 n. 22.

12. Ibid. 93-95. Pádraig Ó Riain would identify Finnian and Finbarr, Beatha Bharra (ITS, London 1994) ix.

13. Pochin Mould, D. D. C., *The Irish Saints* (Dublin,1964) 41-47. *v.* also W. Stokes, *Lives of the Saints from the Book of Lismore* (Oxford 1890), 198. For a discussion of the various Lives of Brigid *v.* Kim McCone, 'Beatha Mheadarach Bhríde', *Léachtaí Cholm Cille* XV(1985) 34-60 and Órlaith de Buitléir, 'Beatha Mheán-Ghaeilge Bhríde'; ibid. 98-114.

14. Ryan, John SJ, *Irish Monasticism* (Dublin, 1931) 15-24.

15. Ibid. 125-32.

16. Meehan, D., *Adamnan, De Locis Sanctis* (Dublin, 1958).

17. Anderson, A. Orr, and Anderson, M., *Adomnan's Life of Columba* (Edinburgh, 1961) 18-30. The psalter known as the *Cathach* is often attributed to him but it dates from c. 630. Klett Cotta, *Ireland and Europe* (Stuttgart, 1984) 34 n. 57.

18. Pochin Mould, D. D. C.. 'Naomh Colmcille', *IER* (1963) 388-9.

19. Anderson, *Adomnani Vita II*, 37 and 411-13.

20. *IER* (Jan 1963) 389.

21. Anderson, 283-87.

22. Ibid.421 ff., 253-59, 497-507.

23. Ibid. 527-29.

24. Bernard, J.H., and Atkinson, R., *The Irish Liber Hymnorum*, 2 vols. (London,1898) I, 62-89, II 22-28, 140-72. Henceforth *LH*.

25. *LH* I, 67.

26. *LH* II, 150.

27. *LH* I, 88. As he offered himself to God he begged three boons, chastity, wisdom and pilgrimage. Stokes, W., *Lives of the Saints from the Book of Lismore*, (Oxford, 1890) 173.

28. *Monumenta Germaniae Historica* (1889) *Epistola II*, 331.

29. Walker, G.S.M., *Sancti Columbani Opera* (Dublin 1957) 182-5.

30. 'Columbanus and The Antiphonary of Bangor', *Peritia* 4 (1985) 104-16

31. Walker, xxxii.

32. Ó Fiaich, T., *Columbanus in his own words* (Dublin, 1974) 82-4

33. Walker, 119-121

34. Ibid. 121.

35. Ibid. 169.

36. Ibid. 171-3.

37. Ibid. 181.

38. Ibid. 181.

39. Ibid. xlvi-xlviii.

40. Ibid. xlviii.

41. Ibid. 126.

42. This is a rather negative approach to the virtue.

43. Walker, 131, 5.

44. Ibid. 133.

45. The role of the *anamchara* is well described here.

46. I am deeply indebted to Walker's work in making this resume.

47. Ó Fiaich, op. cit. 109-10. I have altered his translation of the final line *Omne quod est nimium* which he renders 'whatever is too much'.

48. Except perhaps in the case of St Gall. *v* Ó Fiaich op. cit. 56-7.

49. Walker, xxxi-xxxii.

50. Leclercq, J., Vandenbroucke, F., Bouyer, L., *The Spirituality of the Middle Ages* (New York, 1968) 39.

51. O'Dwyer, P, *Célí Dé*, (Dublin, 1981) 177-8. Henceforth *CD*.

52. Ó Néill, P. P., 'The date and authorship of Apgitir Crábaid', *Ireland and Christendom*, Ní Chatháin, P., and Richter, M. (eds) (Stuttgart, 1987) 203-15.

53. *CD* 113.

54. Hull, V., 'Apgitir Chrábaidh', *Celtica* 8 (1968) 44-89.

55. *CD* 182.

56. Ibid.

57. Breen, A, 'Pseudo–Cyprian De Duodecim Abusivis Saeculi', *Ireland and Christendom*, *v.* n. 24. More than 200 copies of the text have survived.

58. Bede, *A history of the English Church and People*, translated by Leo Shirley-Price (Mx, 1955) 142. Henceforth *Hist.Eccl.*.

59. Stokes, W., *Lives of the Saints from the Book of Lismore* (Oxford, 1890) 288-9. Henceforth *BK Lismore*.

60. *A Golden Treasury of Irish Poetry 600-1200* (London, 1967) 81.

61. *The Antiphonary of Bangor* (Dublin, 1984) and his article 'Early Irish Monasticism', *Irish Spirituality* (Dublin, 1982) 14-18. Henceforth *Ir. Spir.*.

62. Healy, J., *Ireland's Ancient Schools and Scholars* (Dublin, 1902) 81.

63. *Ir. Spir.*, 17-18.

64. O'Dwyer, P., *Mary, A History of Devotion in Ireland* (Dublin, 1988) 34. Henceforth *Mary*.

65. Ibid. 36.

66. Byrne, J., *Ériu XXI* (1980) 111-112.

67. Kenney, J. F., *The Sources for the Early History of Ireland. 1. Ecclesiastical* (Dublin, 1979) 379-80. Henceforth *Kenney*.

68. McNamara, M., MSC, 'The Bible in Irish Spirituality', *Ir. Spir.*, 36.

69. McNamara, M., MSC, 'Tradition and Creativity in early Irish psalter study', *Ireland and Europe*, Ní Chathain, P., and Richter. M., (eds), (Stuttgart, 1984), 380.

CHAPTER 2

The Eighth and Ninth Centuries

'They sang in secret and paid the debts of sinners.' (*Célí Dé*)

By 640 most of the monasteries in the south of Ireland had changed over to the Roman dating of Easter. Armagh seems to have been the first in the north to follow suit, while Iona and its confederation of monasteries was the last to conform. Before the great plague in the middle of the seventh century, celibacy had been the rule for ecclesiastics. By the time of the compilation of the *Hibernensis*, an abbot did not need to be in Orders. By c. 750 succession to abbacies had become hereditary in some cases.

The Viking invasion and the reforming movement of the *Célí Dé* were the outstanding events of the eighth and ninth centuries. The ninth century saw the Vikings make a number of attacks on Ireland. From 800-825 twenty-six plunderings by them are noted while in the same period eighty-seven attacks were made by Irishmen on fellow-Irishmen. It is necessary to maintain a proper proportion in attributing the degree of disruption of monastic life caused by the Vikings. Historians often tend to telescope them and paint a picture of widespread ravaging. The year 906 has the interesting notice that Congal, Abbot of Slane, a wise man, died in virginity, as succession of abbacy from father to son occurs in the eighth century in Monasterboice.[1] From 837 Viking activity was stepped up. They had sixty ships on the Boyne and a further sixty on the Liffey causing widespread destruction. In 840 they burned Armagh with its church. Feidlimid, King of Munster, was wreaking havoc on monasteries in the southern half of the country and yet the annalist describes him as the 'best of the Irish, scribe and anchorite' when he died in 847.[2]

Bede, in his *Historia Ecclesiastica*, refers to the important contribution made by Ireland to the English church in the late seventh and early eighth century:

Many Englishmen, both of noble and of yeoman blood, had gone there for the sake of sacred knowledge and of stricter rule of life. Some of them yielded themselves to keep monastic discipline; others rejoiced in study, passing from cell to cell of the masters of learning. All of them the Irish welcomed most gladly and zealously gave them their daily food, with books and the teaching of scholars, entirely free of charge.[3]

Alcuin, writing c. 800, tells us that Willibrord went to Ireland 'because he heard that scholarship flourished there and also because he was attracted by the reputation of certain holy men.' In his metrical life of the saint, he expresses the trend of the times:

Quem tibi jam genuit fecunda Britania mater
Doctaque nutrivit studiis sed Hibernia sacris.

Though born in mother Britain
he was educated in sacred studies in Ireland.

Boniface, though not too enamoured of the Irish monks on the continent, testifies that Willibrord acquired 'wonderful self-control and holiness in Ireland'.[4] While allowing for a little holy exaggeration, these references give a very good idea of how the British appreciated the Irish free and generous contribution in preparing their future missionaries.

In the eighth century, Cúcuimhne, a monk of Iona (+747), collaborated with Ruben of Darinis near Lismore in collating the ecclesiastical text known as the *Hibernensis*.[5] His early life saw him fail in his monastic pursuits – 'he had a wife and lived badly with her'. Through the poem he sought to make amends by singing Mary's praises. His *Cantemus in omni die* is considered to be the finest Hiberno-Latin hymn in honour of Our Lady:

In alternate measures chanting daily we sing Mary's praise
And in strains of glad rejoicing, to the Lord our voices raise.

His theological and succinct treatment of Mary's role recalls her timely help, her faith and her part in salvation. No mother like her has ever appeared, 'nor was she of fully human origin' seems to have an echo of the Immaculate Conception.

> By a woman's disobedience, eating the forbidden tree,
> was the world betrayed and ruined – was by woman's aid set
> free.
>
> Clad in helmet of salvation-clad in breastplate shining bright.
> May the hand of Mary guide us to the realms of endless light.[6]

A second notable poet, Blathmac, who was of the Fir Roiss in East Monaghan and probably a monk also, composed several poems in Mary's honour c. 700-750.[7] The first of his two longer poems, which were each 150 stanzas, begins:

> Come to me, loving Mary, that I may keen with you your very dear one. Alas! that your Son should go to the cross, he who was a great diadem, a beautiful hero.[8]

In the second long poem he mentions her virginity and adds a profound spiritual observation:

> No wonder that my verses mention it, that you were a true virgin after the birth of Christ. He enters pious hearts and leaves them full and whole. (st.162)

The *Cambrai Homily*, the earliest homily in Old Irish, is dated seventh century.[9] In the phrase 'let him take up his cross' the homilist indicates three ways in which one rejects sin: abstinence or self-denial, fellow-suffering and martyrdom. The approach to the Mystical Body found in the homily is from St Paul:

> If there be any little ailment on a man's body, if it burns a place whether in his front or in his hand or in his fingers, the disease inflames the whole body. Thus it is fitting for us ourselves, that every suffering and every ailment that is on his neighbours should inflame every part, for we are all members unto God.[10]

He treats of the three types of martyrdom which are noted as red, white and blue (green). Red signifies the shedding of one's blood for Christ's sake, white entails separation for God's sake from everything one loves, although it entails fasting and labour. Blue (green) is seen 'when by means of fasting and labour one separates from one's desires or suffers toil in penance and repentance'. He concludes with 'there are three types of

martyrdom which are precious in God's eyes, for which we obtain rewards if we fulfil them, chastity in youth, temperance
(*continentia*) in abundance.[11]

The homilist uses the first person plural, allowing the reader to
identify with him and showing considerable skill in the art of
homiletics in the Irish church in the seventh century.[12] Since the
homily is in Latin, interspersed with Old Irish, his audience was
probably familiar with both or perhaps it was a mixed audience,
some of whom only knew Gaelic.

St Patrick's Breastplate may have been composed in the eighth
century. The writer was familiar with Patrick's devotion to the
Trinity and realised God's special providence in his regard:

> To-day I put on
> God's strength to steer me,
> God's power to uphold me,
> God's wisdom to guide me,
> God's eye for my vision,
> God's ear for my hearing,
> God's word for my speech,
> God's hand to protect me,
> God's pathway before me,
> God's shield for my shelter,
> God's angels to guard me.[13]

The Célí Dé

The period of the *Célí Dé* (culdee) reform, c. 750-900, is marked
by what has been called the anchorite movement and its origin is
to be sought in Ireland.[14] The leaders, Maelruain and Dublittir,
Abbots of Tallaght and Finglas, were obviously inspired by the
spirit which they found in religious such as Ferdácrích, Abbot of
Darinis (+747), MacÓige of Lismore (+753)[15] and Samhthann,
Abbess of Clonbroney, Co Meath (+739).

One notes that the annals indicate that there was a considerable
increase in violence, the murder of abbots, bishops and the burning of churches in the eighth century.[16] While it is true that the
annalists begin to expand the number and content of entries

around the middle of that century, the ninth century does show a very notable increase in violence.

The eighth century saw the introduction of the lay abbot. Among the early instances was Moenach, Abbot of Slane, who was son of Colman, who had been abbot of the same monastery.[17] This practice tended to increase and naturally had an adverse effect on monastic life. The reform aimed at restoring monastic studies to the rightful place. It also insisted very strongly on poverty and forbade members of the reform to hoard goods. But the church elsewhere was also experiencing similar difficulties with local rulers, while the papacy itself was being dominated by Italian family interests.

In its broad sense, the term *Céle Dé* is the equivalent of *servus Dei* and was convertible with the term *manach*. But in the Milan gloss 30C3, dated c. 800, we find a more precise meaning. 'He whom anyone loves and helps is thrown afterwards into the possession of the man who helps him, as it is said, that man is a servant of God' (*Céle Dé*).

While Maelruain was the principle leader of the reform, its initial inspiration began in the south of Ireland in the district round Darinis-Lismore-Daire na bhFlann (near Cashel), probably in the second quarter of the eighth century. The canonical collection known as the *Hibernensis* had Ruben of Darinis and Cúcuimhne as its compilers. It is a collection of aphorisms and enactments, arranged without any special order in sixty–seven books, each subdivided into a number of chapters. It deals with matters pertaining to Christian discipline, the religious life and the care of souls. Its material is drawn chiefly from scripture, from the decisions of foreign and local councils and from the works of the Fathers. It is the most important of the canonical collections of Celtic origin so far known.[18] Maelruain's tutor was Ferdácrích, his mother's brother, from Daire Eidnech, or Daire na bhFlann as it is later called.[19] The Tallaght documents look back with great respect to him as Abbot of Darinis, to MacÓige, to Mocholmóc Úa Líatháin of Lismore and to Caencomhrac, who was also from this district. These men were noted for their sincerity and wisdom in spiritual matters.

Oentú Maelruain

An *oentú* or union was a close relationship between communities or between particular persons. Maelruain founded his reform monastery of Tallaght in 774 and his 'unity' in the *Book of Leinster* has twelve names in addition to his own, probably based on the grouping of Christ and the twelve apostles. Maeltuile is the second name on the list. The fact that the latter has a *dísert* situated in Co Westmeath is significant. Kenney rightly points out that both *dísert* and anchorite are part of this reform.[20] Maelanfaidh, Abbot of Darinis, lived more than a century before Maelruain and is included probably because the latter had special reverence for him. Flann mac Fairchellaig (+825), Abbot of Lismore, Emly and Cork, is contemporaneous with the reform movement.[21] Flann mac Duibthuinne is most likely the Flann mac Duibhchonna who appears in the Tallaght documents and, in common with his namesake, hails from Daire na bhFlann which probably owes its change of name to them. The next Flannan may be from Cill Áird, Co Clare (778).[22] Or he maybe a Flann connected with Daire na bhFlann if we follow the second version of the *oentú* in the *Book of Leinster*.

We know a good deal about the next member, Maeldíthruib, since he lived in the Tallaght community for a period under the direction of the master and returned later to Terryglass. He was a young, enthusiastic and eager questioner who had great respect for his 'hero'. He wished to have access to all the sacred writings which had come to Ireland, to serve in the most perfect community. These wishes are a good summary of the central idea of the movement. He died, anchorite and *suí* (wise man) of Terryglass, in 840.[23]

Dimman was an anchorite in Ara (Limerick/Tipperary) who died in 811 (*AU* 810). Dalbach, who died c. 800, belonged to Cúl Collainge, near Castlelyons, Co Cork.[24] The next member of the unity is a rather strange character, Feidlimid mac Crimthainn, born in 770, who became King of Cashel in 820. His marauding exploits, which included the burning of monasteries, set him apart from the other members and made him a rather unlikely model,[25] though Professor F.J. Byrne classes him as 'a powerful champion of the *Céli Dé*.[26] Diarmait, the founder of Dísert Diarmata (Castledermot, Co Kildare) in 812, was probably very deeply motivated by the reform.[27] The monastic school, with its scriptural crosses, and the probability that he was the scribe of the Milan glosses, suggest that it was an important centre of scriptural studies and Christian art.[28]

The last name in the 'unity' is Oengus, a very gifted man. A considerable number of his writings still survive. It is quite probable that he received his early training in Cluain Eidnech in Co Laois. He came to Tallaght to benefit from Maelruain's direction. He had a *dísert* near the river Nore in Co Kilkenny. The story tells us that on his way to Tallaght he stopped at Cúl Beannchair, Co Laois, where he got the idea of writing a martyrology.[29] Having arrived at Tallaght, he concealed his identity and was given heavy work in the kiln. Finding one of Maelruain's pupils who could not learn his lesson, he helped the boy to such an extent that Maelruain found out who he was and chided him for concealing himself.[30] Oengus had great respect for his master as we see in his writings. Some time later he returned to Cluain Eidnech where he died on March 11, possibly 830.[31]

These names point to a Munster origin. With the advent of Maelruain the reform found a firm base in Tallaght and influenced Finglas. He attracted disciples from other parts of Tipperary, Laois, Cork and Westmeath and it spread to Kildare, Clonmacnoise, Iona and Loch Cré, near Roscrea. Louth and Clonfert are also quoted in the documents. The culdees found their longest duration in Clonmacnoise, Terryglass and Armagh.[32]

The period of the reform is marked by what has been described as the anchorite movement, the aim of which was to give the monk the opportunity for solitude close to the monastery, often in the *dísert*. His life was a poor one. Prayer, work, reading and especially growth in charity were his daily occupations. The core of the anchorite rule was charity, self–denial, useful occupation and perseverance. This useful occupation took the form of intellectual labour or of scribal work frequently. In the ninth century we find twenty-one anchorites, who were also scribes, listed in the annals. Though Armagh and Clonmacnoise are the most frequently mentioned, it is obvious that the production of the *Martyrology of Tallaght* and the *Martyrology of Oengus*, not to mention *The Stowe Missal* required considerable scribal activity among the members of the reform.

The *Irish Penitential* is probably a work of the reform.[33] Most of the document is taken up with lists of penances for various sins. The listing of sins follows the division into the seven or eight capital sins.[34] In addition to the list of penances, each chapter has a body of positive and very helpful teaching. To overcome gluttony it recommends moderate fasting, remorse of heart, sparse meals, frequent self-examination, watching, feeding the poor and hungry, confinement at certain hours with a specified allowance and finally patience. Similar positive practices and mentalities are recommended to overcome the other vices.[35] An interesting example of the manner of spiritual direction is seen in Maelruain's statement to Maeldíthruib, who came to him from Terryglass to be guided by him:

> The first year that a man comes under our guidance is treated by us as a year of purification, and you will have to spend three periods of forty days on bread and water, except for taking a drink of whey on Sundays and mixing the water with milk-whey in the Summer Lent only.[36]

Study, and in particular, study of the psalter was of prime importance.

> This is the most excellent of all labours, to wit, labour in piety; for the kingdom of heaven is granted to him who directs study and to him who studies, and to him who supports the pupil who is studying.[37]

The considerations of the matter of food occupy almost one third of the Tallaght documents. Excessive mortification was discountenanced and a regular measured pittance was recommended. Each one was to regulate his own allowance and if the general diet regime was too strict the abbot was to see that the quality was improved. They ate together in community and the meal was accompanied by the reading of the gospel. The reading also included *The Rules* and *The Miracles of The Saints*. From the maxims on which the diet regulations were based and also from the concession made to those who had heavy work or who were sick, the rule was tempered to the individual so that each person's allowance was sufficient to enable him to perform his duties. This was specially the case for priests who experienced difficulty in offering Mass.[38]

Closely allied to the question of food was the acceptance of gifts. The benefactors often expected easier terms of forgiveness. Monks or anchorites had doubts as to whether they should accept food from their laxer brethern. But Hilary, a reform monk in Loch Cré, received bread from the less strict monks of Roscrea, and Maelruain was also of the opinion that the culdees had a right to this support. Others accepted gifts but gave them to the poor.[39]

In the matter of apartments, each member had his own cubicle and the monastery provided facilities for taking a bath.[40] Monks were warned by Samhthann of Clonbroney to be very careful in their association with women, religious or lay.[41] Maelruain told Cornan, an anchorite and a piper 'on whom lay the grace of God', that he could not listen to his music as his ears are not lent to earthly music, that they may be lent to the music of heaven'.[42] This sounds a little puritanical and unappreciative. On the other hand there was general festivity in the paschal season and relaxation in the matter of food and vigils. The visit of a venerable ecclesiastic might also be the occasion for a more wholesome repast.[43]

Liturgy and the spiritual life

Mass was offered on Sundays, Thursdays and great feasts. All were expected to attend and the penance for absenting oneself from Sunday Mass was the recitation of the 'three fifties' (psalms or more likely *Paters*) standing with eyes shut in an enclosed house.[44] Weekly reception of the Eucharist was the norm for the *Céle Dé* but this was achieved only on a gradual basis over a period of some seven years. There was a difference of opinion as to whether *Viaticum* should be given in *articulo mortis* to those who had lived bad lives even though at the end they did renounce their sins. The old fathers used to say that the repentance was mere dread of death. Others, notably Colcú, held that it should be given if the sorrow seemed to come from the heart. 'Let God be the judge' was his advice.[45]

In the matter of confession one must distinguish between sacramental and minor confession (*min-coibsiu*) which was made to an elder who might not be in Orders on the lines of 'Confess your sins to one another' (Jas 5:16). Maelruain wished his monks to consult their confessor (*anamchara*) at least once a year.[46] Columbanus had advised that confession should precede the reception of the Eucharist.[47] Bad confessions seem to have been fairly frequent, so much so that Hilary of Loch Cré abandoned the office of confessor. The Old Irish *Table of Penitential Commutations (De Arreis)* which allowed for substitute penances was helpful where the sick were concerned. This document also gives valuable insights which should be taken into account when reading the *Penitential*. The final commutation 'atones for every (kind of) sin (if) accompanied by keen and heartfelt repentance ... and heals him who transgresses against his clerical Orders provided there be keen repentance'.[48] The *min-coibsiu* was a very valuable exercise. If the confessor were not at hand it could be made to a *mac-légind* (ecclesiastic) or to a *mac-clérech* (cleric) provided the penitent performed the penance prescribed. In these documents it is very difficult at times to distinguish between sacramental confession and the exercise of 'confession of faults'.[49]

Columbanus had stated in his *Rule* that a man became a monk *uni Deo adhaerere hac in tellure* (to unite himself on this earth to the one God).[50] As the culdee reform expressed it: 'Three profitable things in the day: prayer, labour and study.'[51] Maeldíthruib asked Maelruain how he should rule himself. 'I bid thee,' said Maelruain, 'to abide always where thou art wont to be. Meddle not with worldly disputes. Go not with any man to a law court ... but continue in prayer and pondering thy reading and in teaching, if there be any that desire to receive instruction from thee'.[52] For the monk prayer, *par excellence*, was the Divine Office and in the reform it consisted of eight hours, *iairmhéirghe* (night-vigil), *maiten* (morning), *anteirt* (prime), terce, sext, none, vespers and compline (*fadg*). Michael Curran has given us a good description of the Divine Office in the early Irish church.[53]

Several, if not all of these Hours were accompanied by the cross-vigil (*lúirech léire*) which was a penitential manner of praying with arms outstretched.[54] The *Hymnum dicat* was said several times in the day as was the *Benedictus* canticle. The *Canticle of the Three Youths* (Dan 3:57-58) was also said daily along with the ferial Office which was recited on feastdays when a saint's Office was also said.[55] The penitential touch experienced in attending the Office is found in the lines:

> The wind over the Hog's Back moans
> It takes the trees and lays them low,
> And shivering monks o'er frozen stones
> To the twain Hours of night–time go.

> (That is, the wind is keen when men go to church at Glendalough for vespers and matins.)[56]

Each monk recited the psalter in private daily. Various divisions of the psalms were used by different leaders along with postures of standing or sitting or reading or praying them by heart. Two members kept night–vigil in the church and recited the psalter from nightfall till matins. Special predilection was shown for Psalm 118, commonly called the *Beati* from its opening word. It was considered to have special efficacy as was the *Magnificat*.[57] Maelruain had a special devotion to St Michael known as *cuairt coimhge Mhichíl* (safe-conduct of Michael).[58] The feast of St Michael had a special celebration in Tallaght where it was treated as a Sunday. When a member of the community was at the point of death, they used to sing the *Canticle of Canticles*, thereby signifying the union of the church with the Christian soul. Prayers for the dead were frequently offered both in public and in private and penances were also performed on their behalf.[59]

Vows

The reform did lay down that the resolution to do any good deed should be vowed and proclaimed openly.[60] The ideal of perpetual chastity may easily be gauged from the severity with which breaches of it were punished. One of the offences which could not be sufficiently punished was when those in higher Orders failed in its observance.[61] It is noticeable that the positive aspect of the vow is not emphasised and the approach to marriage in the documents is very negative and limited. Needless to say, great stress was laid on poverty: 'As for him who desires to reach the pitch of perfection, he distributes all he has to the poor and goes on pilgrimage or lives in a communal church until he goes to heaven.'[62]

Penitential practices

The penitential aspect of Celtic spirituality has always been especially noted. The cross-vigil, praying with outstretched arms for a considerable length of time, was a common practice. Genuflections and prostrations were also very much in vogue. Dublittir genuflected after each of the 150 psalms.[63] Castigation was regularly practised. Among the culdees it was inflicted by another member and was never performed on a Sunday. Standing in cold water might be undertaken to crush evil desires or as a labour of piety. Penances were inflicted for breaches of discipline or for carelessness, especially if waste resulted from it. But excessive penance was not encouraged. Normally monks were not to perform more than 200 prostrations daily. An anchorite from Clonard was accustomed to genuflect 700 times daily. The matter was reported to Maelruain who said that a day would come when the anchorite would not be able to genuflect at all. His words proved true as in time this man became a cripple. The external practices of penance were, to their minds, a vital condition for attaining God's friendship and indicated that they were sincerely contrite for their offences.[64]

Pilgrimage, as we have seen, was an important aspect of early Irish spirituality. It was an ascetic exercise to part from home and friends for the love of Christ in order to bear witness to the gospel values. But by the eighth century the practice of leaving Ireland on pilgrimage was being criticised, probably because some were more wanderers (*vagabundi*) than pilgrims. Samhthann of Clonbroney had firm ideas on the subject:

> A certain teacher named Dairchellach came to the virgin and said to her: 'I propose to lay aside study and give myself to prayer.' To whom she replied: 'What then can give your mind stability that it wander not, if you neglect spiritual study'? The teacher continued: 'I wish to go across the sea on

pilgrimage,' he said. She replied: 'If God could not be found on this side of the sea we would indeed journey across. Since, however, God is nigh unto all who call upon him, we are under no obligation to cross the sea. The kingdom of heaven can be reached from every land.'[65]

Maelruain gives the general opinion of the elders that anyone who journeyed outside Ireland was 'a denier of Patrick in heaven and of the faith in Erin'. But he was quite favourable to going on pilgrimage within Ireland.[66] MacÓige of Lismore was once asked what was the best point in the clerical character and he replied that it was steadiness (foss). 'Whatever task a man has set his hand to, it is best for him to persevere in it.'[67]

The feasts of St Michael, Patrick and Colum Cille were celebrated in Tallaght along with Cainnech of Finglas who was held in special reverence.[68] Sermons were preached on Sunday, and on Maundy Thursday there were two sermons, one after the washing of the feet, the other on the Eucharistic Supper.[69] Great respect was show to the altar because of the sacrifice of the Body and Blood of Christ.[70] There was a very interesting point with regard to the ceremonies of baptism. If an expectant mother became sick so that she was in danger of death, the baptismal service was read aloud over a vessel of water. The woman made confession (of faith) on behalf of the unborn child. She then drank the water which passed over the child and baptised it.[71]

Respect for the observance of Sunday was, to say the least, puritanical. A journey of more than a 1,000 paces, whether it was to visit the sick, to bring viaticum, to celebrate Mass or hear a sermon, was discountenanced. It was even forbidden to lift an apple from the ground. Sunday was to be a day of prayer and rest.[72] The main apostolates were the work of the confessional, direction, preaching, study, teaching and writing. As one would expect, the community exercises laid stress on the celebration of the sacred mysteries, the reception of the Eucharist and frequentation of the sacrament of penance. Special predilection was shown for the canticles of the New Testament and certain hymns, especially the Hymnum dicat and the Cantemus. Sundays and feastdays had special celebrations, some of which lasted even three days. Parts of the year, such as the three Lents, were marked by fasting and cross-vigil, while others, such as Eastertide and Christmastide were marked by relaxation in the matter of food and penance. Their life is summed up in the words 'They sang in secret and paid the debts of sinners.'[73]

Though we cannot call these documents a rule in the strict sense of the word, since they are neither formulated nor complete, they give us a very interesting, if incomplete, picture of the monastic life in eighth- and ninth-century Ireland. Though the life is strict and some of its practices strange to our way of thinking, still the general observance is not unduly harsh. It is, to my knowledge, the most detailed picture we can get of life in any period of early Celtic monasticism and so serves not only for its own period but also to fill in for earlier or later periods in its history.

Literature associated with the Célí De movement

In addition to the Tallaght documents, we have noted the tradition that Oengus, the author of the *Martyrology* or *Félire*, found inspiration for his work at the tomb of a man who had great devotion to the saints. Another tradition tells us that he showed his *Félire* to a monk named Fothad na Canóine of Fahan, Co Donegal (+818) and that the latter also showed his work to Oengus.[74]

The poem entitled *Anmchairdes Mancháin Léith* (the Spiritual Direction of Manchán Liath) also derives from this period and its subject matter would indicate it was partly influenced by Mochutu's *Rule*.[75] The section of the latter's *Rule* prescribing the duties of the culdee – the triple prostration on entering the choir, the duty of celebrating each Hour and the general tenor of the poem, show a certain similarity with culdean practice.

Another poem of the period, *Dúthracar, a maic Dé bí*, which describes the natural and supernatural recompenses of the anchorite life, mentions thirteen as the ideal number for a monastic community.[76] *Ceilebram, léighim, lubrum* also echoes parts of the culdean writings.[77] The first duty of the monk is to pray. Superfluity is to be avoided 'as the culdees are content without superfluity, with no excess, without importunate requests for food, without a life of comfort, without wealth, without cattle'. It seems to have a strong connection with the movement.

The *Rule of Mochutu*, also attributed to Fothad na Canóine, which has a section on the *Célí Dé*, is, to my mind the best *Rule* in the Irish language both as to order and content. The writer begins with the two great precepts of the Law and a brief summary of the Decalogue as the introduction. It must be borne in mind that each monastery had its own set of customs. The author knew this and concentrated on giving more of the theory underlying their religious observances, thus helping their interior development. The Irish idea seems to have been that a *Rule* was designed to regulate the interior life. Custom regulated external practices. The combination of *Mochutu's Rule* and the Tallaght documents are the best approximation that one can find to form a picture of the interior and exterior aspects of the reform.[78]

Two martyrologies from the monastery have been preserved for us. The *Martyrology of Tallaght*,[79] which is contemporaneous with *The Stowe Missal*[80] was compiled in the early decades of the ninth century. The second is the *Martyrology* or *Félire of Oengus*.[81] The former is ascribed to Maelruain and Oengus by John Colgan OFM.[82] Both provide lists of saints' feasts. The former gives a list of Roman and Irish saints for each day except for some six weeks which are missing. The latter has a stanza of poetry for each day commemorating the saint(s) of the day. Until recently it was held that it was composed between 797-808 but Professor Pádraig Ó Riain has put forward good reasons for a later date.[83] Dr John Hennig suggests that *The Martyrology of Tallaght* was read during the Canon of the Mass and that the *Félire* was read in the chapter-room.[84] Oengus' work is more a composition for private devotion. He tells us that he searched earlier martyrologies and 'Ireland's host of books'.[85] There are varying judgements on the literary merit of the work. Stokes held that it has 'not a trace of imaginative power or observation of nature and human life as they really are'.[86] David Greene agrees with him but admits of 'an occasional flash of inspiration' in the *Félire* itself but points out that Prologue and Epilogue have deep religious and technical virtuousity.[87] On the other hand, Hennig writes that it is the largest and most highly developed work of early Irish religious poetry.[88]

Oengus divides his work into three parts, the Prologue, the *Félire* proper and the Epilogue, or as Oengus entitles it 'the final Prologue'. The whole work being in metrical form could be memorised or possibly sung. In the Prologue he has some reflections on the vanity of earthly power and of kings as compared with the love of Christ.

> The might of the world is a lie
> to all who within it live;
> this is the (true) strength –
> great love of Mary's son.

> Naught is nearer to you than God's love
> if you can win it –
> adoration of the King of the clouds
> does not bring sadness with it.[89]

Here and there some beautiful stanzas break a long list of comparisons which tend to become wearisome:

> Maelruain after his pious service
> the great sun of Meath's south plain –
> visiting their tombs
> heals the sighs of my heart.

> Donnchad the wrathful one, ruddy, chosen
> or victorious Bran of the Barrow,
> visiting their tombs
> dispels not my weary weakness.

> Let our will be firm
> let us strive after what is dearest
> since this is the noblest –
> let us all love Jesus.[90]

The *Félire* itself is copiously annotated with poems and marginal notes, partly mystical, hagiographical or historical. This tends to show that Oengus, while in Tallaght, had a large collection of these materials. In the Epilogue, he acknowledges Christ's help in compiling the Calendar and prays for eternal life in union with the saints whom he has commemorated. Significant are the lines:

> May the copious blessing of the king,
> with his beautiful hosts

descend over your assemblies
on Maelruain before all men.
May my tutor bring me unto Christ
dear beyond affection
by his pure blessing
with his heart's desire.[91]

Hennig has the interesting remark that 'this whole idea originated from the fundamental conception of the precariousness of life without the assistance of the saints, or, conversely, is expressive of an extremely realist conception of the efficacy of the intercession of the saints'.[92] Here and there in the Epilogue Oengus reveals his inner self to us and one is struck by his humility and his intense desire to be united with those whom he has commemorated:

Hear Thou, O Jesus, Thy feeble exile
to leave the world I would rather than stay.

If you possess charity in good measure
you may exercise it meetly on this poor deserving wretch.

If you be compassionate your succour is timely,
Here is one of the loneliest, a weakling of Jesus.

Hearken Thou, O Jesus, whose servant (céle) I am
Mayest Thou grant every prayer of each son of piety.[93]

One of the most important products of the reform was *The Stowe Missal*. It is the oldest missal of the early Irish church known to have survived. It contains extracts from the gospel of St John, the rite of baptism, visitation of the sick, Extreme Unction and *Viaticum* and a short treatise in Irish on the Mass. This latter deserves special consideration for its spiritual content. It is dated c. 800-830.[94] It is a symbolic or mystical commentary on the Mass. The altar is the figure of the persecution, the chalice is the figure of the church founded on persecution and martyrdom. The water poured into it signifies the people poured into the church. The host is the turtledove, Jesus. So we have the figure of Christ's Body set in the linen sheet of Mary's womb. The wine poured in represents Christ's godhead on his manhood. The elevation of the chalice after the full uncovering is a commemoration of Christ's birth and of his glory. At the consecration the priest bows thrice in repentance and the people kneel. The three steps which the priest takes backward and again takes forward are the triad in which everyone sins and by which everyone is renewed – word, thought and deed.[95] The treatise points out that the Mass symbolises the Old and New Testament and recalls the principal mysteries of Our Lord's life, his birth, passion, death and resurrection, concentrating particularly on the sacrifice of the cross. The idea of the Mystical Body is seen in the confraction for Communion.[96]

Other ninth-century writings

The lighter side of the scribe's life is beautifully expressed in the well-known poem by the scholar on his cat, *Pangur Bán*, which is dated as ninth century. It appears in the margin of a manuscript which contains a commentary on Virgil, Greek paradigms, astronomical notes and selections from Latin hymns. Stanzas 4 and 7 are indicative of the writer's sense of humour and reality:

> Oftentimes a mouse will stray
> in the hero Pangur's way;
> oftentimes my keen mind set
> takes a meaning in its net.

> So in peace our tasks we ply
> Pangur Bán, my cat and I;
> in our arts we find our bliss
> I have mine and he has his.[97]

Naturally scribes found their works tedious at times but it had its recompense:

> Over my head the woodland wall
> rises; the ousel sings to me;
> above my booklet lined for words
> the woodland birds shake out their glee.

> There's the blithe cuckoo chanting clear
> in mantle grey from bough to bough;
> God keep me still! for here I write
> a Scripture bright in great woods now.[98]

The poem *M'oenurán im aireclán* is a pilgrimage-retirement prayer-poem to prepare for death. It portrays the anchorite life:

All alone in my little cell without a single human being along
with me. Such a pilgrimage (retirement) would be dear to my
heart before going to meet death …

I should love to have Christ, Son of God, my Creator, my
King, visiting me,
and that my mind should resort to Him in the kingdom in
which He dwells.
Let the place which shelters me amid monastic enclosures be
a delightful hermit's plot
hallowed by religious stones, with me alone therein.

This little poem, three quarters of which dwells on the penitential aspect of the anchorite life, may well have expressed the
ideal of many people mentioned in the annals as dying after
penance and pilgrimage. Professor Ó Corráin makes the observation that 'this poem can be read as prescriptive verse rather
than a descriptive personal lyric concerned … with what one
could call the details of a retirement package'.[99] I think that he
misses the point as the poem is important in placing the ideal
conditions for 'good repentance' (a term often found in the annals) just as *Rules*, sermons and prayers point to the ideal, which
is never fully realised.

Though the following poem is well-known, it must be included
here as one of Ireland's treasures. It occurs in the notes to
Oengus' *Félire* commenting on St Ita's feast, January 15. One
feels that this is one of the few compositions we can be reasonably sure was written by a woman, though Ita was dead for
three centuries. The story ends 'Christ came to Ita in the form of
a child and then she said':

Baby Jesus lying
in my little cell lonely –
though a cleric have stores of wealth,
all things lie save Jesu only.

Fosterling in my home I nurse Thee,
no son of base churl Thou art;
Jesu with the angel–hosts above Thee,
nestlest nightlong in my heart.

> Jesu noble, angel–like
> no common cleric art Thou,
> Child of Hebrew Mary's bosom
> in my cell I'm nursing now.
>
> Virgins, sing your tuneful numbers,
> pay your little tribute so,
> on my breast babe Jesu slumbers,
> yet in heaven His small feet go.[100]

Daniel Úa Liathaite, Abbot of Lismore, spoke the following verses c. 850 when a woman was soliciting him, though he was her confessor. He reasoned with her that the outcome would be tragic:

> I will not sell heaven for sin; if I do so retribution will follow. O woman, give not for wrongdoing that which thou shalt never recover here. Abandon that which shall injure thee. Sell not thy share in heaven; under God's protection go to thy home; take from me a blessing, O woman.

His advice was successful and she said: 'Thus it shall be. She vowed him perpetual purity as long as she lived.'[101]

An unusual but very touching poem, written c. 875, describes the love of Líadan, an early seventh-century princess, for the poet Cuirithir. The accompanying story and poem suggests that after Líadain had promised to marry him, she decided to become a nun. He then became a monk. Líadain changed her mind but Cuirithir, wishing to remain faithful to his vocation, left his cell in the Dési when she pursued him there and sailed across the sea from her. Later she died praying on the stone on which Cuirithir used to pray. The ninth-century poet expresses her feelings:

> Unpleasing is the deed which I have done; What I have loved I have vexed. Were it not for fear of the King of heaven, it would have been madness for one not to do what Cuirithir wished.

> Not profitless to him was that which he desired – to reach heaven and avoid pain. A trifle vexed Cuirithir in regard to me; my gentleness towards him was great.

> I am Líadain: I loved Cuirithir; this is as true as anything told. For a short time I was in the company of Cuirithir; to be with me was profitable to him.

> Forest music used to sing to me beside Cuirithir together with the sound of the fierce sea. I should have thought that no arrangement I might make would have vexed Cuirithir in regard to me.

> Conceal it not; he was my heart's love, even though I should love all others besides. A roar of fire has split my heart. Without him for certain it will not live.

A note added at the end of the poem says 'Now the way she vexed him was her haste in taking the veil.'[102]

The folly of the Cross does not exist without the love of the crucified. A short hymn on the Cross of Christ (*Comad croiche Críst*) dates probably from the ninth century. It may have provided the fashion for the many bardic hymns on the Cross. It begins:

> I believe in Christ who has risen and suffered the tree of the Cross and who was three days in the stone sepulchre.

He refers to the piercing of the lance which turns up frequently in Irish medieval prose and poetry. Nature sympathised with him on His death and the treachery of the Jews is lamented. But it ends on a very positive note:

> Every hardship which He suffered for the race of Adam, 'twas to part us from the devil. Woe to him who will not believe in Him. His birth, His baptism, His crucifixion, His burial without strife, His resurrection, His ascension, His advent – it is right to believe in them.[103]

A prayer for help, dating from c. 900, commits the poet's soul into Christ's hands to be protected from the devil. His appeal has a very personal touch:

> Make smooth the road upon which I am intent, unless it be folly, unless it be harm, O Prince of Adam's race, O Christ with the Orders of heaven. Let if not be many years till Thou lift me up with Thy saints, till I come to enter the heavenly abode after being snatched away from vile demons.

> What I have been saying to Thee before I pray Thee, Son of Mary, whether I be long or short upon the road, be there to help me, O heart![104]

Sedulius Scottus and John Scottus Eriugena

Sedulius and Eriugena are names which mark the ninth century. Between 650 and 800 at least forty commentaries (now in European libraries) on parts of Scripture were written by Irish either at home or on the continent. Sedulius and Eriugena added to these texts, the former commenting on St Mark's gospel and the Pauline Epistles, the latter on the prologue and sections of St John's gospel. We know very little about Sedulius prior to his appearance round Liege in 845. The high quality of his Latin and the depth of his scholarship won him immediate recognition. As the manuscripts belonging to his particular circle have devotion to St Brigid he may have come from the neighbourhood of Kildare. He and his companions approached Hartgar, the local bishop, offering learning and looking for bed and board in exchange. He made his request in Latin poetry and in time he got a favourable hearing:

> Then Hartgar, powerful prelate, raise the weak,
> cherish the learned Irish with gentle heart.
> So, blessed in heaven's high temples may you walk,
> celestial Jerusalem and enduring Zion.

> Great prelate, his mercy and his quiet mind
> conquered the blasts and tamed old Boreas' pride;
> kindly took he the weary in, and bountiful
> snatched three scholars from the howling winds,
> clothing us and honouring all three,
> so we became the gentle shepherd's sheep.

Finding that the house did not give adequate light for their work, he took pen in hand again using a touch of mild sarcasm:

> Oh Hartgar, all such that cannot see
> gather together and bring them here to me –
> for this dark house a fitting use we'll find.
> We'll christen it: ASYLUM FOR THE BLIND.[105]

Sedulius' most important and original work is *De Rectoribus Christianis*, composed for Lothaire II (855–69), a treatise on the duties of the Christian ruler. He deals with the question of the relation of church and state which was problematic even in the middle ages. The work had considerable influence on later writings on the question. The Irish flavour may be seen in these lines:

> For, as the wise hold, there are eight pillars which sustain the
> kingdom of a just king. The first pillar is truth in all matters
> pertaining to kingship; the second pillar is patience in every
> affair; the third, generosity in gifts; the fourth, gentle persua-
> siveness or affability in words; the fifth is the correction and
> suppression of evildoers; the sixth is friendship towards and
> exaltation of the good; the seventh pillar, the exaction of light
> taxes from the people; the eighth is equal judgement between
> the rich and the poor.

James Carney attributes the well known lines on pilgrimage to
Rome to Sedulius:

> Pilgrim, take care your journey's not in vain,
> A hazard without profit, without gain,
> The King you seek, you'll find in Rome, 'tis true,
> But only if He travel on the way with you.

It is on the margin of a manuscript commenting on the Epistles
of St Paul which Carney connects with the circle of Sedulius. The
Irish were great believers in piety based on understanding. A
sentence from his work on Christian Rulers might be used to
sum up his ideal: 'God has willed the nature of man to be such
that he should be desirous of and seek two things: religion and
wisdom.' The fully human Sedulius appears in his summary of
his own way of life:

> I read and write and teach, philosophy peruse,
> I eat and freely drink, with rhymes invoke the muse,
> I call on heaven's throne by night and day,
> Snoring I sleep or stay awake and pray.
> While sin and fault inform each act I plan –
> Ah! Christ and Mary, pity this miserable man.[106]

In a review on the book *Eriugena*, Myles Dillon writes 'Eriugena
(c. 810-875) was far better acquainted than any of his contempor-
aries with the works of the Greek theologians such as Gregory of
Nyssa, Maximus the Confessor and above all, the remarkable
Christian neoplatonist who shelters beneath the name of
Dionysius the Areopagite. These, together with authorities near-

er home, Augustine and Boethius, form the basis of Eriugena's inheritance ... Eriugena was the greatest philosopher of his time, and the greatest philosopher to come out of Ireland up to the present except perhaps for Berkeley.'[107]

A poem entitled *Colman's Farewell to Colman*, and dated between the seventh and ninth century, is unusual as it is a farewell of a Colman remaining in Europe to a Colman who wishes to return to Ireland. It is the only example I have found of a returning missionary in these centuries:

> Go freely to your country since care torments you
> may the all-powerful Creator, sole hope of our life,
> who governs the dread-sounding waves and winds,
> give you now safe waves of the curling abyss.
>
> May it return you to the shores of your chosen homeland of
> the Irish!
> Then farewell, may you live in fame and in happiness for
> many year
> achieving the rewards of a distinguished life.
> Here, therefore I wish you the joys of the present life so that
> the joys of everlasting life may reach you.[108]

The *Book of Kells*, which is generally dated as ninth century, represents the highest attainment of Irish writing and illumination. It contains the four gospels, the Eusebian canons, the *breves causae* and *argumenta*. Grants of land made at Kells in the eleventh and twelfth centuries are also entered on blank pages. The gospels and the ornamentation are its most noteworthy features.

> The pictures in the *Book of Kells* helped those who read the four gospels to understand the Christian message, even if the book, written in Latin, was difficult to read. And to those who could not read at all, the pictures were very important. The illustrations bring out the meaning of the text. The book is full of drawings that teach us and explain the words being read. For example we can see a cock and a hen and a chicken in between the lines of the parable of the sower. These pictures make us think of the fowl picking up the seeds that fell by the wayside.

In another place the capital letter N, standing for 'no man' (*nemo* in Latin), is shaped out of two little men. Their bodies and legs are twisted and turned to make the outline of the capital N. The two figures face each other. They are not at all friendly. In fact they are tugging at each other's beards! This letter N begins the well-known sentence: 'No man can serve two masters. He will either hate the one and love the other, or hold to the one and despise the other.' The little picture of the two men struggling gives us the clue to the words of Jesus which need to be thought about. Nothing seems to be going right for these two men! When books about the Bible are printed to-day, the words that are difficult are often explained in written notes. Those who gave us the *Book of Kells* made the deep meanings of the gospel clear by using lively pictures that we will not easily forget.[109]

Notes

1. *CD* 6-7.

2. *AU* 846, FM 845. The annals prove conclusively that Clonard had a reputation as a house of studies in these times. In 830 Cormac, abbot, scribe and bishop died (AU). Similarly Suairlech abbot and best teacher of religion in the whole of Ireland died 870. Ferdomnach, an excellent scribe, died 932. Maelmochta, scribe, abbot and head of piety and wisdom in Ireland, died 940.

3. *Hist. Eccl.* 111 c. 27.

4. Janssen, H. OSB, 'St Willibrord and Ireland', *IER* LXX11 (1952) 356-65.

5. Kenney, 247-9.

6. A fuller treatment of this and the following poem is to be found in *Mary*, 48-56. The verse translation is taken from Moran, P., F., *Essays on the Origin, Doctrines and Discipline of the Early Irish Church* (Dublin, 1864) 226-7. He has taken it from Fr Potter. The verse gives the feeling but it is not a literal translation.

7. Carney, J., *The Poems of Blathmac son of Cú Brettan together with the Irish Gospel of St Thomas and a Poem on the Virgin Mary* (Dublin, 1964) xix.

8. Ibid. 3.

9. Stokes, W. and Strachan, J., *Thesaurus Palaeohibernicus* (Cambridge, 1901-3) II, 244-7. Henceforth *Thes.Pal.*

10. Ibid. II, 245-6.

11. Ibid. 247. The third which is omitted is *largitas in paupertate* (generosity in poverty). P. Ó Néill, 'The Background of the Cambrai Homily', *Ériu* XXXII (1981) 143. The trait 'generosity in poverty' is found in the phrase *Nuair is gann an chuid is fial é roinnt*.

12. *Ériu* XXXII, 147.

13. Kinsella, T., *The New Oxford Book of Irish Verse* (Oxford, 1986) 13.

14. cf. Kenney 468-74. *CD* 1–4.

15. *AU* 752.

16. *AU* 732, 734, 743, 745, 759, 763, 774, 782, 785, 794, 798 and many others could be added.

17. *AU* 772, *FM* 768. *v.* also *CD* 6-7.

18. Gougaud, L., *Christianity in Celtic Lands* (London, 1932) 278-81.

19. Plummer, C., *Vitae Sanctorum Hiberniae*, (Oxford, 1910) 2 vols. II, 250. Henceforth *V.S.H.*. It was at this site that the Derrynaflan sacred vessels were found.

20. Kenney, 468.

21. *AI* 825.

22. Ibid. 778.

23. *FM* 840.

24. *CD* 40 n.6.

25. Ibid. 41-43.

26. Byrne, F.J., *Irish Kings and High-Kings* (London, 1973) 226.

27. *CD* 43-4.

28. McNamara, M., 'Psalter Text and Psalter Study in the Early Irish Church 600-1200'. *PRIA* Sect. C (1973), 221-2.

29. *Félire Oengusso*, ed. Stokes, W. (London, 1905) 2nd edition. Henceforth *FO*(2), 8, 10.

30. Ibid. 12.

31. Ibid. xxiv–xxvi. *v.* also P. Ó Riain 'The Tallaght Martyrologies Redated', *Cambridge Medieval Celtic Studies* 20 (1990) 38.

32. *AU* 921, 1164, 1479.

33. *Ériu* 7, 122-3. *Ir.Pen.* 258.

34. Eight basic sins were distinguished by the fourth-century Evagrius: gluttony, luxury, love of money, sadness, anger, acedia, vainglory and pride. John Cassian was influenced here by Evagrius. Bouyer, L., *The Spirituality of the New Testament and the Fathers* (London, 1960) I, 384.

35. P. J. Payer has a very interesting article, 'The Humanism of the Penitentials and the Continuity of the Penitential Tradition', *Medieval Studies* XLVI (1984) 340-54.

36. *CD* 66. For a description of the Tallaght Documents *v. CD* xiv–xv and Chap II.

37. Ibid. 66-7.

38. Ibid. 68-81.

39. Ibid. 81-2.

40. Ibid. 84.

41. Ibid. 84-5.

42. Ibid. 85.

43. Ibid. 85-6.

44. Ibid. 88.

45. Ibid. 88-90.

46. Ibid. 90.

47. *Pen. Columbani can.* 42. *Ir. Pen* 106, 30 cf. *ACL* III, 319 n. 82.

48. Binchy, D.A., *Ériu* XIX (1962) p. 67 par. 37.

49. *CD* 93-4.

50. Walker, 168, 12-3.

51. *CD* 95.

52. Ibid. 96.

53. *The Antiphonary of Bangor* (Dublin, 1984) Chap. 19.

54. *CD* 108-9.

55. Ibid. 97-8.

56. *Ir. Trad.* 53.

57. *CD* 100-1.

58. Ibid.

59. Ibid, 102-3.

60. Ibid. 104. 'Through a vow a man comes into membership of God's family.'

61. Ibid. 104.

62. *Ériu* VII, 154 n. 6.

63. *CD* 109.

64. 110-1.

65. *V.S.H.* II, 260, xxiv.

66. *CD* 112.

67. Ibid. 113 n.1.

68. Ibid. 88.

69. Ibid. 115.

70. Ibid.

71. Ibid.

72. Ibid. 116.

73. Ibid. 120.

74. *FO*(2) 5.

75. *ZCP* VII, 310-12.

76. Murphy, G., *Early Irish Lyrics* (Oxford, 1956) 28-31. Henceforth *EIL*.

77. *ZCP* VIII, 231.

78. *CD* 138-9.

79. Best, R.I., and Lawlor, H.J., (London, 1931). Henceforth *Mart. Tall.*

80. Ed. G.F. Warner, (London, 1906).

81. An earlier edition by him (Dublin, 1880) is referred to as *FO* (1). P. Ó Riain dates it 828-833. *v.* n. 31, 21-38.

82. *Mart. Tall*, based on Colgan *AA.SS. Hib.* 5.

83. *ZCP* VI, 6 *v.* Ó Riain n. 31 dates it also 828-833. I see no reason for dating it so late as the latest reference is Dimmán of Ara who died 811.

84. *Medieval Studies* XXVI, 324-5.

85. *FO*(2) Epil. lines 141-2.

86. Greene, D., 'The Religious Epic', in Carney, J., (ed.), *Early Irish Poetry* (Cork, 1969) 75-77.

87. Ibid.

88. *Medieval Studies* XVII (1955) 219.

89. *FO*(2) Prol. Lines 145-8, 185-8.

90. Ibid. 221-4, 225-8, 261-4.

91. *FO*(2) Epil. lines 65-6.

92. *Medieval Studies* XXVI, 324.

93. *FO*(2) lines 365-8, 389-92, 393-6, 425-8.

94. Kenney 697-8. P. Ó Riain dates it c. 830, art. cit. n. 92, 38.

95. *Stowe Missal* II, 40-2.

96. *CD* 154-9.

97. *Ir. Trad.* 25. For a more literal translation *v. EIL*, 3.

98. *Thes Pal.* II, 290, *Ir Trad.* 42-3.

99. *EIL* 19-23. Ó Corráin, D., Breathnach, L. and McCone, K., (eds.), *Sagas, Saints and Storytellers* (1989) 261-2.

100. *Ir. Trad.* 56-7. This is a translation which gives the feeling of the poem. I have emended a few phrases in it more in keeping with the Irish text.

101. *EIL* 7-9.

102. Ibid. 83-5.

103. Meyer, K., *Ériu* I, 41-2.

104. Meyer, K., *Ériu* VI, 14-5.

105. Carney, J., Sedulius Scottus', *Old Ireland*,(1965) 228-41. I have used this article of Prof. Carney very liberally as he had great feelings for Sedulius.

106. Ibid. 241-50.

107. Bamford, C., and Marsh, W.P., (eds.), *Celtic Christianity, Ecology and Holiness* (1987) 137.

108. Meyer, K., 'Colman's Farewell to Colman', *Ériu* III, 186-9.

109. Simms, G. O., *Exploring the Book of Kells* (Dublin, 1988) 24-5.

Addendum

The *Scuab Crábaid* attributed to Colcu Úa Duinechda, who died in 796, should have been included. The reader will find discussion of this text in *CD* 173-7.

CHAPTER 3

The Tenth and Eleventh Centuries

Rules

'Their Father is God, their mother is holy church.' (*Rule of Ailbe*)

The *Martyrology of Oengus* mentions four rules (*cána*):the *Rule of Patrick* which forbade the slaying of clerics, Adomnán's, which exempted women from military service and protected children and clerics, Daire's, which outlawed the stealing of cattle and the *Rule of Sunday* (*Cáin Domnaig*) which forbade work on a Sunday.[1] These are not monastic rules but rather general prohibitions. It is clear that there was an abundance of these latter in Ireland. Mention is found of a monastic *Rule* in the Lives of Brendan, Canice of Achadh-Bó, Kevin, Colman, Comgall, Cronan, Declan, Fechin, and Molua.[2] It is probable that most of the founders drew up *Rules*. Some are still exant, though not always mentioned in the Life of the saint.

In general the *Rules* resemble more closely the ascetic practices of Egyptian monasticism than the orderly type of *Rule* found in Europe in the fifth and sixth centuries as in the case of Benedict's *Rule*. At the close of the eighth century, St Benedict of Aniane wrote his *Codex* which contains about twenty-five such *Rules*. If we include a few which he missed, such as the *Rule of Caesarius of Arles*, there are about thirty writings which might be called *Rules*. However since he had little influence on Irish *Rules*, if we except that of Columbanus, which has been mentioned earlier, it will be more advantageous to concentrate our attention on the *Rules* of Patrick, Comgall, Colum Cille, Mochutu (or Fothad) and of Cormac Mac Cuillenáin. There are also *Rules* of Ciaran and of the Manaig Líatha, both of which have very poor texts and are practically unintelligible.[3]

The Rule of Patrick,[4] which is in prose, lays down that each tribe is to have a bishop. His duty is to ordain clergy, consecrate churches, give spiritual advice to rulers and show pastoral care for families. This is from Patrick's will (*timna*). If there are not bishops to fulfil these duties faith dies, and if people do not have good directors (*anamchara*) they are liable to commit all sorts of sin. A priest incapable of offering Mass or saying the Hours before kings and bishops is not entitled to exemption from taxes, military service, nor is he entitled to his honour-price. A bishop must not confer priesthood or diaconate on one who is unable to give spiritual direction, practice piety and be given to reading, nor on one who does not know the law or the rule, else he is guilty of sin because he insults Christ and the church and causes ruin to people. If he does ordain such a person, a heavy fine is placed on him as penance (seven years and twenty-one milch cows). Children under seven years of age are chastised either with scourge, belt or the palm of the hand. Anyone who transgresses his Orders with a nun pays a fine and is entitled to nothing from the church until he does penance according to the decision of an abbot or of a pious *anamchara*.

A priest in a smaller church is entitled to house, bed, clothing, food, some corn and condiment, a milch cow each quarter and (special) food for feasts. His payment for baptism is guaranteed by the *manaig*. His duties are clearly specified: baptism, communion, intercession, Mass, Office, daily psalter, unless instruction, spiritual direction and anointing do not allow him time. Where priests are few, one may provide for three or four churches, provided baptism, Mass and communion are supplied by him. The *manach*'s due to the priest is set out: one day's ploughing with seed and arable land for the year, half the cloth for a mantle (*étaig*), or shirt or tunic and dinner for four at Christmas, Easter and Pentecost. The greater the dignity of the priest the more is due to him.

A number of *Rules* and spiritual treatises appeared around the time of the *Céli Dé* reform, probably influenced by their spirit. *The Rule of Colum Cille*, which dates from the ninth century, was obviously written for anchorites where the religious is advised to live apart from the community if his conscience bids him do so. He is to have a hermitage. Poverty must be strictly observed. He may eat only when he is hungry, sleep only when fatigued and speak only when necessary. His superfluities should be given to those who need them. His love of God and of his neighbour is shown by his observance of the commandments. Thus he labours unto sweat and prays till tears are loosed. 'Fervour in singing and Office of the Dead as if every faithful dead person was a particular friend of yours' is the ideal.[5]

Comgall's Rule is dated c. 800 and is known as *Riaghal in Choimded*.[6] The religious is bidden to keep the *Rule* and he will run no danger of losing heaven. The essence of the *Rule* is love of Christ and mildness with people. Wealth must be shunned. Three good rules are: patience, humility and the love of God in your heart. Fear leads to love of God which heals every sorrow. Love makes us abide by His commandments and counsel. He is advised to sing the psalter every day since the elders prescribe and recommend it. Here the note of reform, poverty and piety is stressed. Great sin requires deep repentance else his reward in heaven will be small and purgatory will be severe. Genuine peace is a mark of sincerity.

The Rule of Ailbe is written in Old Irish and probably dates from the eighth or ninth century.[7] It is addressed to Eogan Mac Saráin, Abbot of Cluain Coeláin, Co Tipperary. It advises keeping a clean conscience without pride, lies or vanity, working in silence and meeting the needs of the sick. Perseverance (*fossud*) is an anvil for good,[8] doing others' wishes, being responsible for all souls. They occupied themselves with sewing and washing until terce, while each drew strength from prayer in his cell. The tolling of the bell should last a considerable time to allow all to obey it with pleasure.[9] Then comes the beautiful interjection: 'Their Father is God, their mother is holy church' – let them be genuinely humble and have compassion for each other.'

To discomfort the devil each should confess his faults at the Cross in the presence of the abbot. This is probably not sacramental confession. Flagellation and washing after scourging was followed by good food for seniors and a little honey. (Honey seems to have been rare as the *Célí Dé* were allowed it when God sent it.) The bell was rung to thank God for the food from St John's Day till Easter. The allowance of bread was thirty ounces which measured twelve inches. It was taken at None. A wise *airchinnech* should be prudent in the matter of food, remembering that 'as the food is so will the Order be'.

A person who will not endure reproof and who does not confess his faults should be told by his *anamchara* to go to some other place. Warriors and women were forbidden to enter their living quarters. From the Annunciation till October, None is said in a holy place according to the rules (or during which the rules are said). A person visiting the servants of God (*mogada Dé*) should learn from the good he sees. He should be silent about what he hears or sees, avoid calumny, attacking and reviling. The steward (*fertaiges*) should be humble and obedient, welcoming and blessing all who come to him, with a clean house for guests, a big fire, wash and bath facilities and a good couch. The *airchinnech* should be pure, pious, gentle with others' rights, distributing justly to his *manaig* and not be over-demanding on them – neither too generous nor too mean. While saying nothing ill, he 'should point out transgressions and his monks should be well-occupied'.

While the rule was written for Eogan, it must be the writer's experience of what was best in Emly in his day, probably based on traditions and rules which Ailbe had set out some centuries earlier. One notes that there is no strong emphasis on Mass.

The Rule of Mochutu (or of Fothad na Canóine)

Of all the rules written in Gaelic poetry, this is the best at least in format. It begins with a general introduction and devotes sections to the bishop, the abbot, the *anamchara*, the priest, the *Céle Dé*, the student and finally to the king. It is attributed to Mochutu of Lismore and also to Fothad na Canóine of Fahan, Co Donegal (833).[10] If the attribution to Mochutu is to be sustained, then I think that since it is a ninth century composition it may have been composed by a monk in Lismore, based on the ideas which had been trasmitted by Mochutu. Lismore made a considerable contribution to Irish spirituality from the seventh to the twelfth century.

The *Rule* begins with the evangelical maxim to love God with one's whole heart and soul and with one's deeds, and follows with the second evangelical precept to love one's neighbour as oneself. The commandments are recalled by the injunction to avoid idolatry and to make our requests to God with humility. Christ has told us to respect our parents and elders. We are to honour our abbot Christ, and to refrain from adultery, stealing and murder. We should not covet wealth as it is deceitful. We are also enjoined not to swear false witness or to offend anyone. The concluding stanzas again recall the evangelical maxim that we do to others the good we would wish them to do to us so that we may reach heaven. We should not wish anybody what we would not wish for ourselves.

Duties of a bishop

It is to be noted that the bishop is the first to be mentioned. It is a noble Order and the office should be carried out with zeal. He is to submit to Christ and then others will submit to him. He is told to heal diseases and pain. This may be our present sacrament of the sick or a special episcopal grace. His it is to maintain peace and to correct rulers. He must take his pastoral duties diligently in the case of the laity and clergy. As a teacher he must be direct, accurate and constant, taking evildoers to task. He must not fail to emphasise the whole truth. On taking Orders he must be well-versed in scripture, otherwise he will be a stepson of the church since he is lacking in knowledge and an unlearned bishop is not a (real) successor to the Lord, since he does not know His law. It is his duty to condemn every evil and heresy. He should be guileless in word and deed. If people are not obedient to him and follow his bidding, he is to be blamed if he is gentle with them and it is certain that at judgement he must answer for his own sins and those of his flock.

The Céle Dé

'If we[11] are clerics it is a noble calling. We pray each Hour of the Office in church. On hearing the bell we raise our hearts to heaven and cast our faces down to earth. (This was probably to help recollection.) We sing a *Pater* and *Ave* to ward off sorrow and make the sign of the Cross on our faces and breasts. On reaching the church we prostrate thrice except on Sundays when we genuflect. We celebrate the Office directing our prayer joyfully and constantly to the noble Lord. We keep vigil, we read and we pray according to our capacity till Terce. Each grade goes to its proper duty which is laid out for it from Terce till None. Those who are in Orders go to pray and celebrate Mass fittingly; teachers to teach to the best of their ability; the youth to learn obedience and humility to the best of their power since the idle person belongs to the devil. A holy cleric directs manual labour for the unlearned, and the labour of wisdom for others. Each Hour we celebrate in proper manner, with three prostrations before and after celebration. Silence, earnestness and serenity are to be cultivated without deceit, murmuring or mutual rivalry.'

The King

'Be skilful in ruling, avoid falsehood, it is the Lord who ordained you. Be steady, truthful, learned in judgement, heedful of the Lord. If you do not fulfil His will you will be deprived of His kingdom and be punished. Your principal danger lies in deceit and falsehood since it destroys peace between all peoples, and causes suffering and calamity even in crops like corn, milk and fruit. Kings are responsible for dire plagues, storms, monsters and multiple diseases. They are also responsible for losing land when defeated in battle. If a king is false, fruits do not ripen, storms kill them. He destroys tribes and families up to the ninth generation. He is responsible for their sins as a result of his falseness (bad example?). But if he loves truth and exalts the good he will be long-lived and happy. If he is gentle and merciful to the miserable, if he is humble and patient, heaven will be his reward. He must shun pride in whatever good he may possess and (remember) that he cannot add a single day to his lifespan. He should avoid all evil especially greed. Let him allow mercy and truth reign and his rule will be all the longer and heaven will be his reward.'

The Order of Priests

'Be industrious and speak only the truth. You have the noble

Order of offering the Body of the King. Be not unlearned but let your doctrine be exact. Be well-versed in sacred scripture and in the rules and laws. Let your baptism be lawful – the Holy Spirit works with you. In bringing *viaticum* take care to exact a proper careful confession. Give *viaticum* if repentance is sincere. The priesthood is a great strength so you should influence all in word and deed. Do not give it (*viaticum*?) to imperfect people, though you like their company.'

The work of the abbot

'Noble is the authority of the ruler of a church so you should assume fittingly the heirship of the King. It is a noble undertaking. Protect the rights of the church, small and great. Preach diligently to the people all Christ has commanded you and exemplify it in your own life. Love everyone's soul as you love you own. Promote all that is good and banish all evil. Use your learning and your light for God. Heal the hosts whether they are weak or strong. You are to judge all according to their rank and according to their deeds so that you will be able to answer for them at the final judgement. Pray frequently for the elderly, for the sick and the sorrowful, with abundance of tears. Teach the young so that they may not be foolish and that they may avoid hell. Give thanks for everyone who does his duty in the church. Rebuke the foolish, punish boorish misbehaviours and unruly wretches.

'As an abbot, your qualities should be humble patience, mildness, fasting, almsgiving, steadfastness, generosity and calmness. It is your duty to bring all to the truth, showing firmness, simplicity and uprightness in your dealings. Continually preach the gospel to convert people. Offer Mass. Any abbot who does not fulfil this is not an heir to the church but rather an enemy of God, a thief and a fornicator, who is not a shepherd coming through the door of the sheepfold. He is a savage thief and a loathsome enemy. He usurps the church. He then devours it and deprives the people of truth openly and secretly. The person who gives him the abbacy is no better and shall not attain heaven. Young clerics, fearing Christ, should not be associated with him, unless bound by obedience. All who acquiesce in this offence of God will suffer hell for eternity.'

The Anamchara

It begins on a rather negative note:

'Do not kill the soul of your client. Be not like the blind leading the blind. Do not neglect him. Their confessions should be simple and diligent but do not take their alms unless they obey you. Do not be attached to offerings but distribute them fairly to others. Pray and fast for those who give them, otherwise you will be responsible for their faults. Teach the unlearned who come to you for direction so that, as a result of your good example, they may not sin. Do not be mean with gifts since your own soul is more valuable. Give them to guests, rich or poor. Give them to the poor and seek no return. Give them to old people, especially to widows, and always do it secretly so that you do not seek personal glory or recognition. That will be your profit.

'Sing their requiems which are of great value; attend every Hour when the bell calls. When the men of life come to celebrate with victory, you should go there and let each take his turn after the abbot. Sunday and Thursday are suitable days for Mass, though it may be daily after seeking forgiveness for every fault. It should be offered for Christians of all grades, for the suffering, for all who merit or will merit it. It should be offered on solemnities, on feasts of apostles, of great martyrs and holy confessors. Assistance at or celebration of Mass is a noble offering and should be expressed with compunction at heart, shedding of tears and raising of hands, attentively(?), without murmuring and with forgiveness of all injury. At Mass one should be at peace with one's neighbour, having confessed one's sins when going to Communion. The *anamchara* should make 200 prostrations daily with the *Beati* and say the psalter. He should not eat or sleep in a house where are laity. His great love should be for God alone and he should approach the altar with great purity. If a director be a priest it is (only) fitting that he should not be a miserable transgressor.'

The MacCléirech

This is directed to the cleric or monk under discipline (i.e. in training). He should renounce evil and sedulously follow the law of the church. He should avoid haste, ill-will, slander, theft, falsehood and gluttony. He should avoid impropriety, murmuring, slander, envy, pride, contention, self-will, grumbling, anger persecution, private enmity, ferocity and force. He should also avoid ineffectiveness, despair, sluggishness, folly, unsteadiness, loquacity, infidelity to another, destructive violence, gluttony, drunkness, (empty?) joy, idle speech, hesitation, retaliation for evil.

Now come the positive virtues. 'He should be humble with all; have faith, obedience and charity to all. He should be genuinely poor, not mean but honest, awaiting rewards at the graves of the saints. Be modest, calm, persevering and speedy in duty and sincerity, even when offended. Practice these things.'

He should be patient, simple, gentle with all, entreating and praying Christ at every hour. He should spread truth, denounce evil, use frequent confession diligently as holy friends advise. Restraint of both the internal and external senses for the love of Christ should be developed. The thought of his death and the recollection of hell will help him. He should be joyful in suffering, patient always with people, and meditate on the saints. The older members should be revered and obeyed – he should instruct the younger ones for their good. He should pray for his contemporaries that they may avoid hell. He must be willing to forgive all who harm him in thought, word and deed as Christ bids. His command is that he love those who hate him and do good to those who persecute him.'

I have treated the *Rule* of the *Célí Dé* in Chapter III and more fully in my book *Célí Dé* (Chapters II and III).

The section on the order of Meals and Refectory may have been composed independently about the same time or may have been part of the preceding text.[12] The portions are designated for each Order by the abbot. The repast of the workman should be more substantial than that of others. Compassion is to be shown to elders who do not come to their meal, lest they be neglected. Consideration should be shown to the young since they need to build up their strength. They should eat their proper share. But Sundays, feasts of the apostles, of great martyrs and of saints should be honoured. This is also true of the twelve days of Christmas till the Epiphany. Feasts of Christ should always be honoured and celebrated. The fast of Lent should be minutely observed each day but there was no fast on Sundays. Joy, festivity and reverence is the mark of Easter and each day after it till Whit. There are two fast days each week for those who are able (probably Wednesday and Friday) and the praiseworthy fast is from None to None. When the little bell is rung all the brethren go to the refectory quickly or else a penance is imposed. When they come in they make an inclination, sing a *Pater*, beg pardon (ask for food?), prostrate three times. Then they sit at table, the food is blessed and *Alleluia* is sung. The bell is rung and *Benedic* is said. The senior in the house responds and says *Dominus vobiscum (Dia libh)*.

Finally, there is Cormac's *Rule* which is attributed to Cormac Mac Cuillenáin, King and Bishop of Cashel, who was killed in battle in 908. Its language is dated as the end of the ninth century and it is shorter and gentler than the other *Rules*.[13] His wish is for calm, melodious music and great knowledge. He says: 'Let us praise God in the beautiful way your elders did that it may purify us as it purified them.' Love of God demands fear of Him also. The devil is to be avoided. One should never be arrogant but be patient, avoiding hypocrisy and perversity. A holy meal is one without repletion and without meat but consists of a small fair ration. Proper fasting brings excellent restraint, faith in salvation avoids heresy. Piety should be accompanied with gentleness. Pure joyful behaviour, with one's thoughts on heaven, replaces darkness with light. Other desireable things are a thin mortified body, reading with a well-spoken elder, intent study of the scripture, detachment from the world, protection of one's soul, desire of heaven.

'The Body of Christ with the Blood of Mary's Son is a wonderful power to extinguish desire and to foster purity.' 'At the end of my life I will be happy to get the white garment of an elder, satisfying food and bright order from my active King.'

The tenth century

'Let us love justice since it is that which is
the judgement for all in the end'. (*Tenth century*)

By the tenth century, the Vikings had settled along the coast and organised trading communities closely linked to their northern homelands. In 914 a great fleet established a base in Waterford. From here they penetrated as far as Limerick. Once again they became a formidable menace but they were met with stiffening opposition by the Uí Néill of the north. The Eoganacht in the south of the country were unable to cope with them, but the rise of Dál Cais in east Clare caused the turning of the tide. In 964 they defeated the Vikings of Limerick and sacked the city. Mahon, their leader, was killed in 976, but his brother Brian Bóraimhe brought all Munster under his control in a short time. Malachy, king of the Uí Néill, besieged and took Dublin in 981. He realised that Brian's power was growing very strong so he yielded and allied himself with him, thus preparing the way for the defeat of the vikings at Clontarf in 1014.

The fusion of native and continental traditions in literature and art continued. Muiredach's Cross at Monasterboice, dated c .923, and the Cross of the Scriptures at Clonmacnoise, erected early in the tenth century, are excellent illustrations of the art of stone sculpture. Stone churches had been gradually replacing wooden buildings and round towers or bell-houses, modelled probably on Italian belfries, were becoming more widespread. They were gradually adapted as places of refuge from marauders and continued to be used to summon people to church or to safety by the ringing of bells from the top windows.

The tenth-century poem, *Comad Mancháin Léith*, expresses the wish for a little hut in the desert (wilderness), the desire to repent with the aid of the Holy Spirit, the singing of the birds, warm and abundant plant life, a community of twelve (and himself). This poem is a nicely-balanced expression of a reasonable spiritual life catering for soul and body. It does not have the rigour of the early Irish monastery. It does have a slight touch of the Sedulius Scottus mentality but does not wish for as many creature comforts. It might be considered an average tenth-century approach to monastic life in a small quiet secluded setting:

I wish, O Son of God, eternal, ancient King, for a hidden, little hut in the wilderness that it might be my dwelling. A few young men of sense, we shall tell their number, humble, obedient to pray to the King. A lovely church decked with linen, a dwelling for God from heaven, bright lights then above the pure, white scriptures. Raiment and food enough for me from the King whose fame is fair, to be seated for a time and to pray to God in some place.[14]

The middle-aged author of the tenth-century poem ascribed to Moling has a sense of humour as he describes his dull seriousness in the company of the seniors and of his over-identification with the juniors when in their company:

When I am among the seniors I am proof that games are forbidden: when I am among the wild they think I am younger than they.[15]

Protection is a very frequent plea in Irish prayers, especially in Loricas. An early example of this type of prayer is Suffragare, Trinitas unita composed either by Gildas (+570) or Laidchenn (+661).[16] A tenth-century poem, Cros Críst tarsin gnúisse (Christ's Cross over this face), composed by Mugrón, Abbot of Iona 965-81, appeals for protection over his ears, eyes, nose and all parts of his body. He also asks that the Cross may accompany him and help him in every difficulty; that it may be with him sitting or sleeping and that it give him the strength to reach heaven. He prays that it may guard his community (muintir) and his church in this world and in the next.[17] Mugrón has also written a fine litany in praise of the Blessed Trinity. A few invocations give us the approach to nature also found in earlier poetry:

Have mercy upon us, o God the Father Almighty,
O God of the tempestuous sea and serene air,
O God of the many languages round the circuit of the earth,
O God of the waves from the bottomless house of the ocean,
O God who fashioned the mass and inaugurated day and night,
O golden God,
O heavenly Father, who are in heaven.

O Son twice-born,
O true knowledge,

O true light of love that lightens every darkness,
O intelligence of the mystical world,
O Mediator of all men,
O fountain of the faith,
O Redeemer of the human race.

Have mercy on us, O God Almighty, O Holy Spirit;
O finger of God,
O imparter of true wisdom,
O author of the Holy Scriptures,
O septiform Spirit,
O Holy Spirit that rulest all created things, visible and invisible.[18]

A middle-Irish poem on the Trinity, which is found in nine manuscripts, shows the poet's desire to be with them in heaven.[19]

Father, Son and Holy Spirit, abundance according to knowledge,
my own desire, my sun, my love, each One of the Three. However it is my wish to speak of the One in which is this Trio.
The mighty Trinity, its very self, my going into harbour. Going into harbour it is for me to go into their house
from the bitter world where joy has been curbed, feasting perverted and form ignobled. Let us love justice, since it is that which is the judgement for all in the end; let us cause not destruction through weakness or hate; let us consider wisdom.[20]

Airbertach mac Coisse Dobráin

Airbertach mac Coisse Dobráin, the principal teacher in the monastery of Ross Ailithir (Rosscarbery) in west Cork (+990) has left us a poem on the Psalter dating from c. 950.[21] It consists of one hundred and fifty stanzas, and most of the poem deals with the writing of the psalter, translations of it and useful information about sections of it. The opening stanzas are a prayer expressing the poet's love of God:

O God the Creator, I implore You, You are my gracious counsellor, do not turn Your face away from me, for You are my judgement without treachery. You are my King, You are my law, to You belongs my flesh, my body. I love You, O Christ, without duress for my soul is Yours tonight.[22]

The common opinion today is that Airbertach is also the author of *Saltair na Rann* which was written in 985. It is a series of one hundred and fifty poems dealing mainly with Old Testament history, the life of Christ and a good deal of traditional material which does not derive from biblical sources.[23] He added a prayer for forgiveness at the end of the poems:

I am repentant for my transgression, as is right; Christ of Thy mercy, forgive me every sin that may be attributed to me .... For the company of the sinless apostles, for the host of the chaste disciples, for every blessed saint with kingly grace, forgive me my ill deeds. For every holy virgin on the great earth, for the assemblage of the distinguished laywomen, forgive me every sin beneath heaven for wondrous maiden Mary. For those who dwell on earth ... for those who dwell in blessed bright heaven, grant me fullest forgiveness of my sins because I am repentant.[24]

The poem, *Is mebul dom imrádud*, which is also tenth century, laments the flightiness of thought but reflects the experiences of the ordinary human being in the practice of prayer throughout the centuries:

My thought it is a wanton stranger
It skips away;
I fear 'twill bring my soul in danger
On Judgement Day.
For when the holy psalms are singing
Away it flies,
Gambolling, stumbling, lightly springing
Before God's eyes.
'Mongst giddypated folk it rambles,
Girls light of mind;
Through forests and through cities gambols
Swifter than wind.[25]

The *Life of Adomnán*, which is dated c. 960, ends with a picture of
the ideal abbot in the mind of the contemporary writer:

> A just man, indeed, was this man, with purity of nature like a
> patriarch. A true pilgrim, like Abraham. Gentle and forgiv-
> ing of heart like Moses. A praiseworthy psalmist like David.
> A treasury of wisdom like Solomon. A choice vessel for pro-
> claiming truth, like Paul the apostle. A man full of grace and
> bounty of the Holy Spirit. A branch of vine with fruitfulness,
> like John the Younger. A brilliant fire with embers which
> warm and heat the sons of life, kindling and inspiring chari-
> ty. A lion in strength and power. A dove in meekness and
> simplicity. A serpent in sagacity and prudence towards
> righteousness. Mild, humble and gentle towards the sons of
> life, severe and unrestrained towards the sons of death. A
> slave of hard work and service for Christ. A king in honour
> and power for binding and loosing, for releasing and enslav-
> ing, for taking and restoring life.

It continues:

> When the hour of the holy Adomnán's death approached,
> there he yielded up his spirit to heaven, to the Lord whom he
> had served. His body, however, is still here in this world,
> with honour and reverence, with daily miracles. Though his
> honour be great to-day, it shall be greater on the day of
> judgement, when he shall shine like the sun, and shall judge
> the fruit of his preaching, and his good work, his pilgrimage,
> his chastity and his humility towards the Lord of the ele-
> ments, in the union of the nine heavenly grades which he did
> not transgress, in the union of the saints and holy virgins of
> the world, of the patriarchs and prophets, of the apostles and
> disciples of Jesus, in the union of the Godhead and manhood
> of God's Son, in the noblest of all unions, in the union of the
> Holy Trinity, Father, Son and Holy Spirit. I beseech the
> mercy of God, through the intercession of Adomnán, that we
> may enter that union for ever and ever. Amen.[26]

While few pilgrims are noted in the tenth century, Otto I, who
became Emperor in 936, gave the monastery of Waulsort in the
Ardennes in Belgium to Irish pilgrims who wished to live ac-

cording to the *Rule of St Benedict*. The abbot was to be an Irishman *in perpetuum*, if possible. Thus we note Cadroe (978), a Scotsman, educated in Armagh, as the first abbot. Scotus meant Irish at this time. His successor Forannán (982) was also an Irishman. In 975 the famed monastery of St Martin in Cologne was given to the Irish monks. Fingen became abbot of St Symphorian in Metz in 992 and it was hoped that there would be many Irish monks there. He moved to St Vannes in the same city before his death in 1005, and had seven Irish monks under his rule. There was also a colony of Irish pilgrims in Toul before the end of the tenth century.[27]

The anonymous poem *Rop tú mo baile* (Be Thou my vision) belongs to the tenth or eleventh century. The versified translation made by Eleanor Hull, based on Mary Byrne's work, is used very happily in our liturgy. I think that some readers may be interested in a literal translation of the whole poem:

> Be Thou my vision, beloved Lord, none other is ought but the King of the seven heavens. Be Thou my meditation by day and by night; may it be Thou that I behold forever in my sleep. Be Thou my speech; be Thou my understanding; be Thou for me, may I be for Thee. Be Thou my Father; may I be Thy son, mayest Thou be mine; may I be Thine. Be Thou my battle-shield, be Thou my sword; be Thou my honour; be Thou my delight. Be Thou my shelter; be Thou my stronghold; mayest Thou raise me up in the company of the angels. Be Thou every good to my body and soul; be Thou my kingdom in heaven and earth. Be Thou alone my heart's special love, let there be none other save the High-King of heaven ... before going into Thy hands, my sustenance, through greatness of love for Thee. Be Thou alone my wonderful and noble portion: I seek not men nor lifeless wealth. To see Thee alone, may I despise all time, all life, as a stinking corpse. Thy love in my soul and in my heart – grant this to me, O King of the seven heavens. Grant this to me, O King of the seven heavens – Thy love in my soul and in my heart. To the King of all I come after prized practice of devotion; may I be in the kingdom of heaven in the brightness of the sun. Beloved Father, hear my lamentation; this miserable wretch (alas) thinks it

time. Beloved Christ, whate'er befall me, O Ruler of all, be Thou my vision.[28]

These seemingly simple, effortless prayer-poems express a very deep personal spirituality. An evening hymn, also from the tenth or eleventh century, *Torramat do noebaingil*, expresses ideas still commonly found in night prayer, i.e. May the angels tend our sleep and rest, bring us true visions, guard us against the devil or bad dreams, and closes with the wish: 'May our waking, our work and all our activity be holy – our sleep, our rest unhindered and untroubled.[29]

James Carney has provided us with an excellent translation of a tenth-century poem on the inevitability of death:

I walk the lonely mountain road
O King of Suns, and darkest glen,
no nearer death though I be alone,
than fared I with three thousand men.

Signs stop me not from setting out
– Did someone sneeze – for my last breath
will be when foot compulsively
treads the awaiting sod of Death.

It is no paltry little man
that can take my life away,
only the Maker of earth and sky
the shaper of the summer-day.

I fear no more to walk alone
let world which shaped me, gave me birth,
take not untimely back but wait
for nut-ripe falling to the earth.[30]

Eleventh Century

'Deus meus, adiuva me' (Maolíosa Ó Brolcháin)

The eleventh century is marked by the battle of Clontarf in 1014 in which Brian Bóraimhe was killed. The Viking power was no longer a threat. They were christianised and contributed to the spiritual and temporal well-being of the country. Religious reform was sorely needed after a period during which many abuses had crept in and moral standards had dropped. Greater contact with Rome and the emergence of outstanding kings and churchmen towards the end of the century helped to promote this renewal. Cultural activity also came back more fully into its own.

An eleventh-century poem ascribed to Colum Cille, found in eight different manuscripts, is to my mind the finest hymn to Our Lady in this period. He implores her intercession for forgiveness.

> Gentle Mary, good maiden, give us help, thou casket of the Lord's Body and shrine of all mysteries. Queen of all who reign, thou chaste, holy maiden, pray for us that, through thee our wretched transgressions be forgiven....

The title 'Mother of truth' is one not commonly found in Irish writing.

> Mother of truth, thou hast excelled every one ... pray with me to powerful Christ, who is truly thy Father and thy Son.[31]

The phrase 'pray with me' is a nice one and a little unusual in Gaelic literature, if we except Blathmac's invitation to her to come to visit him and his willingness to keen her Son with her.

From this century also comes the poem *Mé Éba, ben Ádaim uill* (I am Eve, great Adam's wife). The anonymous writer takes all the blame:

> It is I who outraged Jesus of old; it is I who stole heaven from my children; by rights it is I who should have gone upon the tree ... It is I who plucked the apple: it overcame the control of my greed; for that women will not cease from folly as long as they live in the light of day.[32]

The prayer-poem *Ropo mian dom menmainse* has been adapted into the present liturgical Office under the title 'It were my soul's desire'. It is a very positive, beautifully balanced prayer expressing the desire for the beatific vision.[33]

Monastic *scriptoria* were busy as we see from the Annals. Armagh, Glendalough and Clonmacnoise are three of the more outstanding ones. Most of the *fer léginn* were in Armagh, Lismore, Clonmacnoise, Clonard, Kildare and Glendalough. There was also a notable increase in the numbers making the pilgrimage to Rome, especially among kings, as we shall see later. The fact that Sulien, a Welshman, spent ten years (1045-1055) studying in Ireland is further evidence of these scholarly interests.

Maolíosa Ó Brolcháin, who died in 1086, is one of the outstanding men of this century. He is described as a very eminent senior, master of wisdom, piety and poetry in Irish and Latin by the *Annals of Ulster*. He was educated in Both Chonais near Culdaff, Co Donegal. Later he went to Armagh. He was related to the Clann Sinaig who held succession to the abbacy there for quite a while. Armagh was not tempted by the movement towards reform which occurred in the latter part of this century. The indications are that temporally and spiritually the monastery was in a poor state, though as we have noted, its fame for learning still continued. Maelíosa came to the south of Ireland and ended his life on pilgrimage in Lismore where he died. That monastery and Toirrdelbach Ó Briain, King of Munster, were anxious to spread the reforming ideas which were taking root there in the last quarter of the century. This probably enticed Maelíosa to go there. Eight poems of his survive. Four others and a *Homiliarium* may also be his.[34]

The poem *A Choimdiu báid* (Beloved Lord) begs God's mercy and forgiveness. The lines 'Give us tribulation which cleanses us' shows a healthy approach. 'Within, without take us in Thy care'.[35] Most of his poems are short prayers. His appeal to Christ to send the Holy Spirit to abide in us, to hallow and protect us, is very simple and spiritual:

> May the Holy Spirit be about us, in us and with us, let the Holy Spirit, O Christ, come speedily to us. May the Holy Spirit dwell in our bodies and souls; may He protect us readily against peril, against diseases, against devils, against sins, against hell with many evils, O Jesus, may Thy Spirit hallow and deliver us.[36]

The bilingual poem, *Deus meus, adiuva me,* is used in our present liturgy. It is the essence of simplicity. One might consider that is was written for the very young since it is quite repetitive. It is an appeal that God would give him the gift of divine love in his heart and bestow it quickly. Christ can do it if He wishes, so Maelíosa asks, seeks and begs that he may get heaven. 'My Lord, hear me. May my soul, O God, be full of love for Thee ... My God help me'.[37]

His poem *A Choimdiu nom-choimét* (Lord, guard me) seeks His protection against falling into the eight great chief sins and shows how carefully he weighed up the dangers. He asks for pure faith that it may keep his eye from covetousness, his ear from listening to slander, his tongue from reviling, his heart from wretched desires, his stomach from gluttony, his feet from flightiness, his male organ from lust. 'Let me not fall into any of the well-known great eight chief sins: O Christ come to me to quell and chase them'.[38] In the poem *A aingil beir* (Michael, plead) he appeals to the archangel to bear his plea to the Lord. He asks him: 'Do you hear?' and asks him to ask for pardon for his many great sins and not to delay.

> Be constantly advising me, protecting me both day and night: the senseless, wild, furious demon, let him not come to me. Strengthen me that I may go after successful penitence into the assembly of Jesus and the angels.[39]

Buaid crábuid, buaid n-ailithre (The gift of piety, the gift pilgrimage) asks four favours of Christ: piety, pilgrimage, repentance and suffering. The poem *Dia hÁine ní longu* (I do not eat on Friday) shows how important fasting was considered in one's spiritual life. Wednesday was also included as a reparation for Judas' betrayal. He seems to be speaking to or writing for students: 'You eat, but as for me, I will be fasting because of the fire which water quenches, not because of the cold that is not thawed by fire.'[40]

The lengthy poem on the eight vices, *Ocht bhfíoch na ndualach*, is the work of an experienced spiritual guide and composed in the tone of master speaking to students. He names the sins: gluttony, anger, impurity, covetousness, acedia, laziness, pride and vainglory (arrogance). Familiarity with the *Penitentials* and with the *Céli Dé* reform may be noted in his treatment of each of the vices. He repeats the earlier teaching on the harm they cause and, in concluding with his treatment on vainglory, he regrets that he has not time to dwell on them for a longer period: 'I think your watch (lecture?) tonight is too short as we enumerate the vices from one to eight.' He continues with positive remedies to overcome the vices. The best aid is to banish these thoughts swiftly by making the sign of the Cross over one's heart and pleading continuously with the Lord to banish them. Then he turns directly to Christ:

O Jesus, I pray You in the name of the Holy Spirit do not allow me to be a slave to these eight crooked, entangled (vices) for the sake of Your gentleness, softness, purity, kindness, and deep humility, for God's sake whose Son You are, for the sake of every excellent labour You did while in this world, for Your teaching, for Your crucifixion ... May your helmet be on my head, Your shield on my side, your breastplate (*lúireach*) to protect me, Your swords in my belt that I may thus defeat the doughty devil with his ignoble challenge and his eight evil ones.

Here we find echoes of Colcú Úa Duinechda's *Scuab Crábaid*. Maolíosa points out that prayer overcomes them, the eight choice Hours banish them. Prime to overcome unbridled gluttony, Terce to conquer anger, Sext to defeat impurity, None to conquer covetousness: 'joyful Vespers to master sloth, Compline to subdue sadness (acedia), cold Matins to control pride, Lauds of the great God to smother vainglory'. He adds that those clerics who reduce the eight Hours to three will be severely punished.[41]

A number of poems have been attributed to Maolíosa. *A Chrínóc, cubaid do cheól* (Crínóc of measured melody) at first sight looks like a love poem. The late Professor Carney was the first to divine the depth of meaning in this poem. *Crínóc* (Old-Young) was a term of affection for a particular psalter which had been used by four different men and finally found its way back to its original owner in his old age. It is interesting that some priests to-day still call the breviary 'the wife'.

Crínóc, lady of measured melody,
not young, but with modest, maiden mind –
together once, in Niall's northern land
we slept, we two, as man and womankind.

Guiltless you are of any sin with man,
fair is your name, bright and without stain,
although I know that when you went from me
each in his turn, four lay where I have lain.

And now you come to me, your final pilgrimage,
weary with toil and travel, grimed with dust,
wise still, but body not immaculate;
time it is that ravished you, not lust.

Again I offer you a faultless love,
a love unfettered for which surely we
shall not be punished in the depths of hell
but together ever walk in piety.

Seeking the presence of elusive God
wandering we stray but the way is found
following the mighty melodies that with you
throughout the pathways of the world resound.

Not ever silent, you bring the word of God
to all who in the present world abide,
and then through you, through finest mesh,
man's earnest prayer to God is purified.

You came and slept with me for that first time,
woman of wise counsel to all fears,
and I a fresh-faced boy, not bent as now,
a gentle lad of seven melodious years …

May the King give us beauty back again
who ever did His will with quiet mind;
may He look on us with eagerness and love,
our old and perished bodies left behind.

It is an extraordinary poem in its metaphors of spiritual love
based on the language of married love. Carney dates it as middle-
Irish and does not hesitate to attribute it to Maolíosa. [42]

Another poem which James Carney attributes to him, *At-lochair duit a mo Rí*, (I thank you, my King) thanks God who works for our good in this world. Maelíosa is like a prisoner and has been six months in bed. His soul is uplifted 'tonight' but his body has fallen to the ground. He is in chains but this is good for his soul. He is like a sightless man leaning weakly against the wall. He prays, 'O Father of hosts, come to me. You placed me in captivity on a cross far away in the good country of Munster.' The poet is clearly a deeply spiritual man and his comparison of the good life in the north and his illness in Munster strongly suggests Maelíosa as the author since he came from the north and died in Lismore. Perhaps this sickness was his last and led to his death.[43]

Rob soraid in sét-sa (Let this path be virtuous) is probably from his pen also. He prays that it may be a curing treasure against the devil, war and destruction. 'May Jesus and the Father and the Holy Spirit bless us – mysterious God who is not dark, the bright King to save us ... The Cross of Christ's Body and Mary to protect us on the road. May it not be at enmity with us, but friendly and agreeable.'[44]

Carney suggests that *Mo chinaid i comláine* (My sins in their fullness) was written by him. It is the short, sincere confession of an old man remembering the sins of his youth:

> Forgiveness, God, for all my sins
> I seek at last,
> the sin in word, the sin in heart,
> the sin compassed.
>
> In heedless youth I broke the rule,
> made grievous slips;
> offered fair women of gleaming teeth
> reckless lips.
>
> But now I am an old, old man
> after sinful years
> I seek no feast but that my cheeks
> be wet with tears.[45]

The practice of inclusion is closely related to going on pilgrimage is. Muiredach mac Robartaig, possibly following the example of Marianus Scottus (1056) and of Anmchad (1043), who had become *inclusi* in Germany, lived in confinement on his own in a cell attached to a church. The cell was provided with windows to enable him to attend church services and receive food. Quite a number of Irish monks lived like this in Germany. In 1076 we are told that Muiredach built an Irish monastery of St Peter at Ratisbon. It is known as Weih-Sanckt-Peter. He died in 1088. His *Life* gives an account of his labours as his contemporary, the father Isaac, a man of 120 years, who lived under his rule, often related:

> Such great talent for writing did Divine Providence confer on Blessed Marianus, that with his speedy pen he completed many extensive volumes. To tell the truth without any dissimulation, among all the achievements which the Divine Mercy deigned to work through the instrumentality of that man, I deem worthy of most praise and admiration, and I myself admire most the fact that, with scanty food and clothing, assisted by his brothers who prepared the parchment, he, for the sake of an eternal reward, wrote through with his own hand, not once or twice, but innumerable times, the Old and New Testament, with expository comments ... Moreover during this same time he had written many little books and manuals of the Psalter for poor widows and clerks of the same city, for the benefit of his soul, without any hope of earthly reward. Moreover many monastic congregations which, recruited from Ireland through faith and charity and the desire to imitate Blessed Marianus, inhabit Bavaria and Franconia 'on pilgrimage', are supplied for the most part with the writings of Blessed Marianus.'

Isaac used *Marianus* for *Muiredach* which was a strange name to him. His *Life* recounts the foundation of similar monasteries at Ratisbon in 1096, at Würzburg in 1134, at Nuremberg in 1140, at Constance in 1142, at Vienna in 1155 and at Eichstätt in 1163.[46] They were known as Schottenklöster and they kept in touch with Ireland even to the extent of seeking aid for their foundations.

Brian Ó Cuív has edited a very interesting late middle-Irish poem, *Aislinge Augustin áin* (Noble Augustine's dream) which recounts the dream that happened after the psalms of Matins.[47] He was pursued by eight wolves and fled to a great wood and climbed up a particular tree which had twenty-two branches. The wolves shook the tree and a shower fell on them. Eight drops fell from each branch on the heads of the wolves and they died immediately. Augustine wrote to Jerome to get his interpretation of the dream. The reply told him that the wolves were the eight principal vices which pursue everybody with ferocity. 'The little wood is pure constant prayer ... the great renowned wood stands for the psalms including the *Beati*.' The twenty-two branches are the number of chapters of the *Beati* and these verses are the eight drops which banish the vices. The recitation of that psalm day and night wards off the devil and invites God's protection. It is a *lorica* and shield for the soul and body against all evil. Ó Cuív suggests that the dream was invented by an Irishman to promote a devotion which was very popular as there is no indication of the dream either in St Augustine's or St Jerome's writings.[48]

Another poem, also from the same period, praises proper fasting. Brian Ó Cuív notes a correspondence between it and a homily found in the *Leabhar Breac* and in the *Liber Flavus Fergussiorum*.[49] Fasting, almsgiving and prayer are called three sisters, treasures beloved of Christ. He gave the example by His own fast as did Moses, Elias and John the Baptist. He then distinguishes between good and bad fasts:

> Fasting through necessity, fasting out of pride, fasting because of avarice, fasting for extreme gluttony, the dear Son of God is not pleased with these. Fasting from the Body of Christ is wrong (as is fasting) from learning and teaching; fasting unaccompanied by almsgiving is the eighth wrong fasting. Fasting of the body from every pleasant food and of the soul from vices brings the soul to high heaven for it is complete fasting.[50]

He continues that gluttony and lust are overcome by work, fasting and solitude. Four sets of people are not bound to fast: an old man, a young child, an ailing man or a man engaged in servile work. Fasting may also be relaxed on major pilgrimages, feast-days and Sundays. The best road to heaven is almsgiving, prayer and moderate fasting.

A poem entitled *Tráth na h-Iairmhéirghe* (The Hour of Matins) stresses the great importance of that Hour. One must rise for it if one wishes to see God and have eternal rewards. The four best things according to Jesus are charity, fasting, pilgrimage and Matins. The latter is of supreme importance and the stress placed upon it may be an indication that the monks were not rising at night for it, or it may be the extraordinary emphasis on the penitential spirit which marks Irish spirituality.[51]

A dialogue in verse attributed to Colum Cille and Baithín (*Mochean duit, a Colaim cáidh*) is also from the middle-Irish period. Dallán Forgaill, the sixth-century poet, welcomes Colum to Druim Ceat. The saint explains that the purpose of his visit was to intercede on behalf of poets, to accept their poems in his honour and to make peace between Aed Ainmerech and Aedán concerning Dál Ríada (Scotland). Dallán has a poem for Colum which he would like to recite. The latter is pleased and offers a reward but Baithín intervenes and reminds Colum that this is worldliness. A goodly section of the poem consists of arguments by Colum in favour of generosity to poets while Baithín stresses that prayer and the church are the only proper considerations. It may well reflect a twelfth-century mentality towards the rise of the bards.

> Tell me, O fair Baithín, eminent, noble cleric, would you wish that God from heaven should take your work without recompense?
>
> (Baithín): Since my labour is holy, the supreme King would not take it without my receiving thereafter from Him a hundredfold in recompense.
>
> (Colum): God from heaven takes no one's labour without recompense. No more would He wish to have another's labour than ours. God created no one of the seed of yellow-haired Adam without the gift of humanity in rewarding men with or without a divine gift.[52]

Echtgus Ó Cúanáin of Roscrea has left us a valuable poem which deals with belief in the real presence in the Eucharist, *A duine nach creit iar cóir* is dated c. 1050-1100.[53] Berengarius' condemnation and recantation with regard to belief in the real presence occurred c. 1050-70. One should also bear in mind that Bernard, in his *Life of Malachy*, refers to a 'cleric of Lismore whose life, as it is said, was good, but his faith not so' since 'he dared to say that in the eucharist there is only sacrament and not the reality signified by the sacrament' (not the real body). Echtgus gives the true doctrine concerning the real presence, based on Christ's own words. Referring to the work of the angels at the consecration bearing the host to heaven he says:

> They bring it without spending a moment, with no interval of time, holily, as I consider, to pray for the sins of all in general. Gregory speaks of three – the priest making a pure sacrifice, Christ judging our hearts and heads, and the heavenly angels giving testimony of it.[54]

Appeal is made to God's power in the Old Testament in creation out of nothing, changing one thing miraculously into another, i.e. clay which cured the blind man – water into wine. He shows the symbolism of the water and wine. 'By the water the believing people are symbolised; by the smooth wine without doubt, is understood Christ, the sinless head of all. As they, the water and the truly lovely wine, have been joined together, Christ is joined together with the church; here lies nobility and perfection of knowledge.'[55] He outlines God's power in the virgin-birth, in the miracle of crossing the Red Sea and that of the manna, and refers to a medieval miracle where the Child appears on the altar instead of the Host. He advises priests:

> If ignorant folk approach them, let them not give the bright Body till right belief has been accepted ... A blessing upon all ordained folk for the sake of the King of heaven and earth. Let them mention what precedes: let them deliver it to the people.[56]

Some time at the beginning of the eleventh century, Brian Bóraimhe sent wise men and masters to teach and to buy books abroad since many copies of the scriptures and other books had been burned in many churches. Aubrey Gwynn has drawn attention to Irish people visiting the continent in this century.[57] In 1026 Maelrúanaid Ó Maeldoraid, King of the North, went on pilgrimage to Clonfert and later to Iona and thence in 1027 to Rome where he died (*AI*). The following year, Sitric, son of Olaf Cúarán, King of the Vikings in Dublin, went with Flannucán Ó Cellaig, King of Brega (Meath), and others, as pilgrims to Rome. Flaithbertach Ó Néill, King of Ailech, known as 'Flaithbertach of the pilgrim's staff'(*in trostáin*) went to Rome in 1031 and returned the following year (*AU*). In 1034, Olaf, son of Sitric, mentioned above, set out on pilgrimage to Rome but was killed in England (*AU*). In 1042 Ó Domnaill, another northern king, went on pilgrimage to Rome (*AI*), as did Laidgnen, King of Gailenga in Meath in 1051. He brought his wife with him but he died on the way home (*AU*). Donnchad, son of Brian Bóraimhe, who lost his kingdom in 1064, went on his pilgrimage to Rome with Echmarcach, King of the Isle of Man(*AU*).

This list of royal pilgrims to Rome is pretty unique by comparison with other countries. It may be safely assumed that many other pilgrims of lesser note made their way there. One such was the cripple Gillemichel who went to Rome six times and then came to King Edward the Confessor (+1066) to be cured.[58] Cellach Ó Selbaig, Abbot of Cork, who had resigned his abbacy in 1025, went abroad on pilgrimage and died in Rome in 1036 (*AI*). There is no record of any Irish pilgrim to Rome between 1064 and 1138 when Malachy Ó Mórgair paid his first visit there. But there is the *obit* of 'Eogan head of the Irish monks in Rome' in 1095 (*AI*). This shows that there was an Irish community in Rome at least in the period of Gregory VII (+1085) and knowledge of his reforming movement which had its effect in Ireland a little later. Gwynn suggests that the presence of the community there may be explained by the personal appeal in a letter of Gregory to Toirrdelbach, King of Ireland, and all the archbishops, bishops and abbots, nobles and other Irish chieftains. 'If any matters arise among you which seem worthy of our help do not fail to send them on to us at once, and, with God's help, you will obtain your just demands.'[59] Cologne also had two small Irish communities in the eleventh century.[60] In passing let us note that Viking influence is to be seen in St Cullean's bell-shrine and the Clonmacnoise crozier, both of which are now in Dublin. They date 1050-1100. The same observation is true of the Lismore crozier, the shrine of St Lachtnán's arm and St Manchán's shrine, which are dated 1113-1130.[61]

Notes:

1. *FO*(l) lxiv.

2. *V.S.H.* I and II.

3. These Rules are mainly in verse and were very probably committed to memory.

4. It is found in 3 MSS. T.C.D. 1336, *Leabhar Breac* 11620 and the *Book of Lismore*. Tigernach's *Annals* refer to its promulgation in 737. It is also interesting that this *Rule* is incorporated in the *Rule* of the *Célí Dé*.

5. *CD* 11-12. Kathleen Hughes, *Early Christian Ireland* (New York, 1972) 91. Henceforth *ECI*. The *Beati* psalm (no.118) had a special efficacy for the dead (*Irish Texts*, I, 44).

6. It is found in 4 MSS. Brussels 5100-4; R.I.A. 23N 10 and 23P3 and T.C.D. 1285. The Brussels MS attributes it to Comgall.

7. Found in the same 4 MSS. *v.* n.6. Joseph O'Neill, 'The Rule of Ailbe', *Ériu* III (1907) 92-115. *ECI* 148. *CD* 134-5.

8. *CD* 113,179.

9. Contrast this with:

> Thou strik'st the bell that calls to prayer,
> The mist dislimns that closed us round;
> Sad cleric! thou art weary there,
> But many listen for that sound. – *Ir.Trad.* 49.

10. Found in Additional 30512; R.I.A. 23NlO, *Leabhar Breac, Yellow Book of Lecan* and Egerton 1782 and 113. For a discussion on the authorship *v.* *CD* 124-5.

11. Note that the text is in the first person plural.

12. Found in R.I.A. 23 N lO, *Leabhar Breac* and *Yellow Book of Lecan*.

13. Found in 4 MSS. Brussels 5100-4; R.I.A. 23N10, 23P3 and 23Nll. It is worth noting that the MS R.I.A. 23P3,a fifteenth-century production, whose scribe was Uilliam Mac an Legha, was written in Melaig Mór on the borders of Tipperary and Kilkenny in the house of Aedh Ócc Magraith (+1491)(*AU*). It has texts of Ailbe's *Rule*, Comgall's, Cormac's and the very poor text of *Riaghal na Manach Liath*. It also has a copy of the *Félire* of Oengus, *The Penitential*, the *Apgitir Crábaid*, the *Life of*

Brendan and the *Life of Ita, inter alia.* One wonders if the Observant movement, which had come into Ireland in the first half of the fifteenth century, had some influence on the owner or on the scribe.

14. *EIL* no. 12.

15. Ibid. no.13.

16. Ibid. p 187.

17. Ibid. no. 4.

18. Plummer, C., *Irish Litanies* (London, 1925) 78-87.

19. Ó Cuív, B., *Éigse* X (1961-3) 305-8.

20. Dr Ó Cuív translates *fath* as 'matter'. It also means 'wisdom'.

21. Ó Neill, P., *Éigse* 17, 19-46.

22. Ibid. stt. 1-2.

23. Greene, D., 'The Religious Epic', James Carney, (ed.), *Early Irish Poetry* (Cork, 1969) 79-80.

24. *EIL* no. 16.

25. *Ir Trad.* 36-7. *EIL* no.17 gives a more literal translation.

26. Herbert, M., and Ó Riain, P., *Betha Adamnáin*, ITS vol. LIV (London, 1988) 8 and 60-3.

27. Ó Fiaich, T., *Gaelscrínte i gCéin* (Áth Cliath, 1986) 37-8.

28. *EIL* no. 18.

29. Ibid. no. 19.

30. 'Old Ireland and her Poetry', *Old Ireland* (Dublin, 1965) 153-4.

31. *EIL* no. 20.

32. Ibid. no. 21.

33. Ibid. no. 26.

34. Ní Bhrolcháin, M., *Maolíosa Ó Brolcháin* (Má Nuad,1986), 13-20. Henceforth *Ní Bhrolcháin.*

35. *EIL* no. 25.

36. *EIL* no. 22.

37. *EIL* no. 23.

38. *EIL* no. 24.

39. *Ní Bhrolcháin* 42-43. B. Ó Cuív draws attention to these 3 stt. which are only in Brussels MS 20979 f. 64., *Éigse* 14, 74.

40. Ibid. 23,50-1, 54-7.

41. Ibid. 60-79. CD 173-5.

42. Carney, J., *Medieval Irish Lyrics* (Dublin, 1967) 74-9 *v.* also *Old Ireland* 155-7.

43. *Ní Bhrolcháin*, 84-7.

44. Ibid. 88-9.

45. Ibid. 78-81. In stanza 2 the text has *boethphócad* which Carney translates 'lascivious kisses', *Old Ireland*, 158-60.

46. Kenney 617.

47. *Éigse* 16 (1975-6) 1-6.

48. cf. Bergin,O .J., 'A Mystical Interpretation of the Beati', *Ériu* XI, 103-6.

49. Atkinson, R., *The Passions and Homilies from Leabhar Breac*, PRIA Todd Lecture Series Vol. II (Dublin, 1887) lines 8353-8424 and RIA23 0 48 f. 21v. *v.* also B.Ó Cuív, *Ériu* XIX, 7-9.

50. Ó Cuív, B., 'Three Middle Irish Poems', *Éigse* 16 (1975-6) 6-8.

51. Ó Cuív, B., *Éigse* 9 (1958-61) 232.

52. Ó Cuív, B., 'A Colam Cille Dialogue', *Éigse* 12 (1967-8) 165-72.

53. Murphy, G., 'Eleventh or Twelfth Century Irish Doctrine concerning the Real Presence', *Medieval Studies presented to Aubrey Gwynn S.J.*, ed. Watt, J.A., Morrall, J.B. and Martin OSA, F.X., (Dublin, 1961) 19-28.

54. Ibid. stt. 13-14.

55. Ibid. stt. 32-33.

56. Ibid. st. 82.

57. 'Ireland and the Continent', *IHS* VIII (1952-3), 201-3.

58. Bethel, D., 'English Monks and Irish Reform in the 11th and 12th Centuries', *Historical Studies* VIII, (1971)119.

59. *IHS* VIII, 201-3.

60. Irish monks also had foundations in Metz, Verdun and Fulda. *IHS* VIII, 204.

61. Ibid. 205.

CHAPTER 4

The Twelfth
and Thirteenth Centuries

'So in the fifty-fourth year of his age, Malachy, Bishop and Legate of the Holy See, was taken up from my arms by the angels of God and blissfully slept in the Lord.' (St Bernard)

The twelfth century is considered a turning-point in the history of Irish Christianity. The church in Ireland came under the influence of the Gregorian reform. Kings like Turlough O'Brien and English bishops, notably Lanfranc and Anselm, were also anxious to bring the Irish church into line with Rome and to extend their own jurisdiction. In 1095 Anselm had consecrated Maolíosa Ó hAinmhire Bishop of Waterford. Though the Bishop of Dublin, who in the eleventh century was normally an Irish Benedictine, was consecrated at Canterbury, he was reckoned more as part of the British church than of the Irish. Murtagh, son of Turlough O'Brien realised after the consecration of the Bishop of Waterford that Ireland was out of line with the church in Europe. Bernard, in his account of Maolíosa of Waterford, comments on his character:

> He was an old man full of days and virtues and the wisdom of God was in him. He was of Irish nationality but he had lived in England, in the habit and rule of a monk in the monastery of Winchester, from which he was proposed to be a bishop in Lismore, a city in Munster, and one of the noblest cities of that kingdom ... He healed a boy who was troubled with a mental disorder in the act of confirming him ... He restored hearing to one who was deaf.... For those and other such deeds his fame increased and he won a great name, so that the Scots and the Irish flowed together to him and he was reverenced by all as the father of all.[1]

In 1096, the year of his consecration but a little earlier than it, a synod was held in Waterford over which Murtagh O'Brien presided. It sent a letter to Anselm:

Holy Father, our blind ignorance has long compelled us to endure great loss to our salvation, for we have chosen rather like slaves to withdraw our necks from the yoke of the Lord than like free children to be subject to the obedience of a pastor. But now we know how profitable is pastoral care: for we call to mind the comparison with other states ... Therefore we and our King Muirchertach and Bishop Donald and Diarmuid, our duke, the King's brother do choose this priest Malchus, a monk of Walchelin, the Bishop of Winchester, who is well known to us, of noble birth and character, steeped in apostolic and ecclesiastical learning, Catholic in his faith, prudent of even temper, chaste in his life, sober, humble, affable, merciful, well-lettered, hospitable, ruling his own household well, no neophyte, but having good testimony in each of the church's orders (*in gradibus singulis*). We beg that he may be consecrated Bishop by your Paternity, so that he may be able to rule over us and help us, and that we may be able to do battle for our salvation under his rule. But that you may know that all our wishes agree on this election, we have each of us, with ready will, confirmed this canonical decree with our signatures with our hands.

I, Muirchertach, King of Ireland, have signed.

I, Duke Dermeth, the King's brother have signed.[2]

I, Bishop Dofnald, have signed.

I, Idunan, Bishop of Meath, have signed.

I, Samuel, Bishop of Dublin, have signed.

I, Ferdomnach, Bishop of the men of Leinster, have signed.[3]

The Synod of Cashel, held in 1101 under Murtagh and with Ó Dunáin as papal legate, was concerned with ecclesiastical reform. The principal decrees condemned simony and ecclesiastical exemption from secular tribute. The synod also insisted that ecclesiastical benefices could be held only by clerics. Another decree tried to prohibit or limit overlapping as well as parallel jurisdictions. The problem of the *comarba* was one which was not catered for in canon law as was the case with the airchinnech, often a layman, who was married and who occupied the church at a nominal rent, and could dispose of it to his heirs. Clerical concubinage, which was common in Europe, was forbidden, but it was to continue in Ireland to a greater or lesser degree till the seventeenth century. The right of sanctuary was to be restored. Clergy were to be exempt from secular jurisdiction. The synod also touched on the question of matrimony.[4]

From the general point of view of the church, public morality with regard to marriage was not in keeping with the Roman canons. Irish brehon law prevailed for many a century still among certain classes. This seemed to turn a blind eye to monogamy and made conditions for divorce and remarriage relatively simple. There was also a general lack of respect of human life, only too clearly evidenced in the savage mutilations among rivals for kingship.

Cellach (or Celsus), Abbot of Armagh, was ordained bishop 1105/6. In 1106 he made the circuit of Munster as one pledged to reform. As it happened, the Bishop of Armagh died so Cellach, no doubt with the whole-hearted agreement of the Bishops of Waterford and Killaloe, under Ó Dunáin, was consecrated bishop according to the Roman ritual.

The synod of Rathbreasail took place in 1111 and Murtagh O'Brien was very much in favour of reform. Gilbert, who had been consecrated Bishop of Limerick was an ardent reformer and was appointed Papal Legate in place of the retiring Ó Dunáin. Cellach was there as was Maolíosa Ó hAinmhire, who had become Archbishop of Cashel, though as yet there were no clearcut dioceses in the country. This synod set up the diocesan and parochial structures in the church and twenty-six sees were established. As this was a very large number by English or European standards, they were poorly endowed. It is worth noting that besides Muirchertach there were a fair number of laity present.

Clonmacnoise did not become a see as yet. It was not ruled by any single family as Armagh was, though it was in need of re-

form. A synod held at Uisnech made it a see a little later than
that of Rathbreasail. At this time, Clonmacnoise was associated
with the *Chronicon Scotorum*, composed by the abbot Gilla Crist
O Malone, who was present at this synod. *Lebor na hUidre* (The
Book of the Dun Cow) had been compiled a little earlier by
Maolmuire, and the so-called *Annals of Tigernach* had been compiled there. It was one of the most important monastic cities at
the turn of the century. We have seen that Ó Dunáin left Killaloe
and retired to Clonard in 1117 where he died, while Murtagh retired to Lismore probably to be in the company of Malchus Ó
hAinmhire who had retired from Cashel and died as Bishop of
Waterford in 1135.[5] Cormac MacCarthy, King of Desmond, was
hopelessly defeated by Turlough O'Connor, King of Connaught
and, to all intents, of Ireland, abdicated and entered the monastery
of Lismore in 1127.

In 1129 Cellach, while on a visit to Munster, died in Ardpatrick.
At his own request, he was buried in Lismore. He had named
Malachy as his successor but the latter was exiled, probably due
to the Cenél Eogain. The Clann Sinaig held on to the abbacy in
Armagh. However the reformers insisted that Malachy should
return from exile in Lismore to the north and, since he had episcopal consecration, take over and continue the work which
Cellach had begun. Malachy, still in the south, did a Patrician
circuit of Munster where he was accepted and the journey probably brought him very useful finances in 1134. By 1137, Niall,
Cellach's brother, who had taken the abbacy in 1135, was having
trouble with the reformers and was forced to vacate the abbacy
in 1137. Malachy entered into the full office of abbot and bishop,
but, being a shrewd man, he saw that his position was going to
cause ongoing trouble before long as he was a *persona non grata*
with the lay rulers. He suggested that he would renounce his
right to the see provided the abbot of Derry, Gilla Mac Liag, a
northerner, sympathetic to the reform and acceptable to the local
rulers, would become bishop and abbot there. He himself would
return to the monastery of Bangor and continue as Bishop of
Down. Gilla Mac Liag entered on the long years of his adminis-
tration (1137-75) without any of the painful experiences which
had made Malachy's brief tenure of office a true martyrdom of

spirit. In 1139 he went to Rome and requested the *pallium* for Armagh and Cashel from Innocent II. He refused to give them until a request should come from a general meeting of the Irish bishops, clergy and nobles but he appointed Malachy Papal Legate. The latter had wished to join the Cistercians with whom he had stayed on the way to Rome but the Pope refused his request. On his return to Ireland, he called again to Clairvaux and to Arrouaise in Flanders, leaving some of his monks in each place to learn the Cistercian and Arroasian Rules with a view to establishing these in Ireland. Mellifont was the first Cistercian monastery founded in Ireland in 1142. There may have been a small number of Benedictines in Ireland before that date but the founding of the Cistercians bore quick results and the Order experienced a rapid expansion in Ireland.

In 1148 a synod was held at Inis Pátraic near Skerries. The Irish secular rulers gave little support to it as they were then at best lukewarm towards reform. There were fifteen bishops and some two hundred clergy at the synod. Having heard Malachy's account of his visit to Rome and of the progress of the reform, it was decided that he should go again to seek the *pallia*. He was now an ailing man and had to travel through Scotland to avoid harassment by Stephen, King of England. He was a dying man when he reached Clairvaux and drew his last breath in the arms of St Bernard on 1/2 November 1148. Bernard describes the death and burial in very moving words:

> We retire but are recalled about midnight. For at this hour it is announced that a light has begun to glimmer through the darkness. The sickroom is crowded, as the whole community are assembled. There also present are several abbots who happen to be on a visit to Clairvaux. 'With psalms and hymns and spiritual canticles' we escort our friend on his way home from the land of his exile. So in the fifty-fourth year of his age, at the place and time he had himself predicted, Malachy, Bishop and Legate of the Holy See, was taken up from my arms by the angels of God and blissfully slept in the Lord …

> When the last rites were all accomplished, the sacred remains were interred in our Lady's chapel, where Malachy had loved to pray, on November 2nd in the year of grace 1148.

That holy body is now in Thy possession, o good Jesus, en-
trusted to our care. It is Thy treasure deposited with us. We
shall keep it safe for Thee and restore it whenever Thou
thinkest it well to demand it back. Only grant that Thy servant may not go forth to meet Thee at Thy coming without
us, his companions, and that, as he shared our hospitality
here, so may we share in his glory hereafter and reign with
Thee and him for ever and ever. Amen.[6]

Dr John Watt sums up his influence on the Irish Church in the
twelfth century:

From whatever angle one views the reform, the figure of
Malachy dominates the scene; whatever the issue involved –
subjection to Rome, the revivification of the episcopate
through emancipation from lay control and constitutional re-
organisation, apostolic endeavour among the people, communication with men of spiritual and intellectual stature at
home and abroad, monasticism in both its traditional and
newer forms – the name of Malachy Ó Mórgair is inseparable
from its history.[7]

Eugene III, a pupil of Bernard's, received a request for the *pallia*
in 1150. He decided to send John Cardinal Paparo to Ireland.
Paparo consulted with Gilla Mac Liag of Armagh and then came
south with Gilla Críst Ó Conairche, the first Abbot of Mellifont,
a disciple of Malachy and Bishop of Lismore. A synod was held
at Kells in March 1152 where twenty-seven bishops were present. The number of sees was increased to thirty-seven. Dublin
and Tuam were raised to the rank of archdioceses and Kells was
included as a diocese. This may have been the result of a reform
among the Columban houses which was brought about mainly
by Flaithbertach Ó Brolcháin, Abbot of Derry. The primacy of
Armagh 'of the whole of Ireland' was ratified. The synod condemned simony and concubinage. The situation seems to have
evolved into the continuation of *comarba*s among celibate occup-
ants of the sees identical in name with the old monasteries. It is
not clear how far the dioceses had been divided into parishes before the coming of the Normans.

Paparo left Ireland shortly after the synod, having appointed

Gilla Críst of Lismore papal legate. In 1152 Dermot MacMurrough, King of Leinster, carried off Dervorgilla, probably not to gratify lust but to get even with her husband and his enemy Tiernan O Rourke. The situation is further complicated by the fact that MacMurrough's own wife was a sister of Laurence O'Toole, Abbot of Glendalough. In 1153 Dervorgilla was restored and taken back by her husband. When the Cistercians' new church was formally opened at Mellifont in 1157 and consecrated by the Papal Legate, Gilla Mac Liag, the Primate and the Archbishops of Dublin and Tuam, one of the most distinguished benefactresses was Dervorgilla, who brought her husband with her. She donated sixty ounces of gold to the new church. The high king gave one hundred and sixty cows and sixty ounces of gold while the local king, Donal O'Carroll, also gave sixty ounces of gold. In 1158 MacLochlainn the high-king chaired a synod at Brí Mac Tadc, near Trim, which ratified Flaithbertach Ó Brolcháin's labours for reform in the *paruchia* of Colum Cille and in 1161 a minor synod at Dervor, near Kells, gave the *paruchia* exemption from the normal diocesan jurisdiction. Aodh Ó Críomhthainn of the monastery of Terryglass and Finn O' Gorman were associated in the composition of the *Book of Leinster*, which contains a great volume of spiritual literature, much of which derived from Tallaght but probably found a home in Terryglass through men like Maeldíthruib and possibly Oengus of Cluain Eidnech.

Professor Pádraig Ó Riain points out that 'Glendalough was one of the more important and richer of the Irish monastic cities at the turn of the twelfth century.' It was also a centre of considerable intellectual activity. The *Drummond Missal* is assigned to it and he holds that Rawlinson B 502 is 'perhaps the most accomplished of the surviving twelfth-century codices and must now be given its correct name, *Book of Glendalough*.'[8]

In 1162 Laurence O'Toole became the first genuine Irish Archbishop of Dublin. In this year a synod was held in Clane, Co Kildare. It was attended by twenty-six bishops. Training in Armagh was made obligatory on a national basis for clerics who had expectations. It also condemned the descent of the comarbship in Armagh within the Clann Sinaig. Gilla Mac Liag was present and MacMurrough was the synod's lay protector. A great synod was held in Athboy, Co Meath, in 1167. It occupied itself with the immunity of the church and also with the secular government but the warring that took place during the years that followed rendered it ineffective.

While the English Pope Adrian IV, in his Bull *Laudabiliter*, had commissioned Henry II to cross to Ireland and take possession of it and reform the church there, Henry had similar ideas of conquest but had put it on the long finger. However, MacMurrough, when driven out of his Kingdom of Leinster, went to Henry and brought back with him the first of the Anglo-Normans in 1167 when they landed in Glascarrig in Wexford.

* * *

Professor F.X. Martin has written:

> The tragedy of the Norman Invasion was not the conquest of Ireland – for that never took place – but the half conquest. The Normans never came in sufficient numbers to complete the conquest while the kings of England, on whom rested the responsibility for peace and progress in Ireland, were either too jealous to assist their barons in Ireland or too distracted by dangers in England and wars on the continent to turn their minds seriously to the Irish problem ... By the year 1300 there was a drawn battle, with the Normans controlling most of the country but the tide was already beginning to turn against them. The Irish question had become part of the heritage between Ireland and England. (*CIH*, 142-3)

With the advent of the thirteenth century, bishoprics were being subdivided into parishes and monastic chapters were being changed into canonical ones. The church was becoming more European and had some influence in Europe due to the Irish monasteries at Cologne and Rome, to the *inclusi* of the Schottenklöster in Germany and Austria and also to Irishmen like Peter of Ireland, who was one of Thomas Aquinas' teachers, and William of Drogheda, who lived in Oxford and was well versed in law and died in 1244. Thomas of Ireland, author of the *Manipulus Florum*, a collection of quotations from scripture and the Fathers, mainly on subjects such as humility, virginity, etc. and probably used by preachers, was a secular priest who died probably before 1328. He had studied at the Sorbonne and on his death he willed all his books and money to that University, where he had worked.

The Augustinian Canons and Benedictines had strengthened their position in Ireland and the Mendicant Orders had been arriving throughout the century, the Dominicans in 1224, the Franciscans c. 1230, the Carmelites and Augustinians in the second half of the century. By 1336, eighty-six friaries had been founded, many of them by Normans. In the case of the older Irish monasteries, the most persistent abuse seems to have been hereditary possession and succession, e.g. Derry had been in the hands of the Cearbhalláin family from 1185 till 1293. It was practically taken for granted, as is seen in Clement III's ruling in 1190, that the son of an Irish bishop, if born before his father's ordination to the see, could become a priest and hold a benefice in his father's diocese.

Up to this century, church councils included both Irish and Norman higher clergy. The last such council seems to have been in 1217.[9] Naturally enough animosity between the 'two nations' was growing. Attempts by the Normans or by the King of England to exclude Irishmen from the office of bishop were resisted, though not always effectively, by the papacy. Armagh and Tuam generally had Irish incumbents while Dublin, after Laurence O'Toole, was always held by Englishmen. By 1254 roughly one-third of the sees were occupied by foreigners and this state of affairs increased in the second half of the century. The papacy, after Innocent III, seems to have had little influence on Irish affairs. The last papal legate was James the Penitentiary and his mission to Ireland in 1221 seems to have been largely a financial one as 'he collected horseloads of gold and silver from the clerics of Ireland through simony.'[10]

The Mendicants were based mainly in urban areas in the beginning and made a very notable contribution to pastoral care and intellectual achievement. Little could be expected from the lower diocesan clergy since they were poorly paid. Quite a number of Mendicants were educated in England or on the continent and these provided teachers for the *studia particularia* or *generalia* in Ireland which educated not only their own students but probably secular students and students from other Orders.

* * *

From 1169 onwards, the Norman invasion penetrated the south, then to the east and gradually through a good section of the country. Henry II came to Ireland in 1171 and kings and bishops did homage to him. The synod of Cashel in 1171 had Gilla Críst of Lismore as its president. The Archbishops of Dublin and Tuam attended but Gilla Mac Liag was too old to travel from Armagh. The chief matter for discussion was public morality in the matter of marriage, though tithes, bequests and Masses for the dead and baptism were also on the agenda. Once again the immunity of the clergy from tribute and from coshering was asserted.[11]

Laurence O'Toole was a fearless upholder of the rights of the church. While he took very strong action against priests who failed to observe celibacy, sending forty of them to Rome for absolution, when he could have given it himself, he worked very diligently in the pastoral care of his flock. Despite certain prohibitions placed on him by Henry II, he attended the Third Lateran Council in 1179 and was appointed Papal Legate for Ireland. He played an important role as an intermediary between the Irish rulers and the Norman invaders in 1170-71, and in 1175 he negotiated the Treaty of Windsor between Ruaidhrí O'Connor, King of Ireland, and Henry, when the former became a vassal of the latter under certain conditions. He showed great social concern in the severe winter 1179-80 and relieved the hunger-stricken either by aid which he managed to gather in the diocese or by sending some of the poor to his friends in Britian to be cared for till the situation improved. Meanwhile trouble was again brewing between Ruaidhrí and Henry. Laurence took Ruaidhrí's son to England as he tried to treat with Henry. But the king ignored him save for forbidding him to return to Ireland. When Henry went to France, Laurence followed him hoping to make peace between the two kings but he died at Eu in Normandy in 1180. He was canonised by Honorius III in 1226, who summed up his spiritual life in the words 'he was totally dedicated to God, indefatigable in his prayer, stern in his bodily penances, unstinting in his almsgiving.'

It is obvious that the twelfth century used the machinery of Councils to try to promote reform in Ireland. In the majority of cases, we have only the decrees of some and no further detail except in the case of the Council which the Archbishop of Dublin, John Cumin, Laurence O'Toole's successor, opened in Holy Trinity Cathedral on Laetare Sunday in 1186. Giraldus Cambrensis attended and gave two accounts in his autobiography and again in *Topographia Hiberniae*. An account of the proceedings has been given by Dr Watt. The archbishop opened the Council with a sermon on the sacraments. The Council pronounced upon the use of wooden tables as altars, praised clerical celibacy among the Irish and noted that the English clergy failed in this matter. Giraldus himself addressed the Council and, while praising clerical celibacy among the Irish, criticised their lack of pastoral care of the people. Dr Watt concludes:

> The remainder of the decrees show affinity with points made by Giraldus in his sermon. It was ordered under canonical penalty that the tithe be paid 'from provisions, hay, the young animals, flax, wool, gardens, orchards and from all things which grow and renew themselves yearly'. It was decreed that no one should be buried in any churchyard which had not been consecrated by a bishop as a burial ground and that no burials should take place without the presence of a priest. Laity who violated ecclesiastical liberty, especially by introducing priests into benefices, were put under sentence of excommunication, as also were those priests who accepted benefices or ecclesiastical possessions uncanonically.

Giraldus has presented a picture of the rivalries between the native clergy and the invader. But it is clear that though the exchanges were sharp, it was not an antagonism that made co-operation impossible. There is other evidence from this period that prelates of each nation found it possible to work together. In 1192, when the new St Patrick's was consecrated, the occasion was graced by Tomaltach O'Connor, Archbishop of Armagh and Archbishop O'Heney of Cashel. The latter, in his capacity as Papal Legate, presided over another reforming Council. Unfortunately its decrees have not survived, nor have we any account of its proceedings.[12]

Literature

The poem, *Tuc dam a Dé móir*, which is a prayer for the gift of tears, is probably a twelfth-century composition.[13] The anonymous poet asks God for great waves of tears so that he may avoid pain in the next life. He laments that tears do not come to cleanse him both in heart and body. He appeals particularly to God's goodness and pleads for 'a well of tears'. The final stanza is very personal in its appeal: 'O my love, my God may Thy blood flow in my heart. Who but Thee, O God, will give me tears?'[14]

A short poem, *Mo labrad*, probably also from this century,[15] seeks to praise God by the use of speech to express the love of the poet's heart for the King of heaven and earth. 'Make it easy for me to do Thee all service and to adore Thee'. He appeals to God: 'O Father of all affection, hear my poems, hear my speech.'[16]

Quite a number of twelfth-century poems have been fathered on Colum Cille and Gerard Murphy has edited some of them.[17] In general they treat of his great longing for his Irish monasteries and for Gartan, his birthplace. *Robad mellach, a Meic mo Dé* (It would be pleasant, O son of my God) is, as Murphy says, an exile's dream to cross over Lough Foyle, to visit Durrow, to hear the music of the wind in the trees and hear the startled cry of the blackbird, to listen to the stags in the early morning, to hear the cuckoo's call, to pass the night with Comgall and to visit Cainneach.[18] The quatrain 'This is why I love Derry, it is so calm and bright, for it is full of white angels from one end to the other', may voice the sentiments of a twelfth-century Derryman, who was a great admirer of the saint.[19] The last collection, *Is scíth mo chrobh ón scríbinn*, also attributed to Colum but dated eleventh or twelfth century, is often quoted and with good reason as it reveals the mentality of a hardworking scribe, a person frequently mentioned in the annals:

My hand is weary with writing; my sharp great point is not thick; my slender-beaked pen juts forth a beetle-hued draught of bright blue ink. A steady stream of wisdom streams from my well-coloured neat fair hand; on the page it pours its draught of ink of the green-skinned holly.

I send my little dripping pen unceasingly over the assemblage of books of great beauty, to enrich the possession of men of art - whence my hand is weary with writing.[20]

In this period, Derry was gradually replacing Kells as the head of Colum's *paruchia* in the twelfth century. Colum's connection with Derry is stressed especially in poems 29, 31 and 32 in *EIL*, which date from the period when Derry was the more noted of these monasteries. The middle-Irish *Life of Colum Cille*, c. 1150-82, is a more spiritual writing than the ordinary *Vita* and might be better described as a homily. In it Derry appears as a much more important monastery than Kells, which does not seem to have been deeply influenced by the reform. This may be due to the fact that there were frequent wars in the surrounding territory. This *Vita* would have afforded considerable help in justifying the transfer of the comarbship of the *paruchia* to the Abbot of Derry for the first time in 1150. Hitherto it had been the prerogative of the Abbot of Kells.[21]

One also notes a development in the *Suibne Geilt* story which seems to have its literary origins c. AD 800. The twelfth-century poem, *M'airiuclán hi Tuaim Inbir* (My little oratory in Tuaim Inbir), describes his contentment with his natural cell or oratory provided by God who is master of nature. There beauty surrounds him and peace reigns within.[22] Towards the middle of the twelfth century other poems are 'fathered' on him. *Gáir na Gairbhe glaidbinne* (The cry of the Garb) describes his appreciation of this river with its fish and tides. It reminds one of the earlier personal poems and perhaps may be interpreted as a revival of that spirit in the twelfth century.

Musical birds on the shore, music-sweet their constant cryings! Lonely longing has seized me to hear their chanting as they sing the Hours. I love to hear blackbirds warbling and listen to Mass ... Chanting of the pure psalms at Rinn Ross

Bruic ... it is hard to attend the canonical Hours at which loud bells are rung by reason of the noise of Inber Dubglaise and the cry of the Garb.

... Beloved Moling to whom I have come to play the end of my game, may you protect me against hell whose cry is rough.

This poem is dated c.1150.[23] A curious mixture of love and pity is seen in the exchanges between Suibne and Eorann, his wife, who had married Guaire after Suibne's madness had come upon him (*EIL* No 45). The poem *Suanach sin, a Eórann án* (Sleep is your lot, o lovely Eorann) is dated c.1175. One admires Suibne's understanding of her choice and Eorann's reply that she would be his loving wife 'were it in my power'. His hard life and her comfortable life are contrasted but her wish is that she could be with him. A poem from the same period, *Mór múich i túsa in-nocht* (I am in great grief to-night), portrays Suibne lamenting his sad lot in the cold, wind and rain, frost and snow.

Gloomy is the life of one who has no house; it is a wretched life, good Christ ... falling from the tops of withered branches, going through furze, shunning mankind, keeping company with wolves ... hearing neither voice nor speech ... Son of God, it is a cause of grief.[24]

An Irish litany of Our Lady is found in the *Leabhar Breac*. It may be earlier but it cannot be later than the twelfth century. It is the oldest Gaelic litany to Mary.

O great Mary,
O greatest of Marys,
O paragon of women,
O queen of the angels,
O lady of heaven,
O lady full and overflowing with the grace of the Holy Spirit,
O blessed and more than blessed one,
O mother of eternal glory,
O mother of the church in heaven and earth,[25]
O mother of affection and forgiveness,
O mother of the golden light,

O honour of the ether,
O sign of gentleness,
O gate of heaven,
O golden casket,
O bed of kindness and compassion,
O temple of the Deity,
O beauty of virgins,
O lady of the nations,
O fountain of the gardens,
O cleansing of sins,
O washing of souls,
O mother of orphans,
O breast of infants,
O consolation of the wretched,
O star of the sea,
O handmaid of God,
O mother of Christ,
O spouse of the Lord,
O beauteous as a dove,
O lovely as the moon,
O elect as the sun,
O repulse of Eve's reproach,
O renewal of life,
O beauty of women,
O chief of virgins,
O garden enclosed,
O sealed fountain,
O mother of God,
O perpetual virgin,
O holy virgin,
O prudent virgin,
O beauteous virgin,
O chaste virgin,
O temple of the living God,
O throne of the eternal King,
O sanctuary of the Holy Ghost,
O virgin of the stem of Jesse,
O cedar of Lebanon,
O cypress of Zion,

O crimson rose of the land of Jacob,
O flourishing as a palm,
O fruitful as an olive tree,
O glorious Son-bearer,
O light of Nazareth,
O beauty of the world,
O highborn of christian people,
O queen of the world,
O ladder of heaven,

We also pray and entreat thee, O Holy Mary, through thy mighty intercession with thine only Son, Jesus Christ, Son of the living God, that He would protect us from all straits and temptations.

And request for us from the God of creation, that we may all receive from Him remission and forgiveness of all our sins and offences, and that we may obtain from Him also by thy intercession an eternal abode in the heavenly kingdom for ever and ever, in the presence of the saints and holy virgins of the world. May we merit it, may we inhabit it, *in saecula saeculorum*. Amen. [26]

Mary's image finds a place in seals from about the twelfth century. An inscription (difficult to read) 'the seal of the fraternity of Blessed Mary of Kyllesse' is found at the foot of her statue. In the centre she is seated under a richly ornamented triple canopy with the Infant Jesus on her right hip or arm.[27] Two other references to her are worth mentioning, *Triamhuin Ghormlaithe*[28] (twelfth/thirteenth century?) and a poem to Colum Cille, *Dia mór dom imdeghail*, (twelfth century?).[29] Gormlaith describes and laments her three husbands at their deaths and concludes: 'O king of the stars, may you forgive Niall, since he no longer lives. O Mary, shelter me since I am sad and broken.' (Stanza 13)

Stanza 80 of the latter has a reference to Our Lady. Professor Brian Ó Cuív suggests this translation: 'Royal is the arrangement which the virgins have for anyone who possesses virginity without doubt (condition); Mary exhorts them, she instructs them, she desires that her Son should have large communities (*muintera*).[30] If it is twelfth century, it may refer to the new communities then making their appearance in Ireland.

Frederic MacDonnacha OFM made a study of preaching between the years 1000-1200 and gives a very valuable summary
of sermons or homilies for the period which are found mainly in
the *Leabhar Breac, Leabhar na hUidhre* and *Leabhar Mhic Carthaigh
Riabhaigh.* He divides the material into five groups:

1: Sermons throughout the year, e.g. for the Circumcision,
Epiphany, Our Lord's fast, Palm Sunday, Spy Wednesday,
the Last Supper, the Passion, The Harrowing of Hell, Easter
and Low Sunday and Pentecost Sunday.

2: Duties of the Christian life, i.e. charity, alms-giving, the
Our Father, fasting, the duties of kings.

3: On our final end: Discussion of the soul with the body at
death, the Vision of Adomnan (preview of heaven and hell),
judgement and resurrection.

4: Passions of martyrs – George, Stephen, Peter and Paul, the
Maccabees, Michael.

5: Lives of the saints – Brendan, Brigid, Ciaran, Colum Cille,
Finian Mochua, Patrick, Senan, found in the *Leabhar Mhic
Carthaigh Riabhaigh.*

He mentions other saints' Lives found elsewhere. One or two excerpts will give us a taste of what the homilies were like. In the
sermon on the Lord's Supper the preacher treats of the Body of
Christ, of the Mass and reception of Holy Communion:

Holy preachers explain the Body of Christ in three ways;
first: His Human Body born of the Virgin Mary without loss
of her virginity; second: the Holy Church i.e. the perfect community of all the faithful – their head is the Saviour, Jesus
Christ, the Son of God: third: Holy Scripture in which the
pure mystery of Christ's Body and Blood is recorded.

Wherefore the question arises – since Christ was crucified
only once for us, what use is it for us to offer the sacrifice of
the Body and Blood of Christ every day? This is the use (reason). Since we sin daily we need to be cleansed every day
from these sins and furthermore that we may not be allowed
by the church to forget Christ's crucifixion since it is recalled
every day in the sacrifice. For who, among the faithful, as
Gregory assures us, doubts that when the priest raises his

voice in the sacrifice heaven opens and the choirs of angels descend and the heavenly and earthly church is united and intimately bonded?'[31]

Speaking of the reception of the Eucharist he says:

We must understand that the Body and Blood of Christ has two enemies – the one who receives it in sin and the one without sin who does not receive it through laziness or weakness of faith. The sacrifice has two genuine friends – the person who receives it frequently in honour of and with respect for the Lord and the person who does not receive it at all because of his humility and poor opinion of himself.

Just as one would not dare to put Christ's Body in a cloth or in a vessel that was not clean, all the more should one fear that it be placed in a body stained by sin or vice.

The following is an excerpt from a sermon on charity where various forms of alms-giving are recommended:

Almsgiving is the third part of holiness and as it is (said) alms, fasting and prayer. There are two types of almsgiving – to one's self and to one's neighbour, and there are two further divisions of this; corporal and spiritual. There are six types of corporal almsgiving to one's neighbour – food to the poor, drink to the thirsty, clothes to the naked, kindness and hospitality to those who need them, visiting the sick, ministering to those in prison.

Spiritual almsgiving, however, is much better for the soul which is made in the image and likeness of God – satisfying it with the food of divine teaching – then succouring the body which is made of earthly clay and relieving it from its earthly needs. It is right, though, to give alms from human consideration even to a sinner if he is poor, since it is not for his sins he is loved but because he is a human being. The person who is without the virtue of almsgiving lacks all virtue; but he who possess it has all goodness, virtue and good deeds. Though the alms is given to the poor it is really Christ who receives it for the breast of the poor today is the chest in which the jewels and wealth of the Lord is kept yonder.[32]

* * *

There were bardic schools operating and others probably under the direction of an *ollamh*, who, while first mentioned in the annals in 1041 (*AU*), begin to be mentioned more frequently in the annals in this and later centuries. The deaths of bards are first recorded in the twelfth century. These schools were well organised. Irish, Latin, grammar, singing, poetry, rhetoric, philosophy and theology were thus available, particularly to the nobility and the future clergy. Poetry is one of modes of praise and also of teaching. In an account written c. 1580,[33] we are informed that the bards fasted and prayed before writing religious poetry. This is evident in men of the calibre of Donnchadh Mór Ó Dálaigh. He was probably a layman although there are some reasons for believing that he may have been a cleric.[34] His poems have left a deep imprint on the Irish mind and heart. Prayer to God is vital for the spiritual life, writes an anonymous bard:

> *Díomhain do dhuine ar domhan*
> *bheith ag iarraidh ealadhan*
> *nó a mheas go bhfuighe sé sin*
> *gan guidhe Dé do dhéinimh.*

He points out that it is useless to seek knowledge or to think that one can acquire it without prayer. This reminds us of the earlier pithy quatrain so well translated by Robin Flower:

> 'Tis sad to see the sons of learning
> in everlasting hellfire burning,
> while he who never read a line
> doth in eternal glory shine.[35]

Donnchadh's spirituality is based on the gospel. 'My prayer (to Mary's Son) at lying down and rising is that He may be my path to God.'

The principal religious subjects treated of in bardic poetry are the mystery of the Trinity, Creation, the Annunciation, the Incarnation and Infancy, the Passion, the Cross, the Crucifixion, the Wounds, especially the piercing of the side with the spear, His Descent into hell, Mary, judgement, heaven, sin and repentance, the angels and saints.

Donnchadh Mór prays both the divine Hours and the Hours of

Mary to protect him against vice. He stresses the necessity of cultivating ascetic practices and the virtues. He appeals to the Passion and seeks union with the angels and saints. He concludes by stating that he seeks to imitate Christ: 'My prayer at lying down and rising is that He be my path to God, be my end peaceful or violent'. Here we see a sign of the times. He gives a nice summary of his devotion to Our Lady:

> Woe to him who neglects the Hours of Mary, white-handed, gold-headed maid; her long hair is as gold thread; all men pray to her at the altar. Altar of the heavenly church, nurse of our God's Son, mother of heaven's noble King, Adam's race beseeches her. Mary's prayer to her Son – may the Virgin guard me to the joy of the chosen household against the dark demons.[36]

Treating of the relationship of body and soul – the former being a dead weight which the latter has to bear – he appeals for help:

> For 76 years I have been misled in folly by it from glen to glen: That I feel no fear is, I think, my danger. By thy power, noble Mary, nurse of the royal Prince, bring me when my term is ended, to the cloud-hidden fort of the wondrous valley. (*Mary*, 83).

The poem *Éisd rem' fhaoisdin, a Íosa* (Listen to my confession, Jesus) is found in seven manuscripts. It is in the nature of a public confession and has a sincerity that is often lacking in bardic poetry. The examination of conscience is very searching: the 7 or 8 deadly sins, the 10 commandments, the violation of church holidays, neglect in paying tithes of cattle and corn, impure deeds, calumny, failure to fast, omission of the Hours, putting off confession till one was old. Having accused himself he says, 'I have now turned my steps to Thee … I call heaven my country … Till to-night I have hidden my sin – a poor kind of religion … May Jesus' mother save me from God's wrath; may the mother of the world's Lord be not angry with His kinsman.' Donnchadh had a very realistic grasp of the gospel when he wrote of charity to the poor as the sign of Christ: 'I was the poor man at the door, thirsty and hungry – without mention of food or drink for me, and you in your comfort … you who saw me in that condition, go to the house of the devil'.[37]

Another poem attributed to him expresses deep feelings:

> Wrens of the lake, I love them all,
> They come to matins at my call,
> The wren whose nest lets through the rain,
> He is my goose, my cock, my crane.
>
> My little bard, my man of song
> Went on a foray all day long;
> Three midges were the poet's prey,
> He cannot eat them in a day.
>
> He caught them in his little feet,
> His brown claws closed about the meat;
> His chicks for dinner gather round,
> Sure, if it rains they'll all be drowned.
>
> The crested plover's lost her young,
> With bitter grief my heart is stung,
> Two little chicks she had – they're gone;
> The wren's round dozen still lives on.[38]

Lines like these bring one back in the tradition of the early nature poetry. From the same period or perhaps a little later come these lines:

> Sadly the ousel sings. I know
> No less than he a world of woe.
> The robbers of his nest have ta'en
> His eggs and his younglings slain.
>
> So in my anguish I complain
> All day for wife and young ones slain;
> They go not out and in my door,
> No marvel, my sad heart is sore.[39]

Rarely do we find lines like these in medieval Gaelic poetry. A short poem of five stanzas, *Día do bheatha-sa a Mhuire*, has recently been attributed to Donnchadh. It seems to be an early Christmas carol composed on Christmas night. Donnchadh Mór died in 1244 and was buried in the Cistercian abbey of Boyle.[40]

Another member of the Ó Dálaigh clan, Muireadhach Albanach, had slain a steward of O'Donnell's and had to flee to Scotland – hence the epithet Albanach. From here he seems to have visited the continent and possibly the Holy Land. Eventually he was able to return to Ireland with O'Donnell's forgiveness and blessing. His poems date from the first half of the thirteenth century. *An foltsa Dhuit, a Dhé Athair*, is attributed to him. It seems to have been written on the occasion of his receiving the tonsure. It shows the appreciation of a man's locks and what a thirteenth-century man considered as personal physical beauty.

This hair I offer Thee, O God, the Father; 'tis a slight gift yet one hard to give; grievous till now have been my sins: I offer my hair in their requital.

I feel sorry for this fair hair ... shorn from its curly head, I should be resigned to this for it would have withered (in any case) of itself.

The two of us offer Thee, O Son of Mary, our comely yellow locks ... But Christ's Body was more comely, more beauteous the head, greyer the eye, whiter the foot.

Brighter was the foot and the slender body, smoother the breast like to a bush-blossom; whiter the pierced foot and brighter the hand, more gleaming the teeth, darker the brow, smoother the face ... greater the beauty of the curling tresses, smoother the cheek, more wavy the hair.[41]

In another poem, *Déana mo theagosg, a Thríonóid*, he seems to be a (Franciscan) friar. He asks the Triune God to bless and teach him. He describes the Incarnation very beautifully:

Pure camest Thou on earth as the flower comes on the streambank or as the ice comes on the water ... Virginal was Thy conception and Thy Baptism, nobly did'st Thou take a Body; pure wert Thou conceived in Mary's womb; no other conception befitted Thee.

In the poem, *Éistidh riomsa a Mhuire mhór*, which Dr Bergin attributes to him, he expresses the thought that Mary is closest to the Trinity: 'O Trinity, O gentle Mary, every glory but yours is passing; listen to my poem, O four persons, no reward of gold will be accepted from you'. Muireadhach also uses the words *Eó na dtrí tobar* of Christ (salmon of the three wells).[42] Another poem, *Do chros féin duit, a Dhúilimh* (Thy own Cross to Thee, O Creator), considered to be his, suggests the pilgrim crusader.

I am carrying it (the cross) assiduously for Thee ... it has been two years on my back without encountering anyone from Ireland ¬ We have come across three seas to the wave-furrowed Mediterranean Sea, having put out from Ireland's shore ... Since I have put the golden Cross on Thy altar, O God the Father, give me a fringed (pilgrim's) cloak ... Here the miserable body, O Son of the Virgin, O beloved One, is as a crucifier for the Lord, – such is the wrongdoing of a multitude. This head I shall place in Thy yoke and this hand in Thy tapering-topped hand; bring my foot to Thy house according to Thy will, Thy own cross I offer Thee, O Creator.[43]

Giolla Bríghde MacConmídhe, a thirteenth-century poet – the family supplied *ollamhs* to the Uí Néill from an early date – is probably the author of the poem *Fuigheall beannacht brú Mhuire* (Mary's womb is overflowing with blessings) which describes her as 'the key which has saved multitudes and unlocked the door for all in trouble'. He is well-acquainted with the apocrypha as were many medieval poets and writers. He relies on his relationship with Mary to save him: 'May the mother of God raise me up erect – we are of the same blood and earthly flesh – I should be set free for the sake of that fair branch coming from golden fruit'.[44]

Just as in Europe, devotion to Mary developed both among the laity and clergy in this century. It is related in the *Life of St Laurence O'Toole* that he built a church 'St Mary le Dam' on Cork Hill in Dublin with the aid of money promised to him by merchants travelling to England on the same boat, on the occasion of a severe storm.[45] In Gwynn-Hadcock's account of medieval Irish monasteries, fifty-one churches or monasteries are mentioned as dedicated to Our Lady in the thirteenth century. The annals also supply us with the little items relating to this devotion. We learn that Maelbrigte Ó Maicín, Abbot of Ballintobber, built the church, sanctuary and Crosses there in honour of Patrick, *Muire Bantighearna* (Mary the Queen), John and the apostles.[46] Donatus, elected Bishop of Limerick in 1231, declared that the celebration of Mass in honour of Our Lady, the patron, was the first duty of the Chapter.[47] Rejoicing and merrymaking were part of the celebration of her feasts. In 1234, Henry III granted

Luke, Archbishop of Dublin, and his successors a yearly holiday at his manor in Ballimor to last for eight days at the feast of the Assumption.[48] Five years later the annals note: 'Lasarfina, daughter of Cathal Crobhderg and wife of Ó Domhnaill, gave a half townland of her marriage-estate, Rossborne, to Clarus MacMailín, and the community of Canons on Trinity Island in Loch Cé this year in honour of the Trinity and Mary, Queen.[49]

From the liturgical angle, we notice that the *Félire Uí Ghormáin*, written by the Abbot of Louth between 1171 and 1174, served to maintain and increase devotion to the Irish saints as the compiler states that he wrote it because he felt that Oengus had omitted a great number of Irish saints. One notes also the introduction of octaves and vigils with greater frequency. The Normans influenced the liturgy when they introduced the Sarum rite in St Patrick's c. 1220. The Mendicant Orders, especially the Dominicans and Carmelites, brought their own particular rites with them and they gradually included Irish saints in their calenders.

Some sections of the *Leabhar Breac* are dated as prior to 1200. The sermon on the ten commandments belongs to the thirteenth century. Such is also the case with the *Book of Uí Maine* (written 1360-1427), e.g. *Sex Aetates Mundi* and some of the apocrypha and poems. The British Library (Royal 6B III) contains a copy of Gregory I's *Letters* copied c. 1200 which belonged to the Cistercian monastery of Graignamanagh while MS C.5.8. in Trinity College, Dublin, which may have been written in Ireland in the second half of the thirteenth century, has sermons for the year and treatises on Canon Law and the sacraments, on various virtues and vices and on a variety of spiritual topics. As these were in Latin they were available only to the learned.

Another manuscript in Trinity College, B. 3. 5., written in Ireland in the thirteenth century seems to have belonged to the monastery of St Thomas in Dublin. Obviously it was primarily for the Augustinian Canons and had Hugh of St Victor's *Exposition of the Rule of St Augustine* and a work by Richard of St Victor on the same subject. It also contains the *Liber Ordinis S. Victoris* which has rules for monks and clerics, a list of Epistles and Gospels for the year, the Rules of SS. Benedict and Francis and papal decrees from Gregory IX and Nicholas III concerning the Franciscans. It also has rules about the anchoritic life and readings from the Fathers to be read in community throughout the year. It also includes a copy of Innocent III's *De miseria humanae condicionis* and verses on proper behaviour in the church.

The Archbishop of Dublin, Fulk of Sandford (1256-71), drew up a code of 48 laws, many of them borrowed from English legislation, in which the public respectability of the clergy had a prominent place. Watt says:

> They were wont to discuss the matter of correct clerical conduct under four headings: diligence in the performance of the priestly office; moral rectitude, dress and deportment, abstention from unsuitable activities. All these occur in the Dublin decrees in one form or another. Priests must be punctilious about performing the services of the church, about sick visiting, proper maintenance of the fabric and furnishings of the churches and the custody of the Blessed Sacrament and the holy oils. Just as their lives must be separate from the lives of the people, so their dress and deportment should demonstrate that separation. Considerable attention was given to the preservation of chastity, the prevention, detection and punishment of it figure prominently in these decrees. Priests' concubines were to be compelled under pain of excommunication to do penance; if they defied this censure, they would be coerced by the civil power. Priests were required to observe the precept of St. Paul: 'In the army, no soldier gets himself mixed up in civilian life because he must be at the disposal of the man who enlisted him' (2 Tim. 2.4.) ...
>
> The laity figured as subjects (*subditi*) whose vices were to be tracked down and denounced. The clergy were to hold regular meetings to prepare and issue such denunciations. Excommunication *ipso facto* was the punishment for a wide variety of offences against ecclesiastical liberty (i.e. the freedom of churchmen in their own concerns) and public order. The common use of excommunication perhaps in part explains the provision that no parish priest should hear the confession of, or give Holy Communion to, anyone from

another parish, without the licence of the parish priest. The absence of such a check would enable an excommunicate to frequent the sacraments of which his sentence had deprived him.[50]

Another characteristic feature of these decrees as they affected the laity concerned marriage. Clandestine marriages (i.e. those contracted without the presence of a priest) were strictly forbidden; even bethrothals should be contracted in the presence of a priest.[51]

With regard to the knowledge required of priests in thirteenth-century Europe, K.A. Fink says:

Shockingly slight was the indispensable minimum of knowledge which thirteenth century theologians required of the priest and with which perhaps persons were probably satisfied in practice. The Dominican Ulric of Strasbourg (1277) expressed it in the following manner and this was adopted by the canonists: 'To the extent that a priest is obliged to the celebration and worship of God, he must know enough grammar to be able to pronounce and accent the words correctly and to understand at least the literal sense of what he reads. As minister of the sacraments he must know the essential form of a sacrament and the correct manner of administering it. As teacher he must know at least the basic doctrine of faith proving itself effective in charity. As judge in matters of conscience he must be able to distinguish between what is sin and what is not and between sin and sin.[52]

Notes:

1. Lawlor, H.J., *St Bernard's Life of Malachy of Armagh* (London, 1920) 20.

2. Gwynn suggests *dux* may be the equivalent of *Tánaiste*.

3. Gwynn, A., S.J., 'Origins of the Diocese of Waterford', *IER* LIX (1942) 292.

4. cf. Dolley, M., *Anglo-Norman Ireland* (Dublin, 1972) 8.

5. Ibid. 11-20.

6. Luddy O. Cist., A. J., *The Life of St Malachy* (Dublin, 1930) 107-109.

7. *The Church and the Two Nations* (Cambridge, 1970) 19.

8. 'The Book of Glendalough or Rawlinson B 502', *Éigse* XVIII (1977-9) 161-76.

9. Watt, J., *The Church in Medieval Ireland* (Dublin, 1972) 157.

10. *Annals of Loch Cé (ALC)* 1221.

11. cf. Dolley, op. cit. 70.

12. Watt, op. cit. 152-7.

13. *EIL* p 201.

14. Ibid. No. 27.

15. Ibid. p 201.

16. Ibid. No. 28.

17. Ibid. Nos. 29-33.

18. No. 30. Murphy dates it c. AD 1000.

19. Ibid. No. 32.

20. Ibid. No. 33.

21. Herbert, M., 'Beatha Mheán-Ghaeilge Cholm Cille', *Léachtaí Cholm Cille* XV (1985) 127-35.

22. *EIL*. No. 43.

23. Ibid. No. 44.

24. Ibid. Nos. 45–47.

25. This title is used also in Vatican II.

26. *Mary*, 70. This was a common ending. cf *Mary* p 72, no. 134.

27. *JRSAI* (1895) 82-4.

28. Ed. O'Sullivan, A., *Ériu* XVI (1952) 188-199.

29. Meyer, K., *ZCP* VIII, (1912) 198-217.

30. I am indebted to Professor B. Ó Cuív for this.

31. Note that Mass was celebrated daily.

32. Mac Donncha, OFM, F., 'Seanmóireacht in Éirinn ó 1000 go 1200', *An Léann Eaglasta 1000-1200* (eag. M. Mac Conmara MSC) (Áth Cliath, 1982) 77-95, and there is a homily on the duty of constant thanksgiving to God from the ninth century, J. Strachan, *Ériu* III (1907) 3-7.

33. *Arch. Hib.* (1916) 19.

34. *Mary* 75-89.

35. *Ir. Trad.* 46.

36. *Mary* 76.

37. *Di. D.* Poem 29 stt. 25-28.

38. *Ir. Trad.* 80.

39. Ibid. 80-81.

40. *Mary* 75-89 where there is long discussion on him.

41. Ibid. 89-90.

42. Ibid. 89-91.

43. Ó Cuív, B., 'A Pilgrim's Poem', *Éigse* 13 (1969-70) 105-9.

44. *Mary* 91-2.

45. Legris, M. Abbé, *Life of St Laurence O'Toole* (Dublin, 1914) 62-3.

46. Annals of Connacht 1225. *ALC* I, 291.

47. Hand, G., 'The Church in the English Lordship 1216-1307', *History of Irish Catholicism* II pt. 3 (Dublin, 1968) 15.

48. *Journal of the Kildare Archaeological Society* VIII, 425.

49. *Ann Conn*. 1239. cf. Concannon, H., *The Queen of Ireland* (Dublin, 1938) 22, 72 and *Ann. Conn*. 1248, for further indications of this devotion.

50. This smacks of the Inquisition which was in use in Europe at the time.

51. Watt, op. cit. 158-60.

52. Jedin, H., *History of the Church* (London, 1980) IV, 575-6.

CHAPTER 5

The Fourteenth
and Fifteenth centuries

'I parted from Éire for love of God.' (*Tadhg Camcosach Ó Dálaigh*)

Though the Normans occupied a considerable part of the country by the beginning of the fourteenth century, it was becoming clearer that the gap between the two nations was unbridgeable. The fact that the Papacy settled in Avignon from 1305 till 1378 meant that new sources of finance had to be found. The election of bishops had been mainly in the hands of the diocesan chapter, especially in Ireland, though the king of England could exercise powerful influence at times.

When Edward Bruce landed at Larne in 1315 he had unexpected success in his campaign, so much so that the king of England had to support the Normans both in state and church. Hence greater pressure was applied to obtain the appointment of English bishops as the Irish could not be trusted. The fact that 1315, 1316 and 1317 also witnessed the failure of the harvest in Ireland did not help the situation.

The authorities also considered that the native Irish were particularly liable to be preyed upon by bogus questors for alms. It was noted in places that men of dissolute life were selling false indulgences, preaching falsely and using forged documents and false relics and thereby extracting money from a pious credulous people. They were also granting pardon for crimes and thus damaging the sacrament of penance and censures of the church. These practices were to be abolished immediately. A provincial council mentioned a class of religious who did not follow any of the well-known *Rules* but a customary *Rule* (*consuetudinalis observantia*). This may mean pockets of Gaelic monasticism which survived into this century.[1]

The Black Death struck first in 1348 and took a very heavy toll in towns like Drogheda, Dublin and others on the east coast. In these, almost half of the population died. Since the Mendicant Orders were based mainly in towns and cities they lost a large number of members. Twenty-five Franciscans died in Drogheda, twenty-two in Dublin. Eight Dominicans died in Kilkenny.

The only case of doctrinal heresy recorded in Ireland occurred in the first half of the fourteenth century, but the three cases smack of personal and political tensions rather than of doctrinal heresy.[2] We are very fortunate that Richard Fitzralph's sermon diary has survived. He was Archbishop of Armagh. The diary gives some insight into his pastoral life, especially his sermons. Preaching in the presence of Clement VI in Avignon in 1349, he depicted the situation between the Irish and the Normans in the province of Armagh:

> The nations are always opposed to one another from a tradi-
> tional hatred, the Irish and Scots being always at variance
> with the English: so much so that every day they rob and slay
> and kill one another; nor can any man make any truce or
> peace among them, for in spite of such a truce they rob and
> slay one another at the first opportunity.[3]

He condemned the Anglo-Irish who refused to acknowledge the legality of wills made by Irishmen and he also condemned the guilds of Drogheda for excluding Irishmen from membership. There is no evidence before 1354 of any tension between him and the friars of his diocese though he had taken up the cudgel against the friars in general at Avignon as early as 1350. He also castigated the people of Drogheda for failure to pay their tithes and placed the city under interdict. By 1354 he was aware that the friars were not insisting on resitution being made to the sec-ular clergy and in 1355 he described certain exempt mendicants as thieves and plunderers of the monies due to the diocesan clergy. In Avignon he waxed more eloquently:

> I have in my diocese of Armagh, so far as I can reckon, 2,000
> subjects who every year are involved in sentences of excom-
> munication by reason of the sentences I have decreed against
> deliberate murderers, public robbers, incendiaries and such

like; and of all these, scarce forty a year come to me or my pentitentiaries; and yet all these receive the sacraments as other men, and are absolved or said to be absolved; and they are believed to have been absolved by the friars beyond doubt, for there are no others to absolve them.[4]

It is not easy to form a judgement on Fitzralph's contribution to Irish spirituality. In a sermon preached to the clergy at the provincial Council of Armagh in 1355, he reminded them of their priestly obligation in the matter of theological knowledge. Fr Gwynn tries to assess the Archbishop's influence.

Few will maintain that Archbishop Fitzralph was a prudent pastor of souls, and he must have left his diocese in considerable confusion. Yet his appeal was to God's law of charity and justice, even when that law seemed to challenge the King's law, or the accepted customs of the border. The violence of his quarrel with the friars seems to have arisen from his experience of episcopal government in a land that was accustomed to local warfare as a way of life. The text which he chose for his famous *Defensorium Curatorum* was a challenging one: 'Do not judge according to appearances but give just judgement'. There are problems of conscience which vary very little from age to age, and we may perhaps leave the Archbishop's blunt insistence on the overriding claims of God's law to the judgement of those who are prepared to risk a judgement.[5]

He died on 16 November 1360.[6] Six years later the Statutes of Kilkenny were passed. Their purpose was purely defensive, to prevent 'over-assimilation' between the two 'races'. The settlers were being swamped culturally in most of the country. Numerically inferior and lacking a real cultural tradition of their own, assimilation in some degree was inevitable. The tensions between the friars and the diocesan clergy continued after Fitzralph's death and whatever were the rights or wrongs of the case it could only lead to scandal among the laity and to a diminution in the care of souls. At the very end of the century, King Richard II was free from his wars with Scotland and France. He came to Ireland in 1394. Soon all the Gaelic leaders came and made their submission. It looked as if at last the Gaelic revival had been checked. He returned to England and war broke out again. By 1399 Richard had lost his throne and the Norman colony shrank as the Gaelic area continued to expand. Most of the decrees emanating from Councils in the province of Armagh in the early fifteenth century are re-issues of those of the previous century. They are discussed by Watt as follows:

> They are in part a penal code, laying sanctions of excommu- nication and, where appropriate, loss of benefice or suspen- sion, on those who live in concubinage, impede the testamen- tary jurisdiction of the ecclesiastical courts or the appelate jurisdiction of the archbishop's metropolitan court, seize or alienate ecclesiastical property or oppress tenants on ecclesi- astical estates. Property and income matters are the subject of other constitutions, aimed at safeguarding parochial contri- butions to bishops and to ensure due payment of the tithe. A local adaptation of a well known canon law ruling insisted that there should be no lay taxation or levy of any kind on ec- clesiastics or their properties or their tenants without licence of the local Ordinary. The rules laid down for the protection of the sources of episcopal incomes were among the most invoked and the most ignored of all ...

> Another group of canons concerned devotional practices, particularly of the laity. Particular stress was laid on the proper observance of Holy Week, so that the faithful might receive Holy Communion on Easter Day as 'most purified vessels'. On the negative side, some undesirable Easter prac- tices were forbidden: the practice of hunting hares on the Monday of Holy Week because it was thought that the blood of the animal killed on that day was of special medicinal value, was condemned as superstitious and unlawful: the game of galbardy (as yet unidentified) traditionally played on Easter Monday and at other times in the Easter season was condemned as a dangerous occasion of sin. Finally, full observance of the feasts of SS. Patrick, Brigid and Colum Cille were enjoined throughout the province, and of SS. Fechin and Ronan in the diocese.[7]

The celebration of the three patrons may be connected with the entry in *AU* 1293:

> The relics of SS Patrick and Colum Cille and Brigit were revealed to Nicholas MacMaelísu, the successor of Patrick, to be in Sabhall of Patrick. And they were taken up by him and, after their being taken up great deeds and marvels were done and they were placed honourably by him in an ornamental shrine.

* * *

The century prior to the reformation saw Europe as a whole in a bad spiritual state due to the period spent by the Popes in Avignon, to the Great Schism and due to the weakened position of the Papacy. The moral lives of some of the Popes at the end of the century was no headline for the rest of the christendom. There was a great psychological unease, evident in the trial of Joan of Arc, in witch-hunts and in a man like Martin Luther who was overburdened with scruples. It was also evident in Ireland during this century where we find at least fifteen different terms for the day of judgement (*lá an luain, lá an tionóil, lá an mheasa* etc.). Bishops and secular clergy were being blamed for their failure to preach. Church edifices were being neglected and Christianity as a whole was weakening. By the fifteenth century familial control of individual dioceses, parishes and monasteries became widespread again, especially in Tuam and Armagh. The inevitable result was a large-scale abandonment of celibacy, especially in the ranks of the higher clergy.

There had been deterioration among the friars from c. 1350 until c. 1440 while deterioration among the monks and Canons was much more serious and they did not recover from it before the Reformation. The Cistercians shrank in numbers and some of their monasteries came under family control. The papacy frequently gave dispensations allowing members of Orders to hold benefices especially in Gaelic Ireland. Indeed hereditary succession to all manner of ecclesiastical offices was quite common in Gaelic Ireland.

A typical example of such an ecclesiastical dynasty may be

selected from the Fermanagh diocese of Clogher where the Maguires were the ruling family and the MacCawells a leading ecclesiastical family. The union of the two families constituted in a very real sense the essence of the relationship between church and state in that area of Ulster and has its parallels throughout Gaelic Ireland.

The two families between them controlled the see virtually throughout the whole century: Art Mac Cawell, Bishop of Clogher 1390-1432, Pierce Maguire 1433-47, Ross Maguire 1447-83. There was also a Bishop Eugene MacCawell 1505-15. The ecclesiastical implications of the intermarriage of these two families left their first mark on the records, to all seeming, with the marriage of Joan, daughter of Bishop Brian MacCawell (1356-58) to the Archdeacon of Clogher, Maurice Maguire, known in the annals as the 'Great Archdeacon'. Their eldest son, after graduating in canon law in Oxford, succeeded his father as Archdeacon before becoming Bishop of Clogher by papal provision in 1433, in succession to his uncle (?) Art MacCawell. A second son became abbot of the Augustinian house of Lisgoole, and a third, also an Oxford man, prior of the Augustinian house of Devenish. All three married. The Ross Maguire who became bishop in 1447 may have been the son of Bishop Pierce but this is not certain. Pierce Maguire's sons did obtain important positions in the diocese: Edmond became Archdeacon and then Dean of Clogher, William was a Canon of Clogher and Abbot of Lisgoole, while Turloch was prior of the Augustinian house of Lough Derg. The first two of these had sons who apparently had to be content with merely parochial benefices. It is not clear exactly where Bishop Ross fits into the family tree though it is certain that he contributed much to its ramification for he had ten sons. One of them, Cathal Óg Maguire, Canon of Clogher and Armagh, rural Dean of Lough Erne, achieved fame as the chief compiler of the *Annals of Ulster*. He had at least twelve children, one of whom married a daughter of Thomas MacBrady, Bishop of Kilmore (1480-1511).[8]

On the other hand, the four Archbishops of Armagh 1417-70

were models in their moral lives and were also very hard working men. It was hard for them to take any effective action against
bishops or priests who had concubines since Rome did not give
them much support. In fact its influence was almost entirely
negative. The Irish church was, on the whole, in lamentable dis-
order during this century. In the monasteries, the fire of religious
devotion and piety was dead and the will for renewal was too
weak to have any noticeable influence.

As happened frequently on the continent, many Irish benefices
were very poor. This poverty had a number of adverse effects:
the holding of more than one benefice at a time, which in-
evitably led to non-residence and an accompanying neglect of
the care of souls and of buildings, was common. The standard
and even the number of candidates for the priesthood suffered.
Clerics were forced to engage in trades and professions. Many
an English bishop, who was appointed to an Irish see, never
visited it. Dromore is very much a case in point. Donnchadh
MacInerney, a cleric of Killaloe, was practicising medicine c. 1400
to give him subsistence. Matthew O'Mulryan, the Cistercian
Abbot of Holy Cross, was carrying on a trade in wine and often
getting drunk in the process.

The system of lay rulers of churches and monasteries (*comarbas*
and *airchinnechs*), which still prevailed, could be excused in a variety of ways: the chieftain needed the land to help him defend
his territory. Quite a number of communities had a small membership and did not need any great amount of land. There was
also the danger that the land might be given to an English absen-
tee, when it should have been administered by an Irish chief,
who was likely to do more for the people. In Gaelic monasteries
certain families still retained proprietary rights by having a
member of the family in the monastery. This practice, while it is
understandable to a degree, given the Irish approach to the possession of land, militated against both observance and mainte-
nance and many a monastery had to pay the price. In 1516
Clonmacnoise was without a roof and had only one set of vest-
ments, while in 1517, the walls of Ardagh Cathedral were barely
standing.

Unexpected hope came from the continent in a new surge of spirituality called the Observant movement. It was particularly noticeable in the Mendicant Orders. It prescribed a genuine return to a practice as full as possible of the Rule and Constitutions with the aid of prayer, personal and liturgical. This was embraced in Ireland by the friars in predominantly Gaelic areas. The Dominicans in Portumna led the way early in the fifteenth century. The impact was greatest on the Franciscans since most of their friaries had become Observant by the late fifteenth or early sixteenth century. The Augustinians were also well to the fore. There are some small indications that the Carmelites followed suit. But there is a great dearth of documents where that Order is concerned. Among the Mendicant Orders, ninety friaries had been founded between 1400 and 1508. By 1517 most of the Franciscan friaries belonged to the movement and they made a very fine contribution to the Counter-Reformation movement in Ireland during the following two centuries.

A new type of Franciscan Order, called the Third Order, not the lay Third Order which had existed for a century, appeared in Ireland and established forty-three friaries in the country, mainly in Gaelic parts. It seems to have been a movement confined to Ireland and one would dearly love to know more about it but it is, to all intents and purposes, without historical sources. It seems to have made its first foundations early in the fifteenth century. There are indications that diocesan clergy in the western dioceses were attracted and became members. Killeenbrennan, Co Mayo, which was founded in 1426-28, was its centre. It is known that its main work was educational. Practically nothing is known about this Order after the Reformation, but its Franciscan inspiration and its swift spread throughout the Gaelic parts of the country leave much food for thought as it provides such a contrast with the older Orders and with their shortage of vocations. They seem to have been secular priests who had a Rule of Franciscan flavour. They were close to the Minors but they had their own Provincial. The Franciscan Observants or Friars Minor have left a catalogue of their library in Youghal which is in two parts, one dated 1491 and the other 1523. From the document we learn that it was a friary which had both Observants and Conventuals and was the residence of the

Vicar-Provincial and was under the authority of a Gaelic Guardian.

It is not easy to get a general idea of the position and the role of the laity in these centuries. This is due mainly to lack of sources. In general one may say that the laity were expected to keep out of ecclesiastical business but that they should cooperate with the clergy. They were expected to obey unquestioningly. But performance rarely matched expectation. We have evidence of native Irishmen seeking to regularise their 'marriages' according to the norms of Canon Law. Dispensation in cases of consanguinity and affinity were the commonest. Sexual sins were punished but they do not appear very often in the records. Cases of breech of faith, perjury and especially slander were common. Punishments inflicted for ecclesiastical offences were sometimes private, sometimes public. One person found guilty of perjury was ordered to walk round the cemetery of Termonfechin church clothed in white linens on six different Sundays, to fast on bread and water for three days, to pay 12d for the expenses of the court and give 3d to the poor.

The relationship of the diocesan priest to his people is hard to investigate as parishes were coming into existence only from the twelfth century onwards, and even then it was a slow process and differed in Gaelic and Anglo-Norman areas. In the Gaelic areas they were probably divided by family groups and preserved a familial flavour. In the more heavily-populated Anglo-Norman areas they were probably more compact and in line with feudal divisions. In certain parts the hereditary *comarba* or *airchinnech* still played an important role, and in colonial parts the system of the proprietary church endowed by the new landowner meant that he had a big influence in choosing the priest, though strictly speaking it was subject to the bishop's approval.

The relationship of priest to people is aptly expressed in anonymous lines:

Me to spek and you to lere
That hit be worship, Lord, to thee
Me to teche and you to here
That helplich to ure sowles be.[9]

With regard to homilies, and we have a small number from Anglo-Irish quarters, we are in a much better position with ones in Gaelic. They give us some knowledge of what popular preaching was like. Another considerable help is found in the fact that in the diocese of Armagh every priest was bound to have a copy of the document which began with the words *Ignorantia sacerdotum*. The purpose of the document was to provide priests with an outline of the doctrine of faith and morals to be preached to the people four times a year and to have explanations and elaborations to make it readily understood. It began with a short explanation of the Apostles' Creed, taught the unity and trinity of God, Christ's birth, death and resurrection. It stressed that the church, with the sacraments and laws given under the direction of the Holy Spirit, provided the way of salvation for every person, even for the greatest sinners. The Commandments were then dealt with and the final part dealt with the seven sacraments.

It is fair to say that in the fifteenth century conditions prevailing in the monasteries left much to be desired. The educational and moral standards among the dicoesan clergy were, on the whole, poor. But the friars, especially those of the reform, developed popular religion and were in touch with the ordinary people especially in urban areas in the second half of the century. They promoted the Third Order among the laity. Confraternities and guilds, such as the Guild of St Anne in St Audoen's church in Dublin, helped to promote a deeper knowledge of religion and better frequentation of the sacraments. The upper and wealthier classes founded or endowed chantries, which increased in numbers considerably during the century. In addition to deepening lay piety they also had the practical effect of providing charity for the poor. These developments were more or less confined to urban areas, especially in the case of confraternities which normally held regular meetings. But the Third Order was probably quite effective in the country areas where there were friars.

The practice of pilgrimage at home and to places as far away as Rome or Spain was still in vogue. By 1413 Giolla Críost Ó Fearadaigh had visited Rome and other shrines five times and was then about to set out for the Holy Land when he died 1424

(AU). Large crowds went to Rome for jubilee years and 1445 and 1462 were years of special indulgence for Santiago. A pilgrimage to Rome is reckoned to have taken the best part of five months. At home pilgrimages to Lough Derg (St Patrick's Purgatory) enjoyed an international reputation where a man could catch a glimpse of heaven and hell. Alexander VI decreed that it should be closed down in 1497. Perhaps it was too near the bone or because certain superstitions were alleged to be connected with it.

Statues, sermons and pilgrimages played a large part in popular devotion. We are very fortunate to have the catalogue of varying libraries which date from the end of the century. That of the Franciscan friary in Youghal dated 1491 is the more interesting for the history of spirituality. The library had about one hundred and thirty volumes. A list of additions to this catalogue was made in 1523. It is a collection of liturgical books, missals, psalters, graduals, martyrologies, antiphonals, the Bible and some exegetical works, some books on theology and philosophy and a number of reference books. There were also Canon Law books and a number of volumes of sermons. It was geared to a community engaged in the care of souls so the emphasis is on the pulpit and on the confessional. From the practical point of view, the prayerbook and the sermons e.g. those of St Bernard, of Leonard of Udino (who was practically a contemporary), sermons for Sundays, sermons by Januensis, by Robert de Licio, by Dominic of Lausanne, Gregory's *Moralia on Job* must have been very useful to preachers. One would be interested in the short treatise dealing with discipline and the twelve bad customs of the cloister. The collection which friar Maurice Hanlan had is interesting as its shows an individual's collection: a breviary, missal and diurnal, a Summa of Cases of Conscience, sermons on the saints and for Sundays, a Compendium of St Thomas, St Bonaventure's *Breviloquium*, a bibliotheca on the final end of man and books on the Passion.[10]

Literature

The fourteenth century has not left us much in the line of spiritual writing in prose. TCD MS H.2.15. has a sermon on St Michael and one on Mary Magdalene. The *Book of Uí Maine,* written between 1360 and 1427, has some religious poems, a history of the Jews, some apocrypha, which may date from c. 1200, and a text of *Sex Aetates Mundi.* The Passion of Mary is treated in detail in the *Dialogus s. Anselmi* which was written before 1400.[11] But it is in the poem, *Corrach do shuan, a shaoghail,* that we get a very valuable insight into Gofraidh Ó Dálaigh's (+1387) understanding of the spiritual life. Speaking of the need to repent he says:

> Now is no time for remissness, short is the spell left to us, we should despise the world ... Though I know of Christ's words, God's condemnation of the world, not them do I heed most; I am to be pitied for my erring. No time this for folly; my comrades are now clay; ever further recedes my youth; O God what disturbs me now is not my youth (but my old age). Our heads will be prostrate in the priests' choir; this wins pardon for us; it causes the payment of (our) tithes. I will try – 'tis time to plead my cause with God; I know I shall get no other chance; I will do it now at the end of my days ...

> Pride – 'tis certain brought the angels to hell; every flood must ebb; therefore give up thy pride. Give Christ thy heart; do penance for thy sins; set store on tears; heaven shall not be pressed on thee. May I succeed in atoning for my sins as is my duty; my eye was given to me for shedding tears; let me not check them ...

> There are two similitudes for the two houses of Adam's race; day shines in the House of Mercy, the other abode is as Night. Mary's Son, kind Saviour rose, unknown to the Jews, from the close-guarded grave; let me not have to requite the death He suffered.[12]

In another poem of Gofraidh's, *Mairg mheallas muirn an tsaoghail,* he dwells on the idea that earth's riches are shortlived and are not helpful in the quest for heaven. A humble heart and the support of the virgins and angels facilitates the journey to heaven. He makes a contemporary comparison between heaven and earth:

Atá idir neamh na naoi ngrád
is aoibhneas talmhan tonnbhán
a mbí idir uaimh dhorcha dhuibh
agus tolcha i n-uair aonaigh.

Between the heaven of the nine grades and the happiness of the white-waved earth is the difference between a dark, black cave and a hilltop at time of a fair (great gathering).[13]

Towards the end of the poem he renews his trust in Mary:

Nár mhealltar mise, a Mhuire,
léir dom dhíon do dheaghghuidhe;
Guidhe óghMhuire is lór linn,
ógh is glórmhaire guidhim.
Comhairle Muire móire
do-ní mac na móróighe;
ó treise san tigh neamhdha
ní dligh meise mímheanma.

May I not be misled, O Mary, your good prayer is sure to protect me. The prayer of the Virgin Mary is sufficient for us. I beseech the most glorious virgin. The Son of the great Virgin fulfils the advice of the great Mary. Because of her power in the heavenly home I should not lack confidence.[14]

Tadhg Camcosach Ó Dálaigh, a poet of the late fourteenth century, who became a Franciscan, bade farewell to his country and his friends to show his love of God.

Do ghrádh do fhágbhas Éirinn
im bhráthair bhocht beigléighinn
gér deacair fonn fódglas Fáil
's an drong d'fhágbhas d'fhágbhail.
Do fhágbhas Éirinn na ríogh
ar ghrádh Dé 's ní dá díombríogh
ní d'álghas fiadha, badh fearr
do fhágbhas fiana Éireann.[15]

Flower gives a translation of the whole poem but unfortunately it is in prose:

For (God's) love I quitted Ireland, a poor brother of little learning, hard though it was to leave the green-grassed land of Fál and all the friends I left behind me there. I went from Éire of the kings for the love of God, not lack of appreciation of her, not in wild yearning for a further shore did I quit the companies of Ireland.

He then recounts how the only son and heir of the King of Sicily gave up his inheritance to become a Franciscan and though his father and mother were totally against it from the beginning they became reconciled after the son explained the wisdom of his choice. Tadhg continues:

Why should any grieve for a poor man, the son of poor folk, what concern to any that clay should cover him or by what way he should die? It is not that I measure myself with that fresh youthful countenance, but 'tis a holy tale that I have told of the brighthaired, sweet-voiced noble. For Christ's sake – though I make no boast thereof – have I left the people of the Gael whom I longed to have ever at my hand, and for love of Him have I deserted Éire.

But though Tadhg may have been poor and did not have any great opinion of himself we see here the same motive for 'white martyrdom' of pilgrimage with the surrender of all the objects of natural affection to fulfil his vows.

* * *

In contrast, the fifteenth century has left a wider and richer volume of spiritual writing than the preceding ones. Tadhg Óg Ó hUiginn, who died after penance at Kilconla, Co Galway in 1448, is described as the archinstructor of Ireland's and Scotland's poets by profession' (FM). In his poem to St John the Evangelist he stresses that only he and Mary were fully faithful to Christ. He was a man with deep devotion to Mary: 'Since (the day) I have come into the world I am as a salmon gone astray, put me safe from the shore into the water, O daughter of Joachim'. I have dealt with his devotion to Mary comprehensively elsewhere.[16]

In a poem to Uaitéar, 'captain of Clann Riocaird, he combines God's providence and predestination:

> God chooses each man when a child – one sees this by the favours He gives: the Creator knows on each birthday how the child will grow. Heaven's King waits not till a child grow in age, but chooses him when He creates him, when he is born into Adam's race. In His chosen one Jesus places on the day of his birth, the sign (of His choice), though men cannot yet recognize it, the charm of attractiveness will never leave him unregarded.

> To the child He wishes to exalt, He gives as a first gift – He gives others too – beauty of form. God, the builder of heaven, made two models for all His race who have been born, the choice ones and the others. It is known to all Eve's race that God, the world's Creator, saw, when creating men, who He would make illustrious. When the electors do not accept and do not crown a prince, they are not to be chidden; it is from heaven the choice comes.[17]

As has been noted, the Cross and the Passion loomed large in medieval Irish spirituality. The poem, *Slán ar na mharbhadh Mac Dé* (Alive again after death is God's Son) written by Tadhg, gives a fair notion of ideas that were common at the time:

> The fifteen sorrows – dread suffering! – which came on Christ from Judas' plotting – why should I not recall these fifteen sorrows which I tell of in the Passion? The first of them was on Thursday; through dread of His betrayal and the ingratitude of his folk there broke out the sweat of God's red blood, a presage of His coming betrayal.

> The second sorrow was a hard trial; when Christ was in chains the apostles had no regard for Him and denied Him. Of His third sorrow I shall mention the four wounds of the three nails, the wounds in His feet and hands, wounds heavy with torture. There was no limb of Him – this was another of his pains – which was not stretched along the Cross up to the nails and then pierced.

> With few followers, left alone after His apostles had abandoned Him, He was in the power of the world's hosts as a

lamb among wolves. After being pierced by the lance He was seized with burning thirst; may I reflect on that thirst and alleviate it by good deeds. Gall was His drink and bad un-drinkable wine: Heaven's Lord, captured by His foes, was as a wounded man taking a bitter draught ...

But in spite of all, may God give a welcome to the children of Adam and Eve at the end of their course, may He cure all afflicted men. For Mary's sake the man who deserves no mercy is saved; sad is our case for we have no right to be at His right-hand, yet our hope of heaven is not ruined.[18]

Tadhg also has a deep devotion to John the Apostle.

Stand warrant (?) for me with my Master, O John; great the danger from Michael's doom ... without an advocate I cannot be saved ... Thou art the apostle dearest to Him; though he loved them all he fondled thee on His own couch ... He gave thee His secrets ... His knee was thy pillow ... We have two reasons for which we cannot be censured,[19] O John; thou wert Mary's last love, she and I are of the one stock. I am in trouble owing to my body's five senses; do thou in mercy, O dove, care for me in my trouble.[20]

Tuathal Ó hUiginn, a fifteenth-century poet, dwells for quite a while on the necessity of freedom from sin before receiving the Body of Christ in *A dhuine chaitheas corp Dé*. He has some fine spiritual thoughts on the subject:

Alas! we all presume on God ... God's Body descends from heaven only when summoned; when He is invited man should give Him at least the honour due to a guest ... He is the herb who heals ... You cannot grasp the greatness of this Body, with its two natures, those of the Father and of Mary, God's mother ... To all men he left His Body to guard them in love for them; good guard He keeps on men, though they flee from His mercy ... On Thursday He left after Him in His last testament this Body to His children, though ill they deserved it.[21]

In another poem, *Déanam cionntughadh na colla*, he discusses the great difficulty he experiences in subduing the body to the soul or to God's will.

When I yield to the body's will, it desires to attempt my ruin; only when I am hard on it does it serve me … As my body has never been corrected, 'tis hard to check its passions once its own way is given to it; one cannot hold a hound without a leash … If God's son helps me not, it is hard for me to release my body, with its four elements held down by the roots of sin … When sin lies heaviest on me, I, God's foe, have found a way to approach Him boldly – wondrous protection. I should have trusted in Mary for making my peace with God; I had no one to support me till she summoned Him to me.[22]

In his poem *Mór grádh Dé do na daoinibh* (Great is God's love for mankind) Tuathal continues:

One can see it by His gifts: much harm shall come to them by His not being loved in return. Love of us made Jesus enter a virgin's womb when in His generosity He assumed the same body as we have.[23]

He continues with a very detailed account of the Passion and Resurrection. The final stanza returns to a thought very frequently found in Gaelic and European literature: 'What more terrible for Mary than to watch His pain? Yet she stays by Him; sorrow as hers I know not of'.[24]

Cormac Ruadh Ó hUiginn, who lived probably in the fifteenth century also, gives a good idea of the average Irishman with regard to his propensity to sin and his hope in the mercy of God. In his poem, *Cara na h-éigne Íosa* (Jesus is the friend in need), the opening verses express his deep feeling of hope:

Jesus is the friend in need for those who pay His tribute; spite of all sin he shows friendship to him who seeks to deserve it. Benefits corresponding to His friendship He would give me and all men too; not me only would He save. God has saved men as bad as I am, many like me were in the power of him who holds me in stress. Mary Magdalene was sinning inexcusably; yet once, spite of her sin, she got a chance to relieve her sad strait. That Paul became what he was after sin is proof enough that God would help all who merit His mercy. It was easy for God to reject him in favour of one who desired

Him; I never heard that till a man be buried, he could not win salvation from Him.

My heart requires His friendship to help me if I am to get it to serve me, for it and I differ in desires. Till my body had spent its youth contriving evil against me, leash was not bound rightly on it; woe to all who would live as I ... Despair owing to my excessive sin was folly for me; want of hope was therefore wrong, though I should place no hope in evil.[25]

He again portrays the average man in *Atá an saoghal ag seanmóir* (The world is (ever) preaching). He continues:

Its words are but whispers; yet if I understand them aright it never ceases preaching. All things seen in the world and in Eve's race are a sermon; each generation passing, another takes its place. May we listen to the world's sermon, speed on the right road; not one but all of us together have strayed ... I must be humble by checking the glory of my pride; not in the evening of a man's life should a folly be corrected ... Merely as a loan has God given men life; this world is not men's own land, they have it only on lease ... An invitation to heaven all have got; not some only of the race dost Thou invite, but the whole assembly of us ... Enable me, O God, to pay Thee the tribute of penance due Thee, a share in Thy crucifixion stands against me; help me to requite it ... God asks of man no more than a man can give; He does His best for them.[26]

One of the most popular texts and one which had a deep effect on continental and especially on Irish people in the late middle ages was the fifteenth-century translation of *Meditationes Vitae Christi*. It is probably the work of the Franciscan Joannes de Caulibus and the original Latin text dates from the early fourteenth century. It has been translated into Italian, French, English, Irish, Swedish, German and Spanish. The Irish translation, *Smaointe Beatha Chríost*, was made by Tomás Gruamdha Ó Bruacháin, a choral Canon of Killala c. 1450.[27] It is found in whole or in part in thirty-two manuscripts, possibly thirty-eight, and it influenced later writings both in poetry and in prose. This is due in no small measure to its simple, natural treatment of the Infancy, to its heart-touching account of Christ's Passion and to

its profound appreciation of Mary's role in His life. It is sometimes described as the fifth gospel and obviously had an influence that was long and deep on the Gaelic approach to Christ in
His Incarnation and in His Passion. It is a very sober piece of
writing in contrast with contemporary spiritual writing and
makes very effective use of the apocrypha. It is in the form of a
meditation for the days of the week, with helpful practical sug-
gestions for the reader to make Christ a living force in his or her
life. Speaking of the Annunciation the author says that God
called Gabriel to Him and said:

> Go to my own dear daughter, Mary, Joseph's wife, whom I
> love very dearly, more than any other creature, and tell her
> that My Son has found pleasure in her face and her comeli-
> ness and that He has chosen her as a mother for Himself.

The writer explains that God decided to bring about the salvation of the human race through her. Though Gabriel came to her
home very speedily the Trinity was there before him. They were
active in the Incarnation. The Father and the Holy Spirit were as
if someone were between them – they were putting a tunic
round Him and were closing the sleeves and helping to put it
on. This is quite an extraordinary way for expressing the idea of
assuming a body. He describes the Visitation and says that
Joseph went with Mary. Then he introduces the personal
thought:

> Meditate on the house and room where these holy women
> were and think of their children and their husbands. When
> John was born Mary took him up off the ground and gave
> her breast to him. This redounded to his honour. John used
> to look at her as though he knew her. He loved her more than
> his own mother. It was in this little house that the two
> Canticles, the Benedictus and the Magnificat, were spoken.
> Mary did not wish to be seen by outsiders who came to
> Elizabeth's house. She and Joseph bade farewell to their
> friends and returned to their house in Nazareth. Pity them as
> they had no bread, wine or any other worldly possessions
> there before them since they were very poor.

The writer makes very good use of parts of the apocrypha with very telling effect. In the account of the Passion when Joseph of Arimathea, John and the others had buried Jesus we find the following account:

> Joseph asked Mary to come with him to his house and make her home with him. 'All that I have, look on it as yours', he said. Nicodemus said the same to her. Mark her now (o reader), Mary is a true widow. She thanked them both but said that she had been given to John. They asked John what he would do. He said he would go back to Mount Sion to the Supper Room to hear from the apostles and their friends. They bowed to the queen and left. Mary and the others remained at the tomb. At nightfall John said: 'Lady, we can't remain here nor go to the city by night. So let us go now'. Mary rose and bowed to the tomb. She kissed and blessed it saying: 'Dear Son, I cannot remain any longer so I commend You to the Father.' She spoke with tears and great sorrow: 'Father, I commend my only Son to You and I leave my soul with Him in the grave'. They began to leave. Passing the Cross she bowed, prayed and wept. Then they came to the city. Before entering the women put the clothing of widowhood on their heads, covering their whole face except their eyes. Mary, who was between John and Magdalen, followed them. Magdalen asked her to come to her home. They would be comfortable there. Mary said to ask John. But John felt that they had better go to Mount Sion as they had promised their friends. They would be more likely to meet them there. But he wanted Magdalen to come with Our Lady wherever she went. She said she would. The virgins, widows and all who met them on their way, sympathised with them. They accompanied her to where she was going. John told the widows – Mary had thanked them – to go back to their homes and he also thanked them.[28]

Lives of Our Lady were very popular in fifteenth-century Ireland. One in particular, a translation of the *Vita Beatae Virginis et Salvatoris Rythmica*, is found in more than twenty manuscripts, which shows its popularity. It has much apocryphal material which the modern reader would not find very interesting as an aid to personal devotion but it did appeal very much to the medieval Irish mind. There are other Lives and tracts which deal with Mary and especially with her role in the Passion. Another text *Transitus Mariae* (The Passing of Mary) is also apocryphal. In its present form it is fifteenth century but it may date back to as early as the seventh or eighth century.[29]

A very important manuscript of the fifteenth century is the *Liber Flavus Fergussiorum* (RIA 23 0 48). Included in it, in whole or in part are: the finding of the true Cross; the miraculous cure of Constantine, the four kinds of wood of which the Cross was made; the miracle of St Ciaran's hand; the wonders at the birth of Christ, the fifteen signs of Doomsday; the distance from the garden of Eden to the House of the Trinity; wise sayings, the Life of Moling, the two sorrows of the Prince of heaven; the Passio of St Christopher, the Vision of Adomnán; six points of behaviour to be observed by clerics at mealtime; the Rule of the school of Sinchell; the power of holy water; the woman who was accustomed to use bad language; the formula for a general Confession; the Office of the dying; the twelve articles of the faith; Christ's descent into hell, the devil and Moling, a story comparing the death of a sinner and the death of a saint; the story of Adam and Eve; the sojourn of the Israelites in Egypt; and a tale of the devil and his nine daughters. [30]

Works available to preachers were, in addition to the *Leabhar Breac*, the *Liber Scintillarum*, an anthology of quotations on moral subjects which originated in France and was translated into Irish in the late medieval period; the *Manipulus florum*, which is a series of excerpts from the Fathers on a variety of subjects such as *Humilitas, Maria, Necessitas* etc. The Latin text was commenced by John of Wales and completed by Thomas of Ireland in 1308. It was translated into Irish in the fifteenth century at the latest. There is also the Irish counterpart of the *Book of the Miracles of the Blessed Virgin*, dating from the fourteenth or fifteenth century.[31]

* * *

While the poet or bard made the greatest contribution as a medium for spreading current religious trends, and the translator kept in touch with developments outside the country, it was the scribes of these books who had the most laborious task – that of copying manuscripts. We are fortunate that some of them, probably under the pressure of the conditions under which they were working, periodically gave expression to their feelings. A scribe of the *Leabhar Breac* remarks on the margins of his manuscript:

> I am writing at Loch Riach in solitude – A sea salmon now in my net. I give thanks to God ... For the love of God don't damn your soul with profitless chattels ... This is the worst Easter I have heard of yet, though it is without ale it is not without treachery ... O Mary help me. To-day is the feast of the dead ... Twenty nights from to-day until Easter and I am cold and tired without fire or shelter ... Lorrha is being plundered to-day ... As for myself I know not if tomorrow will be mine ... Dearer and dearer will be the food ... The day is growing longer, a pleasant thing ... Alas! Alas! our bolster is hard ... We should go with meditation every day to the place where He and we parted ... They seized my brother yesterday ... They plundered him last year ... I shall remember, O Christ, that I am writing of you, because I am tired to-day. It is now Sunday evening ... The wind from the lake is chilling me ... At Clonmacnoise I am tonight, writing the Commandments of God, after coming from Leinster ... The soul that is dear to God is the one who is constantly praising and contemplating Him.

Other scribes complained:

> Let no reader blame the script, for my arm is cramped through excess labour ... May God forgive the owner of this book for compelling me to write on the eve of Sunday ... On my word it is a great torment to be keeping the Friday of the Passion on water, with the excellent wine there is in the house with us. (Laud. 610).

He is grateful for the hospitality:

> A year and a quarter have I been stopping in this place, and I should like to go for a year's tour in another district; and long and lasting life to the family, to wit, Brian MacEgan and his children and Gormlaith and all of them. (Rawl. B. 506)

Translations like that of *De Contemptu mundi*, a work composed by Innocent III (1198-1216) and translated by William Mac-Diffney into Irish in 1443, found in five manuscripts, probably appealed more to the learned or to members of religious communities. It represents the traditional pessimistic view of human nature and human life, due to original sin and its effects which was relieved in succeeding centuries by the writings of the Scholastics.[32] On the other hand the translation of *Instructio pie vivendi et superna meditandi*, which is probably from the latter part of the fifteenth century and exists in only one manuscript, is a treatise on religious life written for a religious by her spiritual director and is far more uplifting.[33] The *Stimulus Amoris*, which now exists only in part in its translation, and is found in two manuscripts, probably had a greater appeal for the ordinary person since it deals with meditation on the Passion, on the gifts of the Holy Spirit, the Commandments, mental prayer and reflections on common prayers like the Our Father, Hail Mary, the Hail, holy Queen etc.[34]

Triads were always popular in Ireland because of their succintness and they were easy to memorise:

> On the three reasons for which God shortens the life of sinners: to inspire fear into people; that they fall not into sin again; that they pray to their native saints to shorten their lives because of their evil deeds.

> Three things lead a person to heaven: holy thoughts, good words, perfect works.

> Three things that lead a person in the direction of hell: bad thoughts, false words, perverse deeds.[35]

An Irish tract, *Carta Humani Generis* or *Testamentum*, dated c. 1450, is a translation of a middle -English poem, which is found in three manuscripts. It encourages the reader to think of Christ's love for him despite his malice and faults. The four evangelists are witnesses of Christ's love for him and especially for the love of His mother who shed tears of blood 'for the pain which she endured at the foot of the Cross'.

> For she could not speak a word as she was standing under the foot of the Cross and her heart was as though broken. 'It

was no wonder her suffering was so great because of the pain of death ... that I was suffering. That is why I said: 'Hely, Hely, lamasabatany". When Mary heard those words she died as much as she could. Though my personal suffering was great she sharpened it tremendously. When I moved my head from side to side in the pain of death she changed completely, for she wished to die at this time and so to help me. Know that the sword of sorrow sharpely and painfully pierced her heart and soul. And when John accepted her she looked so sadly at me as though I would forget her. Know that my mother had many pains and wounds because of her kindness and charity while this charter was being written.[36]

One of the poems which shows love of the dead and respect for the Rosary is found in *The Book of the Dean of Lismore*. Aithbhreac, the daughter of Corcadail, mourns the death of her husband and thinks of her life with him in the 1460s:

> O Rosary that recalled my tear,
> dear was the finger in my sight,
> that touched you once, beloved the heart,
> of him who owned you till to-night.
> I grieve for the death of him whose hand
> you did entwine each hour of prayer,
> my grief that it is lifeless now
> and I no longer see it there.
> May Mary, mother, the King's nurse
> guard each path I follow here,
> and may her Son watch over me,
> O Rosary that recalled my tear.[37]

In the fifteenth-century *Kilcormac Missal* we find this sequence in the Mass of the Immaculate Conception:

> *Mellis stilla de spina exiit*
> *Maris stella de nube prodiit – tenebrosa*
> *Sed spinosum nil stilla sapuit*
> *Sed nubosum nil stella habuit – radiosa*
> *Stilla, Stella, talis origine*
> *Dulcis ortus et clarae Virginis – sunt figura.*

(A drop of honey flowed from the thorns, a Star of the sea came forth from the dark cloud. But the thorn had no taste of the drop (of honey): the cloud had nought of the radiant Star, (Both) are a figure of the sweet origin of the illustrious Virgin).

The Missal belonged to the Carmelite friary of Kilcormac, Co. Offaly and is now in Trinity College. As far as we know this is the only instance of this Sequence in the world.[38]

Trinity College has quite a number of manuscripts, mainly in Latin, which date from the fifteenth century. Thus T.C.D. MS F.5.3. which was written in Clare in 1455, is attributed to a Franciscan[39] and contains the *Elucidarium* of Honorius of Autun. It also has an account of life after death and recalls the duties of remembering the dead. Sections of the psalter also form part of it and the history of the seven wise men. There are also notes on Canon Law, a subject which was widely studied by people with pretentions in the fourteenth and fifteenth centuries. It also has a short chronicle of Ireland which is dated c.1455. Finally it has a section dealing with moral subjects and an abridged catechism.

The Ms T.C.D. E.3.11. was written in Ireland in 1427. It contains a chronicle by Martin Polonus entitled *Annála Naomh Muire Baile Átha Cliath* and has lives of many Irish saints in addition to a Life of St Louis of Toulouse, Franciscan, and one of St Anthony of Padua also a Franciscan. Four books of Richard Fitzralph's *De Pauperie Salvatoris* are bound into it. This seems to have been compiled under Franciscan influence. F.4.6., which may have been written in Ireland in the fourteenth-fifteenth century, has Jocelyn's *Vita S. Patricii* and Bernard's *Life of St Malachy*. B.2.4. may have been written in Ireland in the first half of the fifteenth century and has theological tracts – Fitzralph's *Summa in Questionibus Armenorum* and Henry of Ghent's *Summa Theologica*. B.4.22, which may also have been written in Ireland in the fifteenth century, has the Sunday sermons of Nicholaus de Aquaevilla, the *Dieta Salutis* of William de Lanicis, the *Abominatio Peccati* which is like a treatise on the dangers to be avoided and the paths to be followed to salvation. C.1.28. was written in Ireland in the second half of the fifteenth century

(1492) and deals with the final end of man. It also has a series of sermons, one set being devoted to the Paschal Octave.[40] Further study on all these texts is needed before one can make any definitive assessment of their influence on Irish spirituality.

Notes:

1. Watt, J., *The Church in Medieval Ireland* (Dublin, 1972) 160-1.

2. Corish, P.J., *The Irish Catholic Experience* (Dublin, 1985) 50-1. Henceforth *ICE*.

3. Gwynn, A., 'The Black Death in Ireland', *Studies* 24 (1935) 31.

4. Gwynn, A., 'Richard Fitzralph, Archbishop of Armagh', *Studies* 25 (1936) 94-5.

5. *Anglo-Irish Church Life in the Fourteenth and Fifteenth Centuries* (Dublin, 1968) 30.

6. ibid. 20. A chronicler records that at his death the friars' chant was *Gaudeamus* rather than *Requiescat*. Watt, op. cit. 169.

7. Watt, op. cit. 162-3.

8. Watt, op. cit. 185-6. The Annals describe hs as 'a gem of purity' (*AU* 1498).

9. Watt, op. cit. 209.

10. For a full list of the Catalogue see MacConmara MSC, M., *An Léann Eaglasta in Éirinn 1200-1900* (Áth Cliath, 1988) 102-38. Francis Cotter OFM has just published his thesis, *The Friars Minor in Ireland from their Arrival until 1400* (The Franciscan Institute, St Bonaventure University, New York, 1994). Chapter IV is entitled 'Preachers and Confessors'.

11. Skerrett, R.J., *Celtica* VII (1966) 168-87. *v. Mary*, 154-60.

12. McKenna S.J., L., *Aith-dioghluim Dana* (Dublin, 1939) Poem 69. Henceforth *Aith. D.*

13. McKenna S.J., L., *Dioghluim Dána* (Áth Cliath, 1938) Poem 37. st. 24. Henceforth *Di. D.*

14. O'Rahilly, T.F., *Measgra Dánta* (Cork, 1927) p 132.

15. *Ir. Trad.* 117-9.

16. *Mary* 100-107.

17. *Aith. D.* Poem 37.

18. Ibid. Poem 78.

19. McKenna has 'escape'. Text reads *iongabtha*.

20. McKenna, L, *Dán Dé* (Dublin, 1922) Poem I.

21. Ibid. Poem XVIII.

22. Ibid. Poem XIX.

23. Ibid. Poem XX.

24. *v.* also *Mary* 107-8.

25. *Dán Dé* Poem XXI.

26. Ibid. Poem XXII.

27. Ó Maonaigh OFM, C., (Baile Átha Cliath, 1944) xiv-xix.

28. *Mary* 150-1.

29. For more specific accounts of these texts *v. Mary* 153-61.

30. This story dates from c. 1437. It speaks of a devil marrying a woman named *Écoir* (evil). They had nine daughters: simony, false piety, force, usury, deception, stealing from the church, false humility, pride and impurity (*drúis*). He found husbands for them all. The clergy married simony, Orders married false piety, knights married force, the bourgeoisie married usury, merchants married deceit, church property chose farmers, servants wedded false humility, pride chose lords and impurity chose no one in particular but married them all. This account is very close to a Latin text of the thirteenth century which was well-known in Europe but the Irish translator may have felt that it had its lesson for fifteenth-century Ireland as well. It is edited by Brian Ó Cuív, 'Cleamhna an Diabhail', *Éigse* IX (1958-60) 261.

31. *Mary* 164-74.

32. Geary, J. A., *An Irish Version of Innocent III's De Contemptu mundi* (Washington, 1931) 14ff.

33. McKechnie, Rev J., *Irish Texts Society* XXIX (London, 1934) Translation 1946.

34. Mooney OFM, C., *The Church in Gaelic Ireland, 13th to 15th Centuries* (Dublin, 1969) 36-7.

35. Ó Cuív, B., *Éigse* IX (1958-60) 180, dated to the fifteenth/sixteenth century.

36. MacNiocaill, G., *Éigse* VIII (1956-7) 216-7.

37. Watson, W. J., (ed.) *Scottish Verse from The Book of the Dean of Lismore* (Edinburgh, 1937) 60-65. The poem occurs on p 148 of the actual MS.

38. T.C.D. MS 82 f. 113. *v. cf Mary* 128-9.

39. *Ir. Trad.* 122-3.

40. Most of this information is taken from Colker's study of the Latin MSS in Trinity College, Dublin.

CHAPTER 6

The Sixteenth Century

'I am a priest anointed and also a bishop, although unworthy of such sacred dignities, and no cause could they find against me that might in the least degree deserve the pains of death, but merely my function of priesthood wherein they have proceeded against me in all points cruelly contrary to their own laws.' *(Dermot O'Hurley)*

The Reformation in England was due to Henry VIII's desire to have his marriage with Catherine of Aragon annulled. Upon Clement VII's refusal to grant it, Henry abolished papal authority in England in 1534 and named himself Supreme Head of the church in that country. In the Irish Parliament of 1536 Henry was also accepted as Supreme Head in Ireland. But that does not mean that the country as a whole accepted it or even understood what was involved. As Canice Mooney OFM has pointed out, Ireland at the time of the Reformation was not as depraved as some who were not Catholics thought, nor as exemplary as some Catholics seemed to believe.

There is evidence of a robust faith, of high regard for the Pope as Vicar of Christ, of a mental outlook almost inextricably interwoven with the Christian way of life, of great personal devotion to Christ, Our Lady and the saints, of friendly relations between clergy and laity. Still on the credit side but not beyond criticism in all its aspects, is the tradition of asceticism, for instance, in regard to fast and abstinence, as well as deep reverence for the relics and images of the saints and the undertaking of toilsome pilgrimages.[1]

But there were complaints about the clergy which were being voiced even in pre-Reformation days:

Some sayeth that the prelates of the church and clergy is

much cause of misorder in this land, for there is no archbishop nor bishop, nor prior, parson nor vicar, not any other person of the church, high or low, great or small, that useth to preach the word of God, saving the poor friars beggars; and where the word of God do cease, there can be no grace, and without the special grace of God this land may never be reformed, and by preaching and teaching of prelates of the church, and by prayer and orison of the devout persons of the same God, useth always to grant His abundant graces; ergo the church, not using the premises, is much the cause of all the said misorder of this land. Also the church of this land use not to learn any other science but the law of canon, for covetice of lucre transitory; all other science, whereof grow none such lucre, the parsons of the church doth despise.[2]

This dates from some twenty years earlier than the Reformation parliament and shows that early in the sixteenth century there was need for an educated and devout clergy.[3]

The penetration of the Reformation does not come any way clear till we reach the reign of Elizabeth I, 1558-1603. No parliament was held in Ireland in the reign of Edward VI and though the Acts of Uniformity were passed in 1549 and 1552 it is not clear what effect they had in Ireland. He was succeeded by Mary 1553-58, a Catholic, who restored Catholicism in both countries. By the end of Elizabeth's reign the new religion was more clearly defined in doctrine and in the obligations which it imposed and thus set to become the religion of England. But by 1600 its failure in Ireland was becoming evident. No steady effort was made to impose it or to re-evangelise. Spenser read the situation and the reason for its failure:

Wherein it is a great wonder to see the odds which are between the zeal of popish priests and the ministers of the gospel. For they spare not to come out of Spain, from Rome and from Rheims, by long toil and dangerous travelling hither, where they know peril of death awaiteth them and no reward or riches to be found, only to draw the people into the church of Rome: whereas some of our idle ministers, having a way for credit and estimation thereby open to them, and having the livings of the country offered unto them without pains and without peril, will neither for the same, nor any love of God, nor zeal of religion, nor for all the good they may do by winning souls to God, be drawn forth from their warm nests to look out into God's harvest, which is even ready for the sickle and all the fields yellow long ago.[4]

By 1570 the reforms of the Council of Trent were being encouraged, especially by the Jesuits and the friars, so that the content of the Protestant Reform was hardly known to most Irish or many Anglo-Irish Catholics. David Wolfe SJ had been sent to Ireland by Pius IV. In addition to sending reports on the state of religion in the country he recommended a number of priests who would make suitable bishops and Rome did appoint them and they participated in the last session of the Council of Trent.[5]

The note of hope sounds clear in the lines:

A Róisín, ná bíodh brón ort fá'r éirigh duit.
Tá na bráithre ag teacht thar sáile 's ag triall ar muir.
Tiocfaidh do phardún ón bPápa 's ón Róimh anoir,
Is ní sparáilfear fíon Spáinneach ar mo Róisín Dubh.

Oh Ireland be not sad because of what has befallen you.
The brothers (friars) are coming across the ocean.
Reconciliation will come from the Pope, east in Rome and Spanish wine will be lavished on my Róisín Dubh (Ireland).

We have seen that the Irish chieftains accepted Henry's supremacy but, whatever they may have understood by it, they continued to live as Catholics. We find little interest in Luther's doctrines. While many were ardent in faith, though perhaps a little weak on good works, the annals report their deaths 'after anointing and penance' regularly. There were good relations between the Irish chief and the clergy, especially the friar, as we see in a man like Mánus Ó Dómhnaill of Tír Chonaill, who not only did not lack self-confidence but was open to continental ideas and remained firmly true to his Catholic values. He was a good ruler and a *literateur* and on good terms with the Franciscans of Donegal, a friary founded by his family in 1474. He could joke about their human failings, as he did on finding Brother Hugh somewhat 'under the weather':

Bráthair bocht brúite ó fhíon
ná dúisgtear é gion gur chóir
gabh go ciúin ceannsa re a thaobh
leigtear d'Aodh an tsreann-so go fóill.[6]

Poor brother overcome by wine, wake him not though one should; go quietly, gently by his side, let Hugh have his snore a little longer.

The Reformation was noticeable only in towns and in the Pale in its early years. Monasteries and friaries, churches and lands were being confiscated mainly in Leinster and Munster from 1538 onwards. In other areas the church fared better. The friars and other priests of Ulster, we are told, 'do preach daily that every man ought, for the salvation of his soul, fight and make war against our sovereign lord the king's majesty, and if any of them die in quarrell, his soul ... shall go to heaven, as the souls of Ss Peter and Paul and others, who suffered death and martyrdom for God's sake'.[7] Chancellor Alen, writing in July 1539, referred to the hostile propaganda of the friars in the independent areas and he was afraid that it might also affect the Pale.[8]

On the whole, the Reformation had little success in Ireland. The resistance which Elizabeth met was far greater than that experienced by Henry VIII. It served to promote greater unity between these two peoples and initiated the mentality of 'faith and fatherland' which was to grow much stronger especially among the Gaelic Irish in the following century. It made much plainer the difference between the 'old English' (Anglo-Irish) and the 'new English' planter colony who got lands in Munster and part of Connacht, though not without considerable opposition in Munster.

One interesting document which has survived from this time describes some Irish customs noted by the writer, who was either Italian or Spanish, who had accompanied the expedition and had managed to remain in Ireland for some time.

1. The use of money is very rare in these regions, barter of goods is the common practice. 2. There are no guesthouses or hostels except perhaps in ports. Whoever is travelling re-

ceives everything *gratis* in whatever house he stays – not immediately but when the father of the family eats. 3. Normally they do not eat before evening time, but they do not refuse drink to travellers in the meantime. 4. There are 8 types of drink: beer made from barley and water, milk, whey, wine, soup (?), wine sweetened with honey, whiskey and pure water. 5. Men cover their heads (?) with mantles, women with very wide linen tiaras. They use very long knives which could also serve as daggers. 6. The most honoured person sits in the middle, the second on his right, the third on his left, the fourth on his right and so on until the whole house is filled following the circuit of the walls. All face the door, no one has his back to it; the reason for this, they say, is so that nobody may be set upon, unprepared, by an enemy. 7. They hold the Catholic faith so firmly that they seem never to have given ear to heretics. They rise at midnight to pray and meditate, some give a whole hour, others a half-hour. They always light the fire at that time. 8. Their language is similar to Chaldaeic and Hebrew; they add aspirations to many letters, which has the effect that they seem to pronounce words different from what is written. 9. They rise to recite the Lord's prayer at Mass, and they hear it standing. 10. Wednesdays they abstain from meat and on Fridays from milk products. 11. Both men and women kiss each other as soon as they meet. 12. Though they lack education in the humanities (*urbana educatione*), nonetheless they live peacefully and lovingly together so that I never saw them or any soldiers come to arms for six whole months. The same peace is found among horses and dogs so that I am led to attribute all this to the excellence of the region and the air. 13. Such is the temperateness of the sky that it varies little so that there is always grass for herds and flocks in the fields. 14. No poisonous animal is found in Ireland; no snake, viper or toad. 15. As they eat copiously when there is plenty, they also fast for two or even three days at a time. 16. They do not violate their oath to their lords and they observe peace or fight according to his wishes. 17. In battle the more courageous will leave his own ranks and penetrate the enemy lines, paying little attention to what his comrades are doing. 18. They are as fast on their feet as horses or even faster. 19. They sit quite freely on grass, turf or straw. They shun benches (stools) completely and also rocks and would choose rushes or straw instead. 20. They mount horses by catching their left ears and with no support for their legs. 21. They do not use metal or any other shin (foot) protection. 22. The more noble wear cloaks made of leather of varied inlaid colours. 23. They cultivate sacred poetry; they learn it without much study. They do not compose religious poems without preparatory prayer and fasting. When dealing with very serious business poets are their negotiators. 24. At supper before they give thanks, bishops or priests deliver a sermon to those present, which is heard with great attention.[9]

A very valuable insight into the life of the friar-bard comes also from this period.

Fr Philip O'Daly, known as the poor (man), a priest and most devoted worshipper of theVirgin Mary, who often enjoyed converse with her, a man devoted to the highest contemplation with frequent ecstasies. At times with his senses suspended, he composed songs in the vernacular idiom in his ecstasy. He died happily in the same monastery (Adare) and was buried there in 1565.[10]

Towards the end of the century it was noted by a state official 'that the mayor, aldermen, merchants and inhabitants of Dublin are notorious papists hating the English nation and government'. The first part of the assertion was correct but there is no question of their hating the English government since they took their politics from England and their religion from Rome. Nonetheless Richard Creagh, Archbishop of Armagh 1564-85, had good reason to dislike the English. Of his twenty-one years as primate eighteen were spent in prisons. 'Worn out by age and the squalor of a prison in the tower of London as a true and strong confessor of Catholic faith (he) departed this life c. 1585'. [11]

Some efforts were being made by rich Protestants to further the Reformation. James Ussher, Protestant Primate of Armagh 1625-56, set up a printing press in his own house to produce and distribute a Gaelic version of a Protestant catechism and other texts, but he had little success.[12] Catholic citizens wished to defend their Catholic heritage. In fact James Eustace, head of a well-known Catholic family in Baltinglass, Co Wicklow, led a rebellion to restore Catholicism in 1580. It was shortlived. It got little support from the Catholic Anglo-Irish though a certain amount of financial aid was supplied by them. This was followed by firm reaction on the part of the government and about twenty men were executed. Religious tension among families of mixed religion increased. Alderman Walter Ball, a convert to Protestantism, took action against his mother Margaret and her chaplain. She gave most valuable service to the church in providing education for some Catholics in her house and she also gave refuge to priests. Though she had been arrested earlier she was released and returned to her former ways. In due course she was arrested again and died in prison in Dublin in 1584. She was seventy years of age.[13]

In the same year, on 20 June, Dermot O'Hurley, Archbishop of Cashel was hanged at Hoggen Green (now College Green), Dublin. He was born near Emly, Co Limerick c. 1530 and his family served the earls of Desmond. He was sent to Louvain in the 1540s, studied law in the university there and in time became dean of law faculty. He was in Rheims from 1567 till 1570 when he went to Rome. Pope Gregory XIII, in the summer of 1581, told him that he was to be Archbishop of Cashel. Obviously Hurley must have been very surprised but he took it as God's will. He received tonsure on 29 July and all the minor and major Orders in a very short time. He was ordained priest on 13 August and appointed to the see of Cashel on 11 September that year.

He returned to Ireland but found that the situation had changed. Though he was circumspect he was soon recognised. The government was recovering control after the revolts of 1579 and 1580. The archbishop could not find the protection which he would have had in Dublin ten years earlier. While staying with Thomas Fleming, Baron of Slane, he was recognised as a Catholic priest by Robert Dillon, Fleming's first cousin. Dillon put pressure on his cousin for receiving a traitor. In the meantime Hurley had gone to his diocese in Munster hoping to be received on friendly terms by the Earl of Ormond.

Thomas Fleming was so intimidated by the threats against him that he followed the archbishop and found him in Carrick-on-Suir. Fleming pleaded with him to return to Dublin and clear himself of the charge of treason. The fact that Hurley did return shows the calibre of the man. The Council in Dublin were sure that he had valuable information about continental conspiracies. But in fact he had none. They could not put him on trial because they had no case. They subjected him to terrible torture. His legs were put in boots filled with oil and he was held over a fire until the flesh melted from the bones. But there was no information forthcoming. Then they tried to induce him to take the Oath of Supremacy but in vain. He was executed early in the morning of 19 June. Despite the secrecy hoped for at that early hour there was some people passing through Hoggen Green. They gathered to see what was happening and he addressed them:

> I am a priest anointed and also a bishop, although unworthy of so sacred diginities, and no cause could they find against me that might in the least degree deserve the pains of death, but merely my function of priesthood wherein they have proceeded against me in all points cruelly contrary to their own laws.

His burial was reported in a Catholic paper:

> And when the report of the execution was spread about the city, certain devout women went forth and had his body brought down which they carried with great respect unto a little church without the city called St Kevin's, where he was buried, and his clothes which he did wear were kept among them, as relics of his martyrdom.[14]

A more vigorous Catholicism was developing in Dublin at the end of the century. The children of the merchant and noble classes got good solid education in Ireland and many were being sent to the continent to colleges like Douai or other seminaries in France. From 1578 onwards Irish colleges were being founded. By 1700 there were more than thirty such colleges on the continent. The result was that priests and laity who had been able to avail of the opportunity of getting schooling in these received a good Catholic education. On their return the laity generally married into Catholic families and thus a solid bastion existed in Dublin. The poorer Catholic was helped and strengthened by their example.

After 1606 the practise of Catholicism seems to have become more open. The government placed obstacles where they could, such as the removal of the exemption from customs and dues. Foreign education was banned. Priests were to leave the country. The Oath of Supremacy was to be demanded of office holders. These enactments served to strengthen Catholics in their beliefs.[15] Pastoral care was improving. Bishops or Vicars and priests set the example. Marriage tended to move more under church control, with the presence of the parish priest and two witnesses. In baptism, godparents were expected to be from the older generation. In the sacrament of penance, emphasis was placed more on contrition and individual repentance. The Ireland of the late sixteenth century was slowly, and at times painfully, recognising that Catholicism could make far-reaching demands on its adherents.

* * *

Literature

The sixteenth century did not produce any great volume of Gaelic prose, even in translations. The *Life of St Catherine of Alexandria*, which is a translation from the Latin, is, at the latest, from the early years of the century.[16] She was a very popular saint in Ireland, especially in the north western part of the country where some churches still have her portrayed in stained glass windows. She was also popular in Europe and her cruel *passio*, which may be unhistorical, probably appealed to Gaelic sympathy. The *Visio Sancti Pauli* was also very popular in Europe in the middle ages and was translated into Irish c. 1513-14. It became one of the chief formative elements in the development of the later legends of heaven and hell which culminated in the *Divina Commedia* of Dante and was one of the sources used in the vision of St Patrick's Purgatory.[17] The *Life of Colum Cille*, which was compiled at Port na dtrí namhad (Portnoo) in Co Donegal in 1532 at the expense of Manus O'Donnell, Chief of

Tyrconnell, is probably the most outstanding work of the century in the religious sphere. Obviously Manus wished to keep Colum's memory ever green.[18] There is a translation of *De cura rei familiaris* in a sixteenth-century manuscript.[19] The Latin original was attributed wrongly to St Bernard. It is in the form of a letter giving advice to a knight . He asks Bernard how he should take care of and govern his family. The author discusses food, clothing, friends, servants, buildings, the art of buying and selling, the use of wine, the careful choice of doctors and hounds! At the end he advises him how to deal with the family and his possessions. Incidentally he does not advise older widows to remarry. A scribal note by Richard O'Connor, who came from a well-known family of physicians in Ossory, is very interesting in regard to Irish medical learning in the sixteenth century.[20] The manuscript has an Irish translation of the *Lilium Medicinae*, of the *Decem Ingenia* and of the *Prognosticon of Bernard of Gordon*. The latter was obviously a very devout man as is seen in the Preface:

> No one can come nearer to God better than by study in the truth and for the truth. To the honour therefore of the heavenly Lamb, who is the splendour and glory of the Father, this book is entitled *Lilium Medicinae*. For in the lily there are many blooms and in each bloom seven white petals as it were seven golden grains. This book likewise contains seven parts, of which the first will be golden, glowing and shining. For it will treat of many universal diseases, beginning with fevers. [21]

The scribe takes Bernard to task:

> Now as regards charms it is a wonder to me that Bernard did not prescribe anything against them in this chapter, since he mentions them in his section on causes, and moreover that he did write a special chapter on them, and more particularly I wonder that Cormac did not do it , unless the reason was that they cannot be cured. And according to my opinion it seems that they can be cured, like every other trial and temptation that the devil and his followers send on human beings. For followers of the devil and devils themselves are those who use them. If so, whosoever is sterile, man or woman, let him not be a heretic etc., but let him believe as the church be-

lieves, and let him make his confession often, and receive the Holy Sacrament of the church, and hear the words and true teaching of God, and restore the things he got wrongly , not have thoughts of committing the same wrong again. And let him give alms and pray and repent and fast, if he be one who can do so. And after this let him pray the merciful Father often that he may have children, for be it known to thee Joachim and Anna, Elizabeth and Zacharias, with whom God was pleased, and who we free from blame, received children from God through prayer. And not that only, but I have no doubt that whatever fitting petition a good Christian is wont to ask of God he will obtain it, ergo, etc. And understand, moreover, that even were there no charms, none the less is it right to do this. For God sends a disease which causes sterility as punishment on the sinner when he does not repent. Therefore until the sin be put away the disease which came by it will not be cured, and until the disease be cured there will be no generation from him ergo, etc. And this ought to be understood in any other disease also. And the physician also should be pure from blame before he begins his works.[22]

The text, *De Disposicione corporis Mariae*, which is part of *Betha Muire* treats of the beauty of her body and refers to her influence during her period in the temple. It is found in a manuscript writtten 1513-14.[23] In October 1538 the shrine of Our Lady of Trim was still intact when the Council held several judicial sessions there and members of the Council affected disgust at Lord Grey's devotion before the image there in view of the known hostility of official policy in England.[24] However the shrine was destroyed a little later and the statue realised £40 for the destroyers.[25]

There is a considerable volume of bardic poetry stemming from this century. A number of poems, composed by Richard Butler of the Kilkenny family, are written into blank spaces of a fifteenth-century manuscript. Flower says that Butler probably lived in the first half of the sixteenth century. A note by the scribe states that 'Richard Butler composed this poem on the day he died'.

Is áille Ísa ina'n cruinne
is ná bláth rós nó lile
is tú a bláth caomh ó Mhuire
dochua a ghnáthghae (1) rinne.

Flower provides a nice translation though it is not literal.

Jesu fairer than earth's fairest
Thou than lily-blossoms more holy,
Mary's winsome blossom, carest
But to join thy kindred lowly.

Sweeter than what else is sweetest,
Than sweet dews that fall from heaven,
Mary's Son that earth completest,
Sweeter than bee's honey even.

Who so longs for Jesu only,
In his secret heart concealing,
To the world's end is not lonely,
Through that heart no new love stealing.

Jesu, Thou hast made for ever,
Sweetest Son of Mary maiden,
every isle in every river,
Every forest-tree fruit-laden.[26]

As I have given a chapter to devotion to Our Lady in sixteenth-century Ireland, the wider aspect of religious poetry will be considered here.[27] Gofraidh Mac Bríain Mac an Bháird is dated by McKenna c.1600.[28] His poem *A Dhé Athar, t'fhaire rum* (O God the Father, attend to me)[29] describes his soul as 'a lamb of Thy flock.' The devil was very real to people: 'In his greed for the trembling soul, hotter and sharper grows Lucifer's attack, that foe's breast presses against the door, his foot within it and his hand on the jamb' (st. 17). 'Swift to attack her too are her own dear offspring, the eight carnal sins, biting her as fierce packs of hounds; pitiful is the attack' (st. 21).

In another poem, Gofraidh cries for help, *Ag so tráth na cabhra a Chríosd*.[30] He asks Him to 'lead me willingly along the true path – whatever may be for my good in this vale of tears' (st. 8). In his poem, *Beir iúl damsha, a Dhé*,[31] he implores God's guidance:

'Doomed in distress ere I die 'neath Thy wrath, my course is a blind man's rushing through life in eager haste' (st. 2). 'The steps of my feet, the deliberate moving of my hands, sting me, alas for the state I am in!' (st. 12). 'The father dwelling above in His household of Three – may He be speedy in course to show me mercy after all. I implore the Son Jesus – if I may express my desire – and the virgin, who bore and nursed Him' (stt. 16-17).

Fearghal Óg Mac an Bháird (+1616) went to Scotland for 'love of the fleeting world', as he thought, but found that he had made a bad decision: 'In this fair-flowered land of bright fields I receive not the Lord's Body. Alas that I came over seas to be without Mass or clergy' (stt, 4-5).[32] The thought of God's avenging anger due to the wounds, especially the wound caused by the piercing of the lance, is very frequently mentioned. The poet's refuge is very often an appeal to Mary, confident in the belief that she is very powerful. In a sixteenth-century poem[33] on Christ's wounds, the anonymous poet says: 'the host of us shall come one day eagerly defending ourselves: the Judge, our only hope, shall be no pleader for us that day. O lady of the fair, bright, golden hair come to guide me on the day of stress, show forth thy power … set about my salvation. Cease not, O virgin Mary, thy urgent prayer to thy Son' (stt. 7-8). A poem by Baothghalach Mac Aodhagáin, *A Athair nua neamhdha-sa* (O bright heavenly Father), is a nice example of a good balanced healthy relationship with God. There are indications in the last stanza that he may have been a Mendicant.

> Power from the Father, Thy wisdom, O dear Son, and Thy love, O Holy spirit – implant these in my heart.
> I am not pious in middle age, I was not chaste in my youth; to cleanse my long perversity may I be innocent in old age.
> I pray for the strength to fight prosperity and not to wax proud; if adversity befall me may I not fall into despair.
> O only God of mercy, O Jesus, Son of the virgin Mary, O Holy Spirit. O Father, save me.
> O Mary, through thy prayer and operation may the Holy Spirit, the Son and His Father wax strong (?) in my heart and mind.
> Mayest thou cleanse me after every fall; wash them with cloth

> and water from the well of penance.
> May St Francis, St Dominic and Patrick of Macha saving me,
> bring my soul to the kingdom where Thou art, O Father.[34]

But fear of the wounds is sometimes replaced by the opposite sentiments, as we find in Fergal Ó Cionga who wrote c. 1560:

> God's Son to save us in spite of the law, forced His way through the nail-points;out beyond the nails were we, His folk. He stepped forward to reach us. (st.3). Many the step – even Thy son's death – Thou did'st take in redeeming us; in pity (for us) Thou didst pay no heed to all the pangs caused by Thy heart's blood (st. 15). If I stay aloof from Christ it is not His (wounded) breast that is the cause; she feels it a shame cast on her Son's wounded breast if men avoid approaching Him. (st. 27).[35]

Towards the end of the century, the Franciscan Florence Conry translated a catechism from Spanish into Gaelic.[36] He finished the work in 1593 and sent it to Ireland in 1598. It seems to be the earliest of the catechisms written by the Franciscans and its purpose was to clarify their faith for the people. It is produced in a very simple manner and is in the form of a master questioning his disciple:

> M. What is your name?
> D. Brian O Domhnaill.
> M. Are you a Christian?
> D. Yes, master, by the grace of God.
> M. Whom do you call a Christian?
> D. A person who believes in Christ and professes Him in baptism?

The main subjects which are dealt with are the duties of a Christian, the Creed, the Incarnation (in detail), the *Pater*, prayer, the *Ave Maria, Salve Regina*, the ten commandments, the five commandments of the church, the sacraments, indulgences, the spiritual and temporal works of mercy, the enemies of the soul (the devil, the world and the flesh), the seven deadly sins, the virtues that are contrary to the vices, the four moral virtues, the three powers of the soul (will, memory and understanding), the five senses of the body, the seven gifts of the Holy Spirit, the twelve fruits of the Holy Spirit, the eight beatitudes, the daily duties of a Christian and the method of keeping a clean conscience.

Brian Ó Cuív has published 'A Modern Irish Devotional Tract' which may also be a translation by Florence Conry. It is from the same period and several copies of it have been preserved. Its main subjects are: How should a Christian work out his salvation? By avoiding evil and doing good, listening to God's word or reading it frequently, receiving absolution and Communion at least once a month or more frequently if the spiritual guide advises it ; by praying and by practising the spiritual and corporal works of mercy. How should a Christian spend his day? On waking he should lift his heart and mind to God, bless himself and say 'Lord, my God, come to my aid. Lord, do not fail to help me. He should try to attend Mass remembering the love of the Lord through His passion and death. One should say the rosary daily. At meals let him or someone bless the food and give thanks. If he can, let him give some alms for God's gift to him. Before going to bed let him pray as he did in the morning and thank God for the good things he received during the day. Then he should examine his conscience carefully, repent of his falls and thank God for His protection which preserved him from worse. He should never go to sleep in mortal sin without genuine repentance as God is severe in His judgements. Then he should commend himself to his angel guardian and sleep in God's name.

In choosing a way of life – priesthood, marriage, religious life, the position or judge of any other post of authority (*uachdarántacht*) let him pray to God and seek advice from his spiritual father or from some competent person. Then he should fulfil the obligation of his state in life, e.g. if it is priesthood, let him say his Hours, have his priestly suit, his tonsure (*corann*).[37]

Every Christian should preserve himself and his people from bad company, from idleness and occasions of sin. He should make his will in good time and not have trouble at his death when he should be occupied with his salvation. Then follows a short method of making an annual confession or general confession of one's whole life. It consists of three parts: heartfelt sorrow, verbal confession and performance of the penance. The writer goes into great detail. He dwells on the ten commandments and the seven deadly sins. The penitent confesses all he can remember and just does not wait for the confessor to question him and merely reply to his questions. The penance should be performed with great devotion as soon as he can and let him thank God for the great gift which he has received.

The manner of making Communion is then discussed. Every Christian should have special devotion to the Trinity, to Christ our Saviour, to his Passion, to the Blessed Sacrament, to Mary, Michael, John the Baptist, Peter, Paul and Patrick, to his angel guardian and to the saint whose name he bears. He should be careful to pray daily for the church, for the strengthening of the Catholic faith, for the suppression of heresy, for peace among Christian rulers, for those in mortal sin and for those in purgatory.[38]

A bardic poem, *Fada h-éisteacht a Mhuire*, recording Reformation times, appeals to Mary:

Do not remain listening any longer; pray earnestly to your Son; O bright apple-blossom, do not allow us to be extinguished. Hundreds are upset after denying their faith, your people are bewildered, your temple is a stable. Shout in the court (of heaven), O mannerly white-bodied virgin, do not bear with no answer, awake Colum and Patrick.[39]

The poem, *Táining ceó tar an gcreidimh*,[40] is attributed to both Donnchadh Mór and to Eochaidh Ó hEoghusa, whose *floruit* is c. 1600. The latter is more likely to be the author. The poem itself is mainly concerned with preparation for death and judgement. But his poem, *Ar th'fhaosamh dhamh, a Dhé Athar*, shows Eochaidh as he stands before God:

O God the Father, I flee to thy protection; acknowledge me for the kinsman I am; my knee that used to bend before thee, behold it now imploring thy favour. Behold me, the foe, who betrayed thee; behold in me a new executioner; behold me the son of guileful ancestors coming to Thee with repentant heart. Long since I should have come to Thee; to be a reckless sinner is my nature. I am a vessel full of evil weeds.

I have not beaten my breast craving pardon; I have not trained myself – what stubborness! to bend my knee to Thee, O God ; now my eyes are streaming tears. I used to wound Thee and crucify Thee daily by my sins; I have behaved as Thy foe, betraying Thee, o dear, loving Son of God. I raise up my hand after raising my heart to Thee and accuse myself; behold me a poor wretch who was ever inflaming afresh Thy wounds, and thus doing the pleasure of my foe, so agressive …

May I not love, for the sake of passing time, this poor earth of short-lived harvest; may I not barter eternal glory for a short spell so that I may indeed dwell in heaven hereafter. 'Tis sad to give up the eternal kingdom for wealth that is not worth loving and fades away; sad for him whom pleasure, ever followed by prick of remorse, keeps from (heaven's) abundant glory. It should deceive no one – the varied beguilement which man's eye sees and gazes on with delight; O short-lived world, 'twere wiser to shrink with horror from thy comely winsome beauty.

Short the enjoyment of thy idle summertime, swift-passing the beauty of thy bright shining, soon passes the white bloom of thy orchards, not far off from me now thy winter. Grief soon follows the beginning of one's exulting in this passing world's deceitful pleasure; this foolish world's fair beauty is but a rainbow's smile. Let me not abandon, for the sake of passing joy, the house of the angels, the everlasting home; O Lord of Heaven, put in my heart (the grace) to earn it in zealousness of will.[41]

Just before the end of the century, we find a moving account of Aodh Rua Ó Domhnaill's devotion to Mary:

A prudent and gracious psalm-singing priest used to be with Ó Domhnaill continually, to offer Mass, the pure mysterious sacrifice of the Body and Blood of Christ, and it was his usual practice whenever he set out on an expedition or hosting, or whenever stress of danger menaced him, to fast for three days and confess his trespass to his confessor; thereafter he would lament his sins before God and partake of the Body of Christ. He requested his army on the occasion[42] to fast on the Golden Friday of the feast of the Blessed Virgin Mary.[43] Mass was offered for him on the next day, for the army generally for everyone who was in the camp, and he received, and the chiefs of the army with him, the Body of Christ with great reverence for the Lord Jesus and his Holy Mother on her feast that fell then. When he took notice of the haughty boasting of the governor, promising to come to his encampment that night, he prayed the Son of the virgin, who was within his breast, and the virgin herself, for whom he had fasted the day before, to beseech the heavenly Father and her beloved Son, first for his soul, and afterwards if it be what God would grant him that on him defeat would fall, that he should be left on the field of battle and that he should never return, but be beheaded by his enemies rather than be disgraced, as was the wish of the governor.[44]

The victory which followed was attributed to Aodh Rua's devotion to the Eucharist and to Mary.

Notes:

1. 'The Irish Church in the sixteenth century', *IER* 99 (1963) 102.

2. State Papers Henry VIII, 1-31. cf. *AU* 1505. Patrick Ó Feidhil, Franciscan, distinguished preacher in Ireland and Scotland.

3. Even the great abbey of Mellifont's church and buildings were so ruinous that the cost of repairs was estimated at £40 and thorns and gorse were eating up the lands of the precinct. B. Bradshaw, *The Dissolution of the Religious Orders in Ireland* (London, 1974) 37. Henceforth *Bradshaw*.

4. Morley, H., *Ireland under Elizabeth and James I* (London, 1890) 203.

5. Brady, J., 'Ireland and the Council of Trent', *IER* 68 (1946) 203.

6. D.B.M. I (Dublin, 1967) 375.

7. State Papers, Henry VIII, Ireland iii,141.

8. Bradshaw 218.

9. Reginald Walsh OP, 'Irish Manners and Customs in the 16th century', *Arch. Hib.* VI (1917) 183.

10. Jennings OFM, B., *Analecta Hibernica* VI, (1934) 183. *v.* also *Mary*, 186, n 68.

11. *Perbreve Compendium*, quoted in *Seanchas Ardmhacha* (1990) 57.

12. de Bhaldraithe, T., 'Leabhar Charswell in Éirinn' *Éigse* 9 (1958) 61-67. McAdoo, Rev H., 'The Irish Translations of the Book of Common Prayer' *Éigse* II (4) (1940) 250-57. de Brún, P., 'Dhá bhlogh de Theagasg Chríostaí ó ré Éilise (?), *Celtica* XIX (1978) 55-58. Williams, N., *I bPrionnta i Leabhar* (Áth Cliath, 1986) which deals with Protestants and Gaelic writing 1567-1724.

13. Moran, P. F., *Spic. Oss.* (Dublin, 1874-84) 105-106. She is one of the seventeen martyrs who were beatified recently.

14. Corish, P. J., *The Irish Martyrs* (Dublin, 1989) 11-13.

15. Lennon, C., 'Recusancy among the Dublin Patricians', *Studies in Church History*, Vol 25., Sheils, W. J., and Wood, D., (eds),(London, 1989) 127-8.

16. Mac Niocaill, G., *Éigse* VIII (1956-7) 231-36.

17. Caerwyn Williams, J. E., *Éigse* VI (1948-52) 127-34.

18. Ed. O'Kelleher, B. and Schoepperle, G., (Illinois, 1918).

19. Wulff, W., 'Contra Incantationes', *Ériu* XII (1938) 250-3, and *Ériu* XI (1933) 174-181.

20. Walsh, Fr P., *Gleanings from Irish Manuscripts* (Dublin, 1933) 2nd ed 123 ff.

21. n 19 *supra* p 251.

22. Ibid. 253.

23. Mac Niocaill, G., *Éigse* VIII (1956-7) 70-73 and 137. It is also found in MS RIA 23B3, 3B22, 24PI and 23C9. The golden Fridays were mainly connected with great feasts in the liturgy. Whoever fasted on the Fridays had his soul borne to heaven by angels. *Éigse* IX (1958-60) 32-33.

24. *Bradshaw* 101.

25. Ibid. 104-5.

26. *Ir. Trad.* 134-5.

27. *Mary* Chap. 5.

28. L McKenna, *Aith D.* I, xix.

29. Ibid. II, Poem 50.

30. Ibid. Poem 51.

31. Ibid. Poem 52.

32. Ibid. II, Poem 53.

33. Ibid. Poem 55.

34. Ibid. Poem 57.

35. Ibid. poem 59.

36. Ó Cuív, B., 'Flaithrí Ó Maolchonaire's Cathechism of Christian Doctrine', *Celtica* I, 2 (1950) 161-206.

37. Obviously the original text was written for continental Catholics since priests at this time in Ireland would have neither tonsure or clerical garb.

38. *Celtica* I, 207-229.

39. RIA 24 P29, 357.

40. *Di. D.* Poem 57. *Irish Monthly* (1922) 416-9.

41. *Aith. D.* Poem 73.

42. His battle was with General Conyers Clifford.

43. This seems to be the feast of the Assumption but *v. Mary*, 188 n 87. Walsh, Fr P., *Beatha Aodh Ruaidh Ui Dhomhnaill* (London, 1948 & 1957) *ITS* XLII, 24-5.

44 ibid. 232-3. Note that he also bought a house for himself on the feast of 'Holy Mary, mother of God' on the preceding year. 15 August 1598 was also the date of Hugh O'Neill's victory at the battle of the Yellow Ford.

CHAPTER 7

The Seventeenth Century

Ní fhuil clíar i n-íathaibh Fódla
Níl aifrinn againn ná órda
Níl baisde ar ár leanbhaigh óga
Gan fear seasaimh nó tagartha a gcóra
(There are no clergy, Masses or Orders, nor baptism for our
children, not any one to stand up for people's rights.)
(*Piaras Feirtéir*)

This century saw a considerable change in the position of
Catholics. In the early decades the Franciscan impact, noted in
the previous chapter, continued. This entailed an effort to inject
tridentine renewal. The Jesuits, though few in number, were not
alone efficient, but were the representatives of Rome and were
men who had received a wide continental education. They did
excellent work both in the pastoral and polemical fields, Fr
Fitzsimon being their leading light in theological discussion.
Though he had lost the faith and become a Protestant at the age
of ten, he later regained it. He says: 'I was overcome by Fr.
Thomas Darbishire an owld English Jesuit long time experienced in the reduction of many thousands to the Catholic religion.'[1] When he was imprisoned later he converted not alone his
gaoler but also the governor of the prison. He was also a very co-
gent defender of the faith in his writings. In the winter of 1641 he
was then about seventy-five years old and was condemned to be
hanged. He fled to the Dublin mountains, where he sought
refuge in a shepherd's hut. Worn out by fatigue and hardship he
was able to return to his brethren in Kilkenny and died there
probably in 1643.[2]

Though small in number, the Jesuits were very effective in

Munster also. In Tipperary they put an end to cattle-rustling and in Kerry they persuaded a thieving farmer to restore 446 beasts, horses and cattle, which he had stolen from his neighbours. Incidentally, in this same province a reward of £40 could be had for killing a Jesuit, £6.3.4 for any other priest trained on the continent and £5 for one who had never left Ireland.[3]

The Capuchins and Discalced Carmelites made their first foundations in Ireland in this century. A small number of secular priests had been able to find the opportunity of getting their formation and education in France and Spain. But the vast majority, especially the clergy of old Irish stock, could get very limited education since they could not manage to get abroad. But from 1578, the year of the foundation of the Irish College in Paris, more than thirty Irish Colleges were set up throughout western Europe before the end of the seventeenth century.[4]

The opening years of the century witnessed some significant persecutions. Dominic Collins was born in Youghal c. 1566 of merchant stock. He went to France c. 1586 and was bereft of funds so he worked in an inn for three years. He then became a soldier in the Catholic League and sometime later entered the Jesuits in Spain. In 1601 he sailed to Ireland with James Archer SJ and arrived in Kinsale. The result of the battle there was disastrous for Ireland and the church. Collins was driven back out to sea and landed in Castlehaven, which was in O'Sullivan Beare territory. In 1602, Dunboy, the stronghold there, was attacked and fell on 18 June. All were massacred except Dominic and two others. He revealed, when interrogated, that he had been a soldier and was now a Jesuit. The two others were executed in Cork but he was brought back to his native Youghal. As he had no information regarding the expedition to Kinsale and refused to serve the Crown as a soldier he was hanged on 31 October 1602. Some half dozen other Jesuits were also put to death about this time.[5]

More significant was the case of Conor O'Devany. He was Bishop of Down and Connor. In 1611 the Lord Deputy was authorised to punish some 'titular' bishops as an example of James I's attitude to Catholicism. The only two bishops in the country

at the time were Conor and David Kearney of Cashel. Bishop
O'Devany was arrested in June 1611 and imprisoned in Dublin.
Quite a number of 'old English' priests were also in prison.
O'Devany was joined by another member of the Franciscan
Order, Patrick O'Loughran, who was of old Irish stock, like the
bishop, and had been Hugh O'Neill's chaplain. Both were tried
for treason in January 1612. The bishop was close on eighty
years of age, while his confrère was about thirty-five. The trial
was transferred from Co Down to Dublin. The bishop showed
considerable skill in pointing out that he was not guilty of treason and consequently the only charge against him was that he
was a Catholic bishop. But the jury was a packed one and it
brought in a verdict of guilty. On 1 February they were taken
from the Castle to the present George's Hill. Thousands gathered round the scaffold while the bishop uttered a brief prayer,
which he also turned into an address to the crowd. He and Fr
O'Loughran were hanged in 1612. Five days later Lord Deputy
Chichester reported glumly to London 'how a titulary bishop
and a priest being lately executed here for treason are notwith-
standing ... thought martyrs and adored for saints.'[6]

Indications of the spiritual life may be found in many texts. Fr
Geoffrey Keating's *Saltair Mhuire*, written 1610-12 elaborates on
the value and manner of saying the Rosary. Each of the fifteen
mysteries is preceded by a short meditation and each Hail Mary
has a short enlightening scriptural sentence leading into it, e.g.
before the tenth Ave of the first joyful mystery he writes: 'the
consecrated virgin answered: "I am the servant of the Lord, let
what you have said be done to me." And then the word was
made man and God and man lived with us in one divine
Person'.[7]

The Franciscans expressed very clearly how they felt about
Catholics who changed their belief and were by no means spar-
ing when members of their Order were the culprits. Bona-
ventura Ó hEoghusa (+1614), in his poem *Truagh liom, a chom-
páin, do chor*, explained to his confrère who had changed his faith
that he was wrong and was to be pitied. He points out that
Scripture alone is not a sufficient guide.

Bheith d'ógh Mhuire riamh 'na h-óigh
Baisdeach leinbh gur chóir do grés,
bheith ar an Domhnach don Cháisg –
san Scrioptúir, fós, cáit 'nar léigh?[8]

That Mary was always a virgin, that a child should always be baptised, that Easter always falls on a Sunday, where did you ever read of this in Scripture?

In the previous century, Eoghan O'Duffy (1590) took a much dimmer view of Myler MacGrath who had been a Franciscan but changed his religion and became a bishop of several dioceses in the Established Church and who had also taken a wife to himself.

A Mhaoil[9] *gan Mhuire, ataoi leamh,*
dul ar neamh ní hé do thriall;
Maol gan aifreann, Maol gan órd
Maol go h-ifrionn is borb pian.
A Mhaoil gan chriediomh, a Mhaoil gan Dia
A Mhaoil gan Íosa, is sia neart,
rachair síos go lasair géar,
's do bhean féin ar leath-láimh leat.

Maol without Mary, you're a fool. Your journey is not towards heaven. Maol without Mass, Maol without Hours is a Maol destined for hell with its savage pain. Maol without faith, Maol without God, Maol without most influential Jesus, you shall descend to the piercing flame and your wife at your side.[10]

We find a welcome change in the Christmas carol written by another Franciscan, Aodh Mac Aingil (1572-1626), who became Archbishop of Armagh:

Coisg a réasúin stad a chiall,
glac an creidiomh, srian do bheól
ní thuigfe, is níor thuig-se riamh
dála an leinbh-si acht Dia beo.
Druid do shúile, a nádúir dhall;
t'eolas annso, is cam an ród;
creidim gach ní adubhairt mé
m'ughdar an té nár chan gó.

Dia do bheatha, a Íosa, arís!
Dia do bheatha i gclí an óigh,
A ghnúis is áille ná an ghrian
na míle fáilte do Dhia óg.

Hold, O reason, stop, O mind. Accept faith, hold your
tongue; you shall not, you never have understood the facts
concerning this Child – only the living God has. Close your
eyes, blind human. Your guidance here is wrong. I believe all
I have heard, and my authority is He who never lied. Hail,
once more Jesus! Welcome to You coming in human form
from the Virgin. A thousand welcomes, Thou countenance
more beautiful than the sun, o young God.[11]

Hugh MacCawell OFM and others stressed the need for spiritual
books in Gaelic. We have seen that Florence Conry translated a
catechism from Spanish into Gaelic. Fr Cathaldus Giblin OFM
has given an excellent short account of Franciscan catechetical
books in the seventeenth century.[12] They printed catechisms on
presses set up in their friaries in Belgium. In addition to using
the question-answer method they also used poetry to sum-
marise doctrine and to help to memorise it. One such poem is *An
Teagasg Críosdaidhe i nDán*.[13] It consists of a short general introduction and gives a metrical Creed, *Pater* and *Ave*, the ten commandments, the five precepts of the church,[14] the corporal and
spiritual works of mercy, the deadly sins, the sacraments, the
vices, the virtues, the gifts of the Holy Spirit, the beatitudes, the
five senses and the four last things. A short excerpt will provide
an idea of simplicity of language and the clarity of doctrine.

Reader of (this) little booklet, look to its source; it is more important than it looks; this work is the fosterer of your soul.
The pearl for which a man renounced possession of his temporal wealth – if the land in which it is, is searched for it, it
will be obtained here for nothing. I have not – it would not be
right for me – dulled with the shine of words, the glistening
array sparkling with gems from heaven – the radiant words
of the Creator. A scroll of debts is due to the Creator; I have
written the charter of your patrimony from Him, without or-
nament for you; inscribe this your charter in your heart.

The Metrical Creed, having treated of the Trinity and their gifts, continues:

> Behold the articles that treat of the holy divinity; now indeed must be expounded the articles dealing with the humanity. First of all we must believe that Mary in intensity of love conceived of the Holy Ghost in her womb, the Son of the eternal Father. That God became man and man eternal God, without these two natures being confused in one person. At the end of nine months after that, the Virgin begot him in Bethlehem without losing her virginity, afterwards, beforehand or at that time. The only Son of God, God and man, suffered in His human nature death on the Cross (and) was buried, through the sins of the children of Adam.

It continues on the ten commandments of God:

> If you wish charity, the third door leading into heaven, [the other two are faith and hope] to open, keep the ten commandments of the King as they are set down here in order. Do not attempt to adore a false God; do not take the name of God in vain; let Sunday, the day of the Lord, be observed always by you. Honour your parents piously; do not commit murder, lust or theft; do not bear false witness against anyone; do not covet for yourselves his property or his wife.[15]

We have already mentioned Hugh Mac Cawell's realisation of the need for spiritual works in Gaelic. In 1618 he published *Scáthán Shacramuinte na nAithridhe* on the Louvain press. Like other European catechisms, it is based on the Catechism of the Council of Trent and sets out to refute the claims made by Protestants in works written in Gaelic and published in Dublin. It is a long treatise on the sacrament of Penance dealing with contrition, the actual confession, absolution and the penance or satisfaction and indulgences. The fact that he was not in the bardic line made his writing perhaps less elegant but more homely and simple. In addition he illustrates his teaching with stories which are always a help.[16]

No study has been undertaken to ascertain how widely these catechisms and spiritual books penetrated among the Gaelic Irish. General catechetics was given by the priest on Sundays at

Mass. That there was profound ignorance in parts is borne out by the report of the Achonry priest, John O'Sullivan, in 1668. While admitting that his experience was only personal, it may easily have been much wider, particularly in backward areas. His problem arose in the matter of giving absolution to people who had very little instruction. He said that many Catholics, even those prepared to suffer for their faith, thought that attendance at Mass was sufficient. On questioning them to ascertain the knowledge they had of their religion, some said that there were three Gods, some four or even more as they added in Our Lady and perhaps some of the apostles and other saints. Some held that the three Persons of the Trinity became man. Personally he did not absolve such people but other priests did, realising the scarcity of priests and the opportunity for confession might not arise very easily again. One of his penitents must have given him food for thought because he met Fr O'Sullivan's questions with the rejoinder that these subtle matters were quite beyond him, adding that he came to confession because he wanted absolution for his sins.[17]

Stapleton in his catechism in Latin, written in Brussels in 1639, says that the catechesis of many unlettered Gaelic speakers consisted in teaching them the common prayers and the rudiments of the faith in Latin which they memorised without understanding what it meant. The sacrament of confession had to be transformed by changing the emphasis on satisfaction as a regulation of external offences among feuding kingroups into an emphasis on sorrow for personal sin in a sacrament of individual reconciliation with God.[18]

Town and cities were reasonably catered for. Tridentine priests were more numerous in cities and less numerous in Gaelic-speaking areas. The fact that books were printed should have made it easier for both secular and regular priests to obtain copies, though some may have been too poor to buy them. Everywhere the clergy were dependent on the laity for material support. This naturally led to conflicts between secular and regular clergy in poorer areas. In cities or in the bigger towns Catholic merchants still supported the clergy and for a time funds were still available from guilds. In the early part of the century, priests were appointed to localities rather than to the old parishes but from c. 1630 onwards the priest system and the role of the parish priest, deriving from Trent, was being more widely developed.

The Jesuit Sodality of Our Lady was able to function more freely and in 1617 a branch in Cashel was the first to be aggregated to the Roman Sodality. By 1621 it had prelates, priests and many lay people who observed the rules carefully and encouraged others to piety and to a deepening of their spiritual lives. Confession and Communion were received more frequently by the members. Peace was fostered and prisoners were relieved. Clonmel had a branch in 1617 as had Limerick, Cork, Kilkenny and Carrick-on-Suir by 1620. In 1641 Drogheda, Dublin, Galway, Wexford and New Ross had branches. All these catered principally for the 'old English' or for Irish Catholics who knew English. These were generally middle-class or more prosperous members of the community. Writing in 1661 Fr William St Leger SJ remarks:

> In all these cities (which we have already named) Congreg-
> ations or Sodalities of the Blessed Virgin were established.
> Crowds of better citizens and young men entered them to the
> great edification of all, and it is well-nigh impossible to tell
> how much, by their works of mercy and frequentation of the
> sacraments, they strengthened the cause of the Catholic religion
> … It is owing to these Sodalities that the seminaries beyond
> the sea were kept supplied with qualified students, that bishops
> always had a number of suitable candidates and that the
> various religious Orders in Ireland obtained their best
> recruits.[19]

The Vincentian Fathers arrived in Ireland early in 1647 and set-tled in the dioceses of Cashel and Limerick. They were inundated with requests for missions. They proceeded on the lines which had been successful in rural France. Word of the wholesale mas-sacres by Cromwell in Drogheda and Wexford filtered into Limerick where they had just arrived and concluded a mission attended by 20,000 people. More alarming was the report that Cromwell was marching on Munster. But there was still a greater cause for alarm in the city by the Shannon, for the spotted plague, even a more dread visitant, had made its appearance. It had spread from Galway and had its origin and first victim in the house of Blake, the man who handed Rinucinni the expulsion Order. Just before the outbreak of the plague, Dr O'Dwyer had written to St Vincent de Paul reporting on the good work of the Vincentians in his diocese:

> Through their example and zeal the Catholic gentry, now few in number, have become models of virtue and piety, which was by no means the case before your priests came among us ... Drunkenness, swearing, adultery and other disorders have vanished ... The entire face of this city has been changed. Our Cathedral was full each time the Fathers preached or gave instructions or conducted the other pious exercises of the mission ... I myself owe my soul's salvation to your sons, Father, and I beg of you to write them a few consoling words.

At the close of this mission, the Mayor, Thomas Stritch, and the Councillors, who had led the citizens at the devotional exercises, placed the keys of the city in the hands of the ancient statue of Our Lady of Limerick.

Cork-born Fr. Donatus Crowley, who entered St Lazare in 1643, served the victims of fever in France. Once a band of soldiers drove away the cattle of some poor villagers, who came and complained to Fr Crowley. Off he ran after the marauders, caught up with them and spoke so eloquently of the poverty of the owners and the dependence on their few cows that the raiders gave back all and the priest returned in triumph to the village driving the cows before him.[20]

* * *

Fr Anthony Gearnon OFM was appointed Superior in Louvain in 1644. While carrying out his priestly work in Ireland he realised how ignorant the people were of the truths of their faith. He decided to compile instructions and prayers and this resulted in *Parrthas an Anma* which came from the press there in 1645. It seems to have been the most popular of the Catholic religious books in Gaelic in this country. One section was in the form of a prayerbook and is found in many manuscripts which indicates it popularity and its use.[21] Richard O'Farrell OFM Cap, in his report to Propaganda in 1658,[22] mentions that Florence Conroy's *Sgáthán an Chrábhaidh*, Hugh Mac Cawell's *Sgáthán Shacramuinte na hAithrídhe* and Bonaventure O'Hussey's *Teagasg Críostaidhe* helped to dissipate ignorance and led the people to live a deeper Christian life. The same might be said of Gearnon's work. All these were very practical books. They distilled the teaching of Trent into the Irish situation. The fact that they were in Gaelic also meant that they were simplified and also inbued with an Irish approach to God. St Francis de Sales' *Introduction to the Devout Life* was also translated into Gaelic in this century.[23] This might have been a great help to the laity who could read it as it dealt specifically with their needs. When it was first published in French his friends tried to dissuade Francis from writing any other book as they felt the welcome which this one received could never again be equalled. Some of the prayers in *Ár bPaidreacha Dúchais*[24] date from bardic times and must have had an effect on unlettered people as they were easy to memorise. Diarmuid Ó Laoghaire's publication shows how varied they were.

Though persecution was very severe, especially from 1650-60, parts of the country were able to have even outward displays of devotion. Kilkenny city was able to hold a special solemnity in honour of Our Lady in 1651. For eight days the citizens performed works of piety and mercy and all received Communion on the appointed day. There was a solemn procession through the city in which bishops, earls, magistrates and the whole city assisted with torches and candles accompanying the statue of the Blessed Virgin which was set in the market place for public veneration while the bells of every church in the city rang out and cannons were fired. This happened just after Cromwell's memorable visit to the city which was followed by a plantation.[25] The oath of abjuration was prescribed by the government in 1658. It required the rejection of the Mass and of devotion to Our Lady and the saints. The Superior of the Jesuits wrote to Propaganda in April 1658 stating that 'as yet there had not been one to take the oath with the exception of a stranger in our island, who was afraid to lose the large possessions he had acquired'. In fact he travelled two hundred miles to take the oath so that he would not be known. The account continues with the imposition of the oath in Cork. Roughly five or six thousand people gathered on the day appointed. They formed queues outside Christ Church, which was situated between Tuckey Street and the Western Road.

> In the foremost ranks was young man who entered the church with a light step, and whose looks beamed with joy. The clerk received immediate orders to administer the oath to him first, for the magistrates saw in his joyous countenance a readiness, as they imagined, to assent to their desires. The young man requested that the oath should be translated into Irish, for he feared lest some of those round him, not understanding the English language, might inadvertently take the oath. A crier at once read it in Irish, so that all within the church might hear. 'And what is the penalty,' he then asked, 'for those who refuse the oath?' 'The loss of two-thirds of their goods,' was the magistrate's reply. 'Well then,' he added smiling, 'all that I possess is £6; take four of them; with the two that remain, and the blessing of God, myself and my family will subsist; I reject your oath.'[26]

In the years 1660-1691, the synods of the period note that ignorance of the faith was widespread due to persecution. However, vocations began to increase. Persecution was intermittent. Bishop Luke Wadding of Wexford, who was a fine pastoral bishop and helped the practice of religion by the distribution of manuals, catechisms, beads and medals, was arrested during the 'Popish Plot' in 1678. His good relations with Protestants, however, effected his release. This was the period of Oliver Plunkett's mission, 1669-1681. With his Roman background of more than a score of years, he found it hard to adjust to various practices in the Irish situation. His letters reflect the state of religion in parts of the country. In addition to drunkeness there were problems of celibacy. With regard to the former, Oliver became an abstainer to give the example to his clergy and is reputed to have said: 'Give me an Irish priest without this vice and he is assuredly a saint.'[27] He gave considerable attention to catechesis and tried to control superstition especially the more unseemly practices at wakes. He did a great deal of pastoral visitation. His work was disrupted by the Popish Plot as was Peter Talbot's, then Archbishop of Dublin, who died in prison. A much more serious view was taken of Oliver Plunkett and on 1 July he was executed at Tyburn in England. An Act was passed in 1697 banishing all bishops and regular clergy from the country. This marks the initiation of the penal days.

* * *

In this century, as in many previous ones, there was a certain laxity of morals 'but at no time was the excessive licence associated with the Restoration period in England to be found in Ireland'. Prostitution was common in towns and cities especially in Dublin and Limerick. There is nothing in the purely native authorities of the time to suggest that the moral standard of the people was particularly low. Poets dwell on drink more freely than on sexual laxities. *Parliament Chlainne Thomáis*, a mid-seventeenth century satire on boorishness, provides evidence of sexual laxity in the lowest stratum of the community.

Illegitimacy was not only common but did not constitute a serious handicap in life. The ease with which divorces were obtained was one of the public scandals adversely commented on by writers of the sixteenth and early seventeenth century, though considered by Keating in his *Díonbhrollach* to be exaggerated. In 1634 it was deemed necessary to pass a law through the Irish parliament to enforce monogamy and it was only carried after determined opposition in both Houses, which at the time were composed of Catholics as well as Protestants. Even six years after the Bill became law, the Lords made an unsuccessful attempt to have it repealed. Writing in 1672, Bishop Brenan of Waterford reports some laxity of living and irregularity in marriages but he adds that 'the people, generally speaking, are very religious and pious, leading a Christian life without great faults or many scandals.' McLysaght concludes that there is no evidence to support the idea that chastity was a virtue as highly esteemed in rural Ireland before the penal code as it was later. His evidence is not too clear. Quoting Bourchier's 'Advertisements for Ireland' to give substance to his judgement, he states:

> They generally (be they never so poor) affect to marry timely or else keep one unmarried and cohabit with her as their reputed wife ... Many of the British inhabitants there and natives keep two wives at once in divers places, and the mere Irish ordinarily, after a private contract, or sometimes without any condition but like on both sides, cohabit with single women in public as their wives and never solemnise any other marriage with them.[28]

But Lynch, in *Cambrensis Eversus*, gives an impression that the Irish people of the generation before the Restoration were much less given to loose living than is suggested by Bourchier. Keating and the Jesuits give a similar impression to that of Lynch but McLysaght would hold that, up to the middle of the century, there was some substance to the charges of a more general loose morality.[29] Efforts to incorporate rites of passage, keening, feasting and (over-) drinking and superstitions at patterns, into a Christian way of life had little success. Drinking habits seem to have improved in the half century, 1630-80, despite Oliver Plunkett's severe criticism or perhaps because of it.[30] Bribery and corruption were part and parcel of the system. Almost everyone from the highest to the humblest official had his price. Complaints of crooked dealing and dishonesty in trade are pretty rare. Failure of gentry to meet their debts is noted periodically. Petty thieving was common. The English traveller, Dunton, was much annoyed by this practice in his journeying through the country. After a particularly exasperating experience in Kilkenny, he excalimed: 'The thieves of Drogheda are saints compared to the pickpockets of Kilkenny.' But on the whole Irish people of this period were not very self-indulgent in the matter of food. Abstinence on Wednesday, Friday and Saturday was *de rigeur*. Even on these days eggs were often excluded. While perjury appears to have been quite common it does not seem to have been considered a serious blot on the good name of the country between 1650-1700.

There is a suggestion of a belief in the supernatural punishment of perjurers in Fr. White's account of the trial of Doctor Pierce

Creagh in Cork in 1705, when the floor of the court collapsed, and all the people were precipitated into the cellar. One of the 'false witnesses was crushed to death in the ruins and the other fled, and none escaped falling down with the floor except the judge whose seat was supported by an iron bar and our Prelate whose chair happened to be placed on a beam which did not give way, and he continued sitting, as it were, in the air. The judge cried out that Heaven itself acquitted him and he thereupon dismissed him with a great deal of honours.'[31]

Between 1670 and the end of the century, bishops like Oliver Plunkett, John O Molony (Killaloe), Luke Wadding of Ferns and John Brenan of Waterford laboured strongly to provide adequate catechesis, Sunday Mass and the sacraments. The thatched Masshouse had become the ordinary centre in the south while the Massrock was very common in Ulster. In some places Catholics were allowed to have Mass provided it was not at the same time as the Protestant service and provided they did not appear on the streets during service time. Not all priests were able to preach but they could give basic catechesis. They were obliged to provide a preacher at least every three months. The basic prayers were to be recited at Mass every Sunday and the *De profundis* for the dead was to be said after Mass. The diocese of Ferns under Bishop Wadding (+1691) was probably one of the most active counter-Reformation dioceses.[32]

Towards the close of the century, the short period of James II (1685-88) brought a false glimmer of hope when complete freedom of religious practice was allowed. This was quickly suppressed on the arrival of William of Orange, with the defeats of Derry and the Boyne and the ultimate defeat at Limerick in 1691. It is interesting to reflect that if James had been successful and if a Catholic Stuart monarchy had been established our situation to-day would probably be totally different. Instead of enduring the long intermittent persecution, the church in Ireland might easily have lost contact with the people and become a 'gallican' and fettered church, as happened in many countries in Europe in the eighteenth century, and suffered a similar fate with the fall of those regimes.

Literature

The Gaelic poets of the seventeenth century who have left us memorable spiritual thoughts are Geoffrey (Seathrún) Keating (1570?-1645?), Pádraigín Haicéad OP (1600-1654), Piaras Feiritéir (+1653), Dáibhí Ó Brúadair (1625-1698) and Aodhagán Ó Raithile (1670?-1726?). Keating was educated on the continent and returned to work in Tipperary. Influenced by the words of Christ, 'Daughters of Jerusalem, weep not for me but for your-selves', he writes:

> *Caoin tú féin a dhuine bhoicht*
> *De chaoine cháich coisc do shúil ...*
> *Caoin ar dtús do pheaca féin.*

Repentance, like charity, begins at home. Lament and do penance for your own sins. While he could appreciate pleasure he was well able to relate it to good living and to recognise that it was transitory.

> *Fáidhbhréagach an saol so is ná humhluigh dó*
> *Gearr bhéaras na séada so chnúmhsaighis dó*
> *Níl lá téarma ag aon neach gur buan bhéas beo*
> *Ach mar bláth éadtrom chraobh-ghlas an uair bhíos nódh.*

The world is deceptive so be not influenced by it for in a short time it will take the treasures you have gathered. No one has any guarantee of a long life no more than the light green-branched flower in its freshness.

Later in life he is more cynical:

> *Bhéarthar thú le ceathrar ar ghuailnibh id'róimh*
> *Is gléasfaid duit leabaidh fhuar-chaol dhomhain*
> *Adéarfaidh lucht t'éagnaigh ag crua-chaoi deór*
> *Cuir cré uirthi – créad é a gnó thuas níos mó?*

You'll be borne on the shoulders of four to your grave and they will prepare a deep cold, narrow bed for you. Those who mourn you, shedding hard tears, will say: Put earth on her – what further business has she above?

Following the Old Testament idea when the chosen people blamed their suffering on their sins, an idea which St Patrick also mentions when he blames his captivity on his earlier life,

Keating continues the motif as he blames Ireland for her sad condition:

Éigceart na nÉireannach féin
Do threascair iad d'aoinbhéim
Ag spairn fá cheart gearr corrach
Ní neart na n-arm n-eachtrannach.

It was the misdeeds of the Irish themselves which vanquished them in one blow – fighting about a short uncertain right – and not the arms of the foreigners.[33]

Pádraigín Haicéad has much the same idea in *Óm scéol ar Árdmháigh Fáil* when he says of (mother) Ireland, *mo chlann féin do dhíol a máthair* (my own family sold their mother).

Keating's two books, *Trí Biorghaoithe an Bháis* (The Three Shafts of Death) and *Eochairsgíath an Aifrinn*, probably influenced the more learned among the clergy and laity. The work on the Mass is in controversial mould and is based on the documents of Trent while *The Three Shafts of Death*, which is a treatise on death and purgatory, is more popular in tone. They are the only two prose books of their kind known to exist in Gaelic in the seventeenth century. Tadhg Ó Dúshláine suggests that Keating probably drew his inspiration for these works from the work of *Odo Ceritona*. He also suggests that Domhnall Ó Colmáin, author of *Parliament na mBan*, and some religious poets of this century also used *Odo* as a source.[34] The earliest extant copy of *Eochairsgíath* is dated 1657. It was transcribed regularly down to the nineteenth century. Though controversial in tone, it contained a firm theological foundation expressed in classical modern Irish.[35] Both works fitted in well with the catechisms appearing in the seventeenth and eighteenth centuries though to-day Keating is studied more for his linguistical than devotional value.

Pádraigín Haicéad combines the humorous and the serious in his outlook:

Má bheir Dia do thíghearnas damhsa
bheith slán on láimh seo do leónadh
Do ghéan beart is maith fa dheóidh damh
Leigfead do bhaosradh na h-óige.

Leigfead síos go mín mo sheolta
isleóchad m'uaill, cé truagh leó-san
ní bhead feasta go rabairneach róimhear
ní iarrfad clú ná tús póige.[36]

He made his pact with God. If He cures his wounded hand
Pádraigín will turn over a new leaf and quit the follies of youth.
He will practice humility, turn his back on carousing and will
seek neither honour nor even a peck. He was an interesting character.

A confrère of his, Peter Higgins, who was born in or near Dublin
c. 1600 had greater demands made on him. He was in Spain in
1627 and was ordained there. In the early 1630s he had returned
to Ireland and worked in the area round Naas, Co Kildare. In the
winter 1641-42 this countryside was taken over by rebels but
Peter continued his work and was able to give protection to
many Protestants, some of whom had fled from Dublin. When
the Crown forces came to Naas in 1642 Peter presented himself
and asked for protection as he had no part in the political struggle but had done his best for all sides. But nevertheless he was
hanged on 23 March 1642 because he was a priest.[37]

The appearance of Cromwell just before 1650, with his sweeping
conquest, brought a great persecution of the clergy, and heavy
plantation in Munster and Leinster with the result that only
about 22% of the land remained in Catholic hands. Many priests
were killed, imprisoned or exiled and the era of the priesthunter
took shape. From this time onward the Mass rock and nocturnal
celebration of Mass begins to be noted. To this period belong
both Terence Albert O'Brien OP, Bishop of Emly, and John
Kearney OFM of Cashel. Bishop O'Brien was born in 1601 near
Cappamore, Co Limerick into a well-off farming family. He
studied in Spain and was ordained in 1627 and returned to
Ireland. In 1643 he was elected Provincial of the Dominicans and
in 1648 he was chosen Bishop of Emly. He was captured in
Ireton's siege of Limerick and put to death on 30 October 1651 in
a barbaric manner and was immediately venerated as a martyr.

John Kearney was born in Cashel in 1619, joined the Franciscans

and was sent to their college in Louvain in Belgium. He was ordained in 1642. Though he was captured on his way home in
England he managed to escape. In Ireland he ministered first in
his native Cashel. This territory was taken by Cromwell and he
was captured in 1653. He was taken to Clonmel and accused of
functioning as a priest. He was sentenced to death and hanged
on 11 March. Fr William Tirry OSA, a Corkman, was arrested in
March 1654 in Fethard. He was brought to Clonmel, and hanged
on 2 May that year.[38] These are but a few instances among many
who gave their lives for the faith in this century.

Piaras Feiritéir (+1654) speaks of Cromwell's dispersion of the
clergy and its effects:

> *Ní fhuil clíar in íathaibh Fódla*
> *níl aifrinn againn ná órda*
> *níl baisde ar ár leanbhaibh óga*
> *gan fear seasaimh ná tagartha a gcóra.*

There are no clergy, Mass nor Orders – no baptism for our
young children – no one to stand up for the people's rights.

Dáibhí Ó Brúadair was quite a young man when Cromwell's
plantation took place. As such he offered his gift of poetic composition to God c. 1648:

> *Tionnsnaim tosach is toradh mo scríbhinne*
> *chun lonnradh A thoile 's A mhola go fírinneach.*

He seeks to praise God and to do His will in his writing. His
poem, *Adoramus Te Christ*, shows deep appreciation of Christ's
suffering

> *Is bághach mé re buime an ríoghdhúilimh*
> *i mbráithreas tug re duine an díolmhúineach*
> *láidir, glic do sciob a phríosúnach*
> *um cháisc a broid an chuithe chríonúrlaigh.*

To the nurse of my King and Creator I'm proudly affection-
ate, who united that Champion to man in bonds of fraternity;
in power and wisdom He quickly delivered its prisoner at
pasch from the slavery vile of the faggot-fringed pit.[39]

He uses *coinneal an chuain* (candle of the harbour) as a description of God and praises Mary's virginity: *Glaine mar í níor geineadh i gclí* (purity like hers was not conceived in a womb). His poetic compositions bore little return towards making a livelihood so like many another Irish poet he complains bitterly of the passing of the old order. From 1674 on his life was poor and his lot is reflected in his poems. He criticises the clergy for their avarice (*do goineadh ár gcléir le saint faríor*). In his poem, *A Chráibhthigh seal*, he castigates a priest who had changed his religion. In his long life he experienced most of the hardships of the century including the plantations under Cromwell, the flight of the Wild Geese, the banishment of bishops and Regulars in the closing decade of his life.

Though younger than Dáibhí, Aodhagán Ó Rathile reflects much of his mentality. He voices once again the conviction that the Irish are a part-cause of their own ruin:

Is dearbh gurab é gach éigean íogórach
ganguid is éitheach, claon is díoth-chomhaill
gan ceangal le chéile, acht réabadh, rinn-scórnach
do tharraing ar Éirinn fraoch an Ríogh chómachtaigh.

Chailleadar Gaedhil a dtréithe caoin córach
carthannacht, féile, béasa is binn-cheólta
allathuirc claon dó, thraoch sinn fa mhórsmacht
agallamh Aon-Mhac Dé ar Ghaoidhil d'fhóirithin.

In sooth it is every violence of injustice on our part, deceit, falsehood, treachery and dishonesty, our want of unity, and instead, the tearing of each other's throats, that have drawn down on us keenly the rage of the mighty King ...

The Gaels have lost their gentle qualities – charity, hospitality, manners and sweet music; wicked alien boars it was that forced us under great oppression; I beseech the only Son of God to grant relief to the Gaels.[40]

Attendance at Mass is commonly mentioned and one gets the feeling of communities coming together for Sunday Mass whether it was in townhouses, in country chapels or in the open air. The English traveller. William Brereton, who visited Dublin in 1635 gives a good description of the Mass house in Back Lane under the care of the Jesuits.

The pulpit in this church was richly adorned with pictures, and so was the high altar, which was advanced with steps, and railed out like cathedrals; upon either side thereof was there erected places for confession; no fastened seats were in the middle or body hereof, nor was there any chancel; but that it might be the more capacious, there was a gallery erected on both sides and at the lower end.[41]

Professor T.F. O'Rahilly produced a collection known as *Burdúin Bheaga*, subtitled *Pithy Irish Quatrains*. He says that they date from the seventeenth century onwards and 'are a mirror in which we can see the hearts and thoughts of the ordinary people from the seventeenth till the twentieth century. They are a tasty drink, a healthy potion which will strengthen the spiritual bond between us and our forebears.'[42]

> *Is iungna an toisc an cor 'na bhfuilim i bpéin*
> *Mo thuisgint óm thoil 's mo thoil ag druidim óm chéill*
> *Ní tuigtear dom thoil gach locht dom thuisgint is léir,*
> *'S má tuigtear, ní toil lé ach toil a tuisgeana féin.*

It's strange what pangs I feel from these disputes –
my sense, my will, my will my sense confutes;
my will embraces what my sense disproves
and when it wills, it wills but what itself approves.[43]

Another quatrain spiritualises this thought:

> *A Bhuime na mbocht, ón locht 'na bhfuilim beir mé,*
> *Túir tuigse dom thoil, nú toil dom thuigse, is beam réig;*
> *Os imeacht le h-olc dom thoil, na ligtear mé lé,*
> *Ach cuirig mo thoil led thoil 'na h-inead, a Dhé.*[44]

O Mother of the poor, release me from my fault. Give understanding to my will or will to my understanding and I'll be fine. Since my will heads for evil may I not be allowed to accompany it but unite my will with Your will, O God.

The well-known comparison or contrast appears:

> *Sagairt óir is cailís chroinn*
> *bhí le linn Phádraig in Éirinn*
> *sagairt chroinn is cailís óir*
> *i ndeire an domhain dearóil.*[45]

In Patrick's day there were golden priests and wooden chalices in Ireland – but at the end (of this) sad world there will be wooden priests and golden chalices.

These quatrains are just a few chosen almost at random which portray different aspects of the Irish mind.

Notes:

1. Corboy SJ, J., 'Fr Henry Fitzsimon SJ (1566-1643)', *IER* 32 (1943) 260.

2. Ibid. 261-66.

3. McRedmond, L., 'The Jesuits in Ireland' (part I), *Religious Life Review* 30 (1991) 44-45.

4. Ó Fiaich, T., *The Irish Colleges in France* (Dublin, 1990) 8-9.

5. Corish, P. J., *The Irish Martyrs* (Dublin, 1989) 17-19.

6. Ibid. 24. O'Devany's death was an event of unexpected importance in the development of the counter-reformation in Ireland. More than a dozen accounts of his death, many of them printed, were circulated in Catholic Europe within a few years. Clarke, A., *New History of Ireland* iii (Oxford, 1976) 209.

7. MS RIA 2319, 101-124.

8. Mhag Craith, C., *Dán na mBráthar Mionúr* (Dublin, 1967) Poem 9, st. 59. Henceforth *DBM*.

9. Maolmhuire is the Gaelic for Myler.

10. *DBM* I, 35; II, 61, 1. I have changed the translation of the last line from 'holding your wife by the hand'.

11. Ibid. I, 156, II, 68.

12. *Ir.Spir.* Chap VII.

13. *DBM* I Poem 12.

14. DBM II 29-30 gives them I) observe the Holy Days by attending Mass; 2) fast during Lent and on vigils and Ember days; 3) abstain from meat on Friday and Saturday; 4) annual confession and Communion; 5) no public solemnisation of marriage in Lent of from the beginning of Advent until the Epiphany.

15. *DBM* II, pp 27-29.

16. Ó Maonaigh, C., OFM, (eag.) (Áth Cliath, 1952).

17. Millett, B., OFM, 'Scritture riferite nei Congressi', *Collectanea Hibernica* Nos. 6-7 (1963-64) 144-48. Henceforth *Coll. Hib.*

18. Corish, P. J., *The Irish Catholic Experience* (Dublin, 1985) 108. Henceforth *ICE.*

19. MacErlean, J., SJ, *The Sodality of the Blessed Virgin Mary in Ireland* (Dublin, 1928) 16. Henceforth *Sodality*.

20. Purcell, M., 'St Vincent de Paul and Ireland 1640-60', *IER* Vol 102 (1964) 4-13 *passim*.

21. Ed. Fachtna, A., OFM (Dublin, 1965).

22. *Commentarius Rinnucinianus* (Dublin, 1949) Vol V. 490.

23. Ó Súilleabháin, P., OFM, *Irisleabhar Má Nuat* (1964) 97.

24. Ó Laoghaire, D., SJ, *Ár bPaidracha Dúchais* (Áth Cliath, 1975) p xxiii.

25. Moran, P. F., *Spicilegium Ossoriense* (Dublin, 1874) I, 354. Henceforth *Spic. Oss.*

26. Moran, P. F., *Historical Sketch of the Persecution suffered by the Catholics of Ireland* (Dublin, 1884) 350-1.

27. McLysaght, E., *Irish Life in the Seventeenth Century* (Oxford, 1950) 30 from Moran, *Memoirs of Dr Plunkett*, 78.

28. McLysaght, op. cit. 47-61.

29. Ibid. 49-51.

30. Ibid. 68, 73, 78-80.

31. Ibid.75-6. He cites RIA MS 24 D21 f. 219.

32. *ICE* 108-120 passim.

33. Ó Raibheartaigh, T., *Máighistrí san Fhilíocht* (Áth Cliath, 1939) 7-22.

34. *Tionól* (Dublin Institiute for Advanced Studies, 1990), 'Odo de Ceritona agus scríobhneoirí cráifeacha Gaelige san 17ú haois', 17.

35. Cunningham, B., 'Geoffrey Keating's *Eochair Sgiath an Aifrinn* and the Catholic Reformation in Ireland'. *The Churches, Ireland and the Irish*, Sheils, W. J., and Wood, D., (eds), (Oxford, 1989) 133-44.

36. Ó Canainn, P., *Filíocht na nGael* (Áth Cliath, 1958) 244. There are variations of this *aithrí*.

37. Corish, *The Irish Martyrs*, 25-28.

38. Ibid. 28-31.

39. MacErlean SJ, J., *Duanaire Dháibhidh Uí Bhrúadair*, ITS (London, 1910) I, 20-23. Henceforth *DDB*.

40. Dineen, Rev P. S. and O Donoghue, T., *Dánta Aodhagáin Uí Rathaile*, *ITS* (London, 1911) Vol III. Poem I.

41. Gilbert, J. T., *A History of the City of Dublin* (Dublin, 1861) 242.

42. Cork, 1925. Preface.

43. Ibid. No 35.

44. Ibid. No 36.

45. O'Rahilly, T. F., *Dán fhocail* (Dublin, 1921) 21. St John Chrysostom in his Homily 50 had 'God has no need of golden vessels but of golden

hearts. I am not saying that you should not give golden vessels'. We find the idea also in St Boniface, Thomas More, John Fisher and Oliver Plunkett. The Latin version is '*Quondam sacerdotes aurei ligneis calicibus utebantur, nunc e contra lignei sacerdotes aureis utuntur calicibus.*' Ó Súill-eabháin, P., OFM, *Éigse* X (1961-3) 315-6. *v.* Mansi, *Sacrorum Conciliorum Collectio*, col 142.

Addendum:

The whole corpus of Louvain Franciscan scholarship emphasises the continuity of the faith in a way which contributed to a new sense of the Irish past and subsequently to a sense of national consciousness. The continuity of the Catholic faith was a tenet of the Counter-Reformation movement, and the sense of Irish national identity which developed gradually in the centuries after the Louvain scholars had been active was one focused on the European theme of the continuity of Catholicism and the Catholic community. It featured a sense of unquestioning loyalty to the Pope, and was defined by a sense of grievance against persecution on the grounds of religion. The culture and ideology of the Franciscan scholars at Louvain inspired a corpus of writing, of which the catechisms and theological tracts reached the widest Irish audience, which reflected many aspects of the idea that Catholicism, even in the face of persecution, was 'the fact that makes an Irishman'.

Cunningham, B., 'The Culture and Ideology of Irish Franciscans 1606-1650', *Ideology and the Historians*, (ed) Ciaran Brady (Dublin, 1991) 29-30.

CHAPTER 8

The Eighteenth Century

As trom do chodla, a Mhuire mhóir.
(Heavy is your sleeping, O mother Mary.)
(Seán Ó Neachtain)

The Penal Laws began with the decree banishing bishops and the regular clergy in 1697.[1] In 1703 the Act of Registration allowed one priest per parish provided he registered with the State authorities. A little more than a thousand registered, some managing to revive the names of parishes which were then extinct. But when the Oath of Abjuration against the Jacobite cause was imposed in 1709 the system broke down as only some thirty priests obeyed the law. The idea behind the Act of 1703 was that the priests would be known to the authorities and there was no intention of replacing them after their death. Moreover the Protestant sovereigns were being pressured by Catholic rulers in Europe with the result that, when the clergy began to return from the continent, they were imprisoned or re-exiled rather than executed.

To exclude the laity from political power, a declaration against transubstantiation, imposed on all office holders, was an effective prohibition. Similar restrictions were enacted by municipal corporations and by professional guilds. Succession to Catholic estates operated under a discriminatory law that directed their division among all the male children, which was called gavelkind. As a result, a number of barristers, lawyers and rich landowners changed their religion. Social discrimination, caused by the alleged fear of a Stuart rising, deprived Catholics of the right, customarily conceded to all gentlemen, to carry swords. In local areas levies were imposed on Catholics for damages by

Catholic invading forces in time of war. They were to be kept in a permanent position of subjection – as Lecky has well expressed it – to make them poor and keep them poor. Property, especially landed property, was the basis of power. In 1641 roughly 59% of the land was held by Catholics; in 1688 the figure was 22%; by 1703 it was 14% and in the 1770s it was 5%.

Masshouses, which were common in Leinster and Munster, were interfered with only occasionally and though the priest-hunters were active, like John Garzia, who sought out Archbishop of Dublin, they were not popular even with the government. The Archbishop had gone into hiding in 1712. Finally Garzia found him at 2 a.m. on Sunday 1 June 1719. But the authorities were embarrassed and discharged the archbishop and Garzia received no reward. While the first quarter of the century was harsh on the clergy the Registration Act was not really effective. By 1730 we find the parish system developing and Masshouses were improving from 1730 onwards though they still kept carefully to the back streets.

The Established Church continued to assert its rights for the fees for baptisms, marriages and funerals but the sacraments etc. were conferred by Catholic priests. On Sundays there were sermons or catechesis. Children received their instruction on Saturdays and servants on Sundays. Many parishes had school teachers, some of whom had been going for the priesthood and they also taught catechesis. The entry in the will of Archbishop Luke Fagan (+1733), 'I give Mr Nary for the use of the charitable infirmary £15', shows that though the latter was parish priest of St Michan's and also wrote spiritual books, he seems to have run some kind of a hospital as well. The devotional life in cities like Dublin was quite well catered for. Exposition of the Blessed Sacrament was common among the Orders from c. 1720. Rosaries were on sale publicly from c. 1750. Confraternities were developing. In 1747 some churches had sung Vespers and Benediction in the afternoon on Sundays. In 1761 the Dominicans in Dublin had a sermon in Irish at the 7 a.m. Mass and one in English at the 10 a.m. Towards the end of the century, Dr Carpenter, Archbishop of Dublin (1770–86) was consolidating the position. He was a noted Gaelic scholar and commissioned a valuable Gaelic preparation for Sunday Mass. Parish schools were scattered round the city, numbering 47 and they had 1,770 pupils in attendance. They were also legalised. The Jesuits ran a successful one in Saul's Court under Frs John Murphy and John Austin, who had received encouragement from Dean Swift in his boyhood.

The population of Dublin was growing and violence and drunkeness were endemic, even more so than in country parts. There is the reference to the work of the friars c. 1751 in Dublin on Sunday afternoons. Apparently the inhabitants of the north side used to come to the north bank of the Liffey and those on the south side to the south bank, and pelt stones at each other with consequent damage to persons and property. The government apparently were unable to stop it but the friars were more successful.[2]

There was also a growth of literate Catholics especially among the middle class. We have noted that Dr Cornelius Nary, PP of St Michan's (1700-38), was also busy with the pen. In 1705 he produced a book of prayers and meditations for the laity. Books were imported. Robert Manning's *Moral Entertainments*, John A. Mannock's *The Poor Man's Catechism* are a few cases in point. *An Essay on the Rosary* was published by John O'Connor, an Irish Dominican and *The Christian Directory* by Robert Parsons, an English Jesuit, proved to be a good guide to the spiritual life and was widely known.[3]

Richard Challoner was in Douai College as a professor in the first half of the eighteenth century. He also had the spiritual care of the Irish students there, teaching and preaching to them. This probably led to the popularity of his translation of the New Testament and of the *Imitation of Christ*. Under the penal laws it was forbidden to write or import Catholic books. Thus in 1719 a big box of books was confiscated on arrival from France. Still printers were not interfered with unduly since we find a notice in 1805: 'there is a fund of piety and attachment to their religion among the Catholics and lower class Roman Catholics'. It added 'a strong proof of the prevalence of this disposition is the number of Catholic books of devotion sold to those descriptions. I understand that the supply of this demand constitutes in our country towns the principal branch of the bookselling business.' In Crosskiel, Co Meath two shops took two hundred copies each of *Reeves' History of the Church* (1809). At the beginning of the eighteenth century, Thomas Brown was the biggest publisher of devotional books: *Instructions for Confession, Communion and Confirmation; Office of the Blessed Virgin Mary; Entertainment for Lent; Key of Paradise; Difference between the temporal and the eternal; The Following of Christ; Rules and Godly Instructions* (1716); *A History of St. Patrick's Purgatory* (1718); *An English Translation of the New Testament* (1719); *The Case of Catholics in Ireland* (1724). *The Holy Court,* which was a translation by Thomas Hawkins from the French written by Nicholas Caussin SJ, who was chaplin to Louis XIII, was printed in England in 1652. Editions appeared in Cork in 1767 and in Dublin in 1815 and 1826.

Challoner's *Morality of the Bible* was printed in Dublin in 1765. Among the purchasers we find Michael Byrne of Hell, six books. Hell was a lane near Christ Church where lodgings might be found. One notice ran: 'To be let: furnished apartments in Hell. N.B. They are well suited for a lawyer.'[4] This is no doubt due to the fact that they were close enough to the law courts.

Fr Sean Gother and Fr Robert Manning defended the faith from literary attacks. Interestingly enough they paid Henry Brooke, a Protestant, who lived c. 1750, to put their ideas in print. He was friendly to Catholics and wrote *A Papist misrepresented and represented.* It was printed by George Faulkner, the biggest printer in Dublin at the time. He was also a Protestant who was favourable to Catholics and hoped that they would be liberated from the penal laws. Dr. Hornihold's *The Decalogue Explained* and *The Sacraments Explained* were reprinted several times.

Dr Gallagher (1685-1751), Bishop of Raphoe and later of Kildare, wrote a *Book of Sermons,* the first Catholic Gaelic book to be printed in Ireland. It was translated into English and reprinted at least twenty times. He had been educated on the continent. He also had a good grasp of the needs of the people. In his preface he writes:

In discharge then of this duty, so incumbent on me and on all

pastors, I have composed the following discourses for the use
of my fellow-labourers principally, and next for such as
please to make use of them, that they may preach them to
their respective flocks, since my repeated troubles debar me
of the comfort of delivering them in person... I have made
them in an easy and familiar style and on purpose omitted
cramped expressions which might be obscure to both
preacher and hearer. *Malo ut me reprehendant grammatici quam
non intelligant populi* (I prefer to be reprehended by grammar-
ians than not to be understood by the people).

The sermons deal mainly with Confession, Communion, the
Passion, the Assumption, and the final ends of man.[5] Seán
Máistear Ó Conaill translated *True Wisdom* into Gaelic and it was
printed in Cork in 1795. Apart from a few catechisms, these are
the only two Irish books printed in Ireland in the eighteenth century.

The most popular Catechism was Fr Mannock's *The Poor Man's
Catechism*. It was first printed in England but it was printed in
Ireland in 1782 and the 11th edition was printed there also in
1838. The fullest edition of *Butler's Lives of the Saints* was printed
in Dublin 1799-1800.[6] The Stations of the Cross were introduced
into Ireland in this century.[7] Bishop Hay of Edinburgh wrote
works which were popular in Ireland. In 1799 his house and
church were burned by his enemies. He had been out of the city
and returned to see his furniture and library being sold at the
fire. He was dressed as a layman and he asked a woman standing at the edge of the crowd of onlookers what was happening.
'Oh Sir,' she said, 'we are burning the popish chapel and we
only wish that we had the Bishop to throw him into the fire.' He
wrote *The Devout Christian*, which was published in Dublin in
1784; *The Pious Christian* (1788), *The Sincere Christian* (1791) and
The Doctrine of Miracles Displayed (1789). Padraig Ugan had them
printed at his shop which he named 'The Sign of Dr Hay's
Head'.[8]

Fr Gahan OSA was also active like Dr Gallagher. In 1793 he published *A Book of Sermons* which was reprinted seven times and
also a prayerbook entitled *The Christian's Guide to Heaven or A*

complete Manual of Catholic Piety which was reprinted more than fifty times. To him also belongs the distinction of receiving Lord Dunboyne, the ex-bishop of Cork, back into the church on his death-bed. A complete Catholic Bible was printed in Ireland for the first time in 1791. There were many prayerbooks printed in Ireland in this century and these served to deepen the faith and devotion of the faithful as they were of considerable size and contained an abridgment of Catholic teaching and a vast collection of prayers which related to the important parts of the spiritual life.[9]

Pádraig Ó Fiannachta gives a much more complete list of subjects of sermons in the eighteenth and nineteenth centuries, which he has taken from the MSS in Maynooth:

> Restitution, The Resurrection, the Commandments, Repentance, Good Friday, Death, Life, The Passion and the Death of Christ, Final Judgement, Ash Wednesday, The Hardship of the Just, The Confraternity of Christian Doctrine, Communion, Sunday, Confession, the Assumption, The Glory of Heaven, Love of God, Hell, Satisfaction (Penance), Faults of the Tongue, Michael the Archangel, Patrick, Peter and Paul, Francis, Thomas, The Pain of Loss, The Seven Deadly Sins, Purgatory, the Kingdom of God, The Sabbath, God's Mercy to the Sinner, The Danger of the World, Prayer.

There are also sermons for the Sundays of the year.[10]

In Stapleton's *Catechism*, published in Brussels in 1639, he gives the impression that the Old Irish prayed not alone in Gaelic but also in Latin which they did not understand or pronounce properly. A Protestant Minister, Rev James Hall, in his journey through Ireland in the early nineteenth century notes that:

> … while one of the old Ladies in the house here (Goresbridge) where I slept all night, was repeating her second evening prayer in Latin, so as everyone that passed might hear her, I heard Methodists in the next house, determined not to be outdone, begin and sing one of Watt's hymns louder than necessary or than true piety required.

The same writer noted the use of Latin by a couple in Clare:

> That good woman and her husband, however, came soon after, and occupied the one (bed) next to that on which I lay. Being good Catholics, and seemingly not bad Christians, before they lay down, each of them uttered some Latin prayers, crossing their foreheads, breast and farther down several times, both at the beginning and at the end of each prayer.

But to balance the picture, it should be noted that Dr O'Brien, Bishop of Cloyne and Ross, writing to Propaganda in 1764 for money to publish his *Irish-English Dictionary*, said that most Catholics lived in rural areas and learned their catechism and said their prayers in Irish.[11]

Galway had not been heavily planted. Consequently the civil authorities were not too exacting. The celebration of Mass, though furtive, was relatively easy in the city where there were nine secular priests, three friaries, a Jesuit and three nuns' convents which were also boarding schools. There were eight headmasters. Though the sheriffs made searches periodically, they reported that they could not find any friars. However, there was connivance as the Account books show. On 9 November 1731 we find the entry in the Augustinian cashbook 'a bottle of wine for the sheriffs, 1/1' while we find that the Dominicans spent 2/2 on the same purpose.[12]

Some of the Elizabethan settlers became Catholic but quite a number of the Catholic gentry conformed to the Established Church in the second half of the eighteenth century for fear of losing their lands. Attempts had been made early in the penal days, 1700-50, to track down clergy who had not emigrated. In 1709 the Bishop of Elphin was living in a poor hut on a hillside. He was too poor to have a servant or a horse. He had to pay for water to be brought to him as he was too infirm to carry it. A little milk was given to him but he 'would have liked a little beer'.[13] According to a Report in 1731, the Masshouse was a normal place for Mass though sometimes altars of turf were used due to the poor circumstances of the area. In Connacht the friars were numerous and influential. In some places they had community living though some of them travelled to serve the outlying areas. We are very fortunate to have the *Opusculum de Missione* written by Dominic Ó Brollacháin OP in 1738. He describes this labour:

After the fast and prayer of Lent proceed about Low Sunday to a particular diocese, and having received the necessary faculties and the blessing of the superior, you are to go from parish to parish, village to village and from house to house to teach them what is necessary for salvation. Rise early, say your Office and hear Confessions. About 9 or half-past, having prepared the altar and blessed the water, begin to teach the catechism and continue at this work until 12 o'clock, if necessary. Begin Mass at 12 and, having said the Epistle, resume the catechism until the poor people who are travelling long distances arrive, lest they should be disappointed at losing Mass. When all have gathered, begin the Gospel and finish the Mass. Having concluded with an exhortation, if there are any who wish to confess, hear them patiently … and place their spiritual good before your own corporal refection. Furthermore, if any ignorant or shy people need and ask for individual instruction, give it.

From the Feast of All Saints until Christmas or the feast of the Purification of the Blessed Virgin Mary, gather together every night not only the boys and girls but others as well to the house in which you are staying and teach Christian doctrine until half-past nine, beginning with the more advanced. Teach them how to pray and how to examine their consciences and how to do everything for the glory of God. Conclude with the recitation in the native language of the Litany and other prayers.[14]

Archbishop Michael O'Reilly (+1758), Primate of Armagh, composed two catechisms, one in English and one in Irish which served well into the eighteenth century. They also contained an abridgment of the faith which was used at Sunday Mass and also in family prayer, not alone in Armagh but also in Clogher, while Carpenter devised a similar one for Dublin. This continued to be said in some parishes throughout the country until the 1930's and was read before Mass with the Acts of Faith, Hope and Charity so that many congregations knew them by heart. By the second half of the century, Protestants, on the whole, were more tolerant and Catholic churches could be built. They contributed even to this work. In 1784, on the opening of its first church, the Belfast volunteers paraded in full dress and marched to Mass where a sermon was preached by Rev Mr O'Connell and a sizeable collection made to meet the expenses of erecting the new Masshouse. A large number of Protestants also attended.[15]

While there had been some criticism of the poor formation of the regular clergy in the seventeenth and eighteenth centuries, it came to a head c. 1750.[16] The Bishops and a number of diocesan clergy complained to Rome. The number of regular clergy was about equal to that of the secular clergy, namely 800. The complaints by the latter played a considerable part in causing Benedict XIV to decree that Ireland was not a suitable place for the formation of novices and they were to be sent to one of their houses on the continent both for their novitiate and naturally for their studies. The effect of this decree was to reduce very considerably the number of regular clergy as early as 1775 and it was noted by many, including some diocesan clergy that there was a considerable decrease in the use of the sacrament of penance. It took the best part of a century to remedy the situation. All regulars, but especially those who did not have an Irish house on the continent, suffered very severely.[17] Rural areas of Leinster and Munster contained the greater part of good land of Ireland. Consequently it is not surprising that in the years following 1709 priests were severely harassed there. Many were arrested and many more had to flee to the continent. By 1731, however, the gravity of the situation, as we have seen, eased and Masshouses were far more common than Massrocks or the altar in the field. The parish was beginning to come into its own.

There was also the concern that people would have the basic instruction necessary for marriage. It was decreed that registers for baptisms and marriages should be kept but this was not always obeyed because of the danger involved. By the middle of the eighteenth century, the parish system was reasonably established in most of Munster. Sunday Mass was the principal occasion for instruction. Deanery conferences were held. Parish missions were conducted periodically by the Jesuits or by the friars. The minimum which the Archbishop of Cashel demanded of his clergy was that they should have the constitutions, the *prône* and the catechism of the diocese. The *prône* was a collection of sermons in the French tradition and seems to have been well-known in Munster.

After 1733, Catholic schools developed rapidly in answer to the threat from the Charter schools. This was the case very much in the south and in the south-east and in Dublin. Nonetheless it was felt that in the 1760s many people did not fulfil the paschal precept. De Burgo, Bishop of Ossary, felt that there were not sufficient confessors due to the diminution of the friars. Some dioceses, such as Achonry and Kerry, did not have any great problem in this matter but there was a general concern about the matter in the country as a whole. Baptism was administered normally in the home in Cloyne but towards the end of the century it was generally performed in the chapel or in the priest's house. The pattern of pre-marriage chastity had been growing stronger since the middle of the century and the arranged marriage was becoming the normal thing in the middle-class society.

Stability and good relations existed between Protestants and Catholics from c. 1750. This is seen in their attendance at funerals and particularly in the Protestant contributions to Catholic chapel-building and charities. Chapel-building in Dublin was quite common from 1730 onwards. At first they were merely converted stables or store houses as they were generally in the lanes or backstreets round the Liffey and in the Liberties. There were St Mary's in Liffey Street, St Michan's in Mary's Lane, St Paul's in Arran Quay, St James's in Watling Street, St Catherine's in Dirty Lane, St Audoen's in Cook Street, St Michael's in Rosemary Lane and St Andrew's in Hawkins Street. All these belonged to the diocesan clergy. The Orders had their chapels also – the Franciscans in Cook Street, then in Francis Street and finally on Merchant's Quay where it was popularly referred to as Adam and Eve's, from the sign of a nearby tavern. The Dominicans were in Bridge Street, the Discalced Carmelites at Wormwood Gate, the Calced Carmelites in Ash Street, the Augustinians in John's Lane and the Capuchins in Church Street. The Dominican nuns had a convent in Channel Row, the Poor Clares in King Street, the Carmelites in Arran Quay and the Augustinians in Mullinahack.[18]

After 1750, a Catholic party began to emerge seeking relief from the penal laws. They pointed out that Catholic allegiance to the Pope did not prevent their being loyal subjects of the king but they achieved little till Daniel O'Connell appeared on the scene. This peace was jolted by the outbreak of agrarian violence in Munster in the 1760s, caused by the enclosure of commonages, forced labour and unemployment for which the people could have no redress in law courts. Fr Nicholas Sheehy was hanged, drawn and quartered in Clonmel in 1766 for expressing sympathy with the distress of the peasantry. In general, movements of violence, such as the Whiteboys, tended to drive a wedge between priests and people. Houses and even the persons of priests were attacked in 1785-86. Dr Butler, Archbishop of Cashel, feared that they would lose their hold on the people if the agitation continued. Eventually the violence of the Whiteboys died down. Bishops issued instructions to priests to be moderate in their demands, especially at the Stations. The Rightboys, who were close to the Whiteboys in violence, laid down schedules for priests. Thus in Cork and Limerick in 1786 we find payments insisted on as a maximum: Marriage (5/-), Baptism (1/6), Extreme Unction (1/-), Funeral Mass (1/-), Station confession (6d or 1/-), Christmas and Easter Dues (1/1).[19] It should be remembered that the average wage of a labourer was 6d per week in the summer and 4d in the winter. Many people were not in a position to pay at all. When one thinks of the chapels, schools and the upkeep of the priest, one realises the sacrifices made by the Catholics of this and the next century. In the early years of the nineteenth century the State was not only willing but anxious to pay the Catholic clergy. The offer was not without attractions for both bishops and diocesan priests but, after cautious consideration and O'Connell's opposition, the voluntary system was retained even though Rome was in favour of State payment. This support was another vital factor in the relationship between people and priest, though it was, and often still is, a subject for complaint.

The final decade of the century was a troubled one. There were many Catholic frustrations concerning tithes, relief Acts and the use of arms. The English feared that the American and particu-

larly the French Revolution might add to these feelings of aggra-
vation. The United Irishmen, founded 1791-2, with Wolfe Tone,
though a Protestant, as one of the founders and Secretary of the
Catholic Committee, added to their unease. He had contact with
France and there was danger of a rising. When French frigates
arrived near the Cork coast, Dr Moylan, the local bishop, ad-
monished his flock to have nothing to do with them. In 1798 the
leaders of the United Irishmen were arrested and the rising
which took place, without the obvious leaders, was quickly and
ruthlessly suppressed. In Wexford the clergy were divided in
their reaction. Bishop Caulfield and many of his priests were opposed to it but other priests like, Frs Murphy and Roche, were
moved by the brutality of the yeomen to take the side of the op-
pressed. It is interesting to note that the first native seminaries
were opened in this decade, Carlow in 1793 and Maynooth, the
National Seminary, in 1795, with the blessing and aid of the
English Government.

There is plenty of contemporary evidence regarding the miserable conditions of the rural population. Arthur Young, and
Englishman who toured Ireland in the 1770s, notes:

> The cottages of the Irish are called cabbins and are the most
> miserable hovels that can well be conceived ... The furniture
> of the cabins is as bad as the architecture; in very many con-
> sisting only of a pot for boiling their potatoes; a bit of a table,
> and one or two broken stools; beds are not found universally,
> the family lying on straw.[20]

But in normal times when harvests were good they led a reasonably happy life and were entertained by story-telling, singing,
dancing and music. They also observed religious feasts and patterns though the latter often finished in excessive drinking and
faction fights which the clergy condemned and gradually dis-
couraged.

Literature

The early years of the eighteenth century, when Aodhagán Ó Rathile had perforce to hope for help from Valentine Brown – help which did not materialise – it led him to satirise him. Life for him was hardly worth living. In the poem, *An File ar leabaidh a bháis*, he voices not only his own hopelessness but that of his fellowcountrymen.

> *Do b'fhearrde mise is gach duine atá ag fulang pian Gall*
> *an bás dá sciobadh tá tuille agus fiche blian ann.*

> I and everyone who is sufffering with me the punishments of foreigners would have been better off if death had snatched us more than twenty years ago.

Since he feels that his death is not far away he decides:

> *Stadfadsa feasta, is gar dam éag gan mhoill*
> *Ó treascradh dragain Leamhain, Léin is Laoi.*
> *Rachad-sa a h-aithle searc na laoch don chill*
> *Na flatha fá raibh mo shean roimh éag do Chríost.*[21]

> I will cease now, death is nigh to me, without delay, since the warriors of the Laune, Lein and Lee have been laid low. I will follow the beloved heroes to the churchyard, the nobility whom my forebears served even before Christ died.

He was probably the best of the modern poets and it is fitting that his body is laid to rest in the old Franciscan friary at Muckross near Killarney.

The Trinity College Manuscript 1373, which is dated 1703-10, has a number of poems which treat of Our Lady. Towards the end of the manuscript Seán Ó Conaill has a long poem, *An uair a smaoineam ar shaoithibh na h-Éireann*, which deplores the plight of the country. It concludes with part of the Ave Maria calling on her, the friend of poets, to pray for them since she is sure 'to get a hearing'. A poetic confession by Seán sees him examine his conscience on the seven deadly sins, bad language, lies and oaths. He also confesses:

> Seldom did I go to Mass with desire
> I forgot to read the psalms on my knees,

I did not recite the psalter of Holy Mary to God
and through disrespect for the clergy I seldom listened to
them.

But his hope is not quenched:

Though I be deeper in damnation that any man that ever
walked
I would get pardon and willing hearing,
Let me but cry bitterly with tearful screams and shrieks and
moans to the mother -nurse of the bright child – she has not
refused a wretch.
For that reason I cry out to thee, O woman without blemish,
and the nurse-mother of the only Son will be a supreme star
over them showing them the way to the delightful heavenly
mansions. [22]

A poem to Mary, *A Mhuire óigh fhíonghlan fhíor*, [23] by Seán Ó
Neachtain (+1728) combines the old metre of bardic times with
the new stress metre. In content it also forms a bridge between
the medieval and modern approach. Our Lady is the 'guide of
all human generations', the 'star of knowledge', the 'right covering of Our Lord's Body'. 'Close to you a sad state is not bitter' …
'In earlier times you had great love of Patrick's chosen family …
If you wish you can correct all injustices, nothing is impossible
to you since you can appeal to heaven'. RIA MS 23A22 (dated
1735) is a fine example of a manuscript prayerbook commissioned by an individual. It begins with the Calendar and then
follows the catechism, the *Ave Maris Stella*, *Te Deum*, Morning
and Evening prayers, prayers to the name of the Jesus,
Instruction before Mass, prayers in preparation for confession
and after Confession and Communion, Prayer to Mary, Litany
of St Anne, Litany of the Trinity, the seven penitential psalms,
the Litany of the Saints, the Nicene Creed, the Athanasian creed,
Litany of Jesus, Litany of Mary, Hail holy Queen, the psalter of
Jesus, the Office of the Immaculate Conception, The Rosary, an
explanation of the *Pater* and of the *Ave*, prayer to St Brigid,
Litany of the Sick, the *Dies irae*, *De profundis* and the Litany of St
Francis. It is good to see the balance and variety in the devotion
in second quarter of the eighteenth century.

Cathal Buí MacGiolla Gunna (1666-1756) combines various traits of Irish spirituality and humour. While he was partial to the drop, his conscience would not allow him pass by a dead bird without a lament – *An Bunán Buí*. He is touched by the bird's sad death on the frozen lake due to the lack of a drink:

Ní easba bídh ach díoghbháil dí
A d'fhág in do luí thú ar chúl do chinn.

It was not hunger but the want of a drink
that left you lying on the back of your head.

The word *Buí* (yellow) was common to both their names (*gur cosúil liom féin tú i nós is i ndath*: you were like me in habits and colour). Having finished his laments and admitted his own failings, the manner of the bird's death had its own moral for him. One can see the serious and the humourous blending naturally in him as it often did in the Gaelic poets.

Nil aon deór dá bhfuighinn ná leigfinn síos
ar eagla go bhfuighinn bás den tart.

There's no drop I'd get that I would not lower
lest I should die of the thirst.

He advises his friends:

A chomhursain chléibh, fliuchaidh bhúr mbéal
Óir ní bhfuighfidh sibh braon i ndiaidh bhúr mbás.

Dear friend, wet your whistle
because you'll get ne'er a drop once you're dead.

As his end drew near he showed his genuine self:

Tá mo léagsa caithte, is deimhin nach fada mo shaoghal,
Is nach trua mé is mo lochta sgríobhtha in mo aghaidh;
Ach guidhim thú, a Mhuire, a bhuime 's a mháthair Mhic Dé,
Go n-íocfaidh mo chorp in gach olc dá ndeárna mé. [24]

My race is run – my time is short. My lot is sad with my sins noted against me. But I beseech you, Mary, nurse and mother of the Son of God, that my body may requite all the evil which I have done.

Cathal Buí has style, music, innocence, weakness, humour and happiness in his verses which portray a deep love of God and of Mary. A tradition holds that Mary came to his deathbed. Perhaps the fact that Séamus Dall MacCuarta (1647-1732) was blind endowed him with his great appreciation of nature. His poem, *Fáilte don éan is binne ar chraoibh*, led him to the beauty of nature as a whole which is manifested in *Ceithre ráithe na bliadhna*. Speaking of summer, he says:

> *Bíonn deallradh na gréine gach lá in mo éadan,*
> *an lile is an samharclann's an rós in mo ghruadh.*

The sun shines every day on my forehead;
the lily, primrose and rose are in my cheek.

He holds out hope for Ireland:

> *Tiocfaidh in Éirinn aimsir éigin*
> *is beidh ann athrú*
> *sé deir na naoimh is na fíor-chléirigh*
> *go sgriosfar an Galltacht.* [25]

A time will come when there will be a change in Ireland; the saints and holy clergy declare that oppression will be destroyed.

In his article, *Filíocht Uladh mar fhoinnse don stair shóisialta san 18ú hAois*, the late Cardinal Tomás Ó Fiaich dwells on the close relationship between poets and clergy. He also refers to Patrick O'Donnelly, Bishop of Dromore, who during the hardest times in the penal days used leave his hut on Sliabh Cuilinn, dressed as a harper as he visited his parishes and was known to the people as the Bard of Armagh. [26]

Mac Cuarta's elegy on Somhairle MacDomhnaill shows his appreciation of the church in its splendour and in its compassion:

> *Sé mo chian-sa mar fágadh do bhán-chneas gan chomhráidh,*
> *gan mílte do bhráithribh bheith i ngrádaibh dá thórradh,*
> *An Príomhfháidh ó Árdmach' is alán de na hórdaibh*
> *gach diadhaire dob áirde is do b'fhearr ins an eolas*
> *a bheith ag guidhe ar an ArdRígh atá i bPárrthas 'na chomhnuidhe,*
> *'s ag míniú na Páise ar an mbás sin Mhic Dhomhnuill,*
> *'s ag cantain na salm do rinne Dáibhidh don Choimhdhe.*[27]

My grief that your fair skin was left without speech,
without thousands of Brothers in Orders at your wake;
The primate of Armagh and many of its Orders,
every greatest divine, well-versed in wisdom –
praying the High-King who is living in Paradise
and explaining the passion of that death of Mac Domhnuill
and singing the psalms which David composed for the Lord.

Sean Ó Murchadha na Raithíneach (1700-62) expresses his personal love of God in *Liaigh na ngrás ngrádhmhar*:

Mo Dhia 's mo ghrádh in-áirde, mo shearc, mo bhrígh is m'fhonn
Mo riarthach rán, rábach, le ceart dam síor-shúil.

My God and my great love, my strength and my desire, my noble, liberal Dispenser with justice in answer to my constant quest.

In *Áireamh Eachtra an Ghalair*, where he tells us that he was incapacitated for the whole spring, we find his best poetry in his approach to God in his sickness:

Níor fhág sí achmuinn im bhallaibh im chroidhe ná im'aeibh
is d'fhág sí m'aigne balbh is m'intleacht faon,
d'fhág sí lagtha, leagaithe mé mí-chuíbhseach clé
acht tá an Rí neartmhar, do chasfaidh arís mo ghéag.

It left no strength in my members nor in my heart and liver and it deprived me of my wisdom and left my intellect weakened. It left me prone and weakened, slovenly and awkward but the King is powerful – He will cure my limb.

He laments the sad state of the country:

Ár n-eaglais ciúin gan chealla, gan chiúl,
's ár bhflatha thar triúchaibh tréigthe.[28]

Our church is silent, without cells, without music and our princes forlorn over the countryside.

Piaras MacGearailt (1700-1792) found it so hard to provide for his family that he changed his religion:

Is deilbh liom ceangal le Cailbhin is Liútar claon
ach golfhairt mo leanbh 's a gcreachadh gan triúch, gan tréad,
thug srothanna óm dhearcaibh 'na gcaisibh is túirlint déar.

It is hard for me to unite with Calvin and perverse Luther but the weeping of my (hungry) children and their being robbed of land and flock drew floods and streams of tears from my eyes.

But he remained a Catholic at heart:

Óm namhaid is ó dhamaint an anma réidhtigh mé
Sásuigh t'aigne is masluigh mo chréachta anois,
Gach crádh, gach peannaid, gach anfaithe, péin is bruid
go sásta geanmnach glacfadsa is géillfeadsa.
Ó thréigeas Do phairt, is Do dhlighe
Lem' shaoghal béad léanmhar le crádh is caoi
Fé dhéar-chneadh i ngéibhinn le grádh do Chriost. [29]

From my enemy and the damnation of my soul deliver me. Satisfy your mind and reproach me for wounding You now. I will willingly accept with pure heart every affliction, penance, pain and torture. I will submit peacefully and happily to Your holy will because I abandoned Your love and Your law. As long as I live I will keep lamenting it with tears and anguish-wounded and in bondage because of my love for Christ.

A very dim view was taken of a priest who changed religion, and a dimmer one still if he took a spouse.

Tadhg Gaelach Ó Súilleabháin (1715-95) was the most influential religious poet of the century. His contribution to the piety of the faithful in his own and succeeding generations cannot be stressed too strongly. The fact that his poems have seen at least forty editions between 1802 and 1929[30] puts him poles apart form any other writer, cleric or lay, of the eighteenth century. He seems to have undergone a deep spiritual conversion c. 1767. Tomás Ó Míodhcháin wrote a poem on his renunciation of the wickedness of the world and of his conversion to piety as a pilgrim. His pilgrimage took him to the Decies and it seems that most of his religious poetry was composed in Dungarvan, Co Waterford. His poem, *A Mhór-Mhic Chailce na soillse aoibhinn*, is considered to be one of the best religious poems in Gaelic literature. It is a very genuine opening of the soul to God:

A Íosa, dhealbhaigh talamh is tréan-mhuir dúinn,
A NaomhSpiorad bheannaighthe cheannaigh go daor mé ar dtúis,
Díbir, m'ainbhfios damanta, a Dhé na ndúl,
Is dírig m'anam gan pheannaid, gan phéin id' chúairt.

O Jesus, who created the land, the mighty sea for us, O blessed spirit, who redeemed me at great price banish my cursed ignorance, O God of the elements and guide my soul without pain or penance to your court.

Then he remembers his sins:

Amen, a Rí na ndúl,
Cé thugas leat mo chúl,
Do ritheas uait ar siubhal,
Do thréigeas, do shéanas Do ghnúis.

Amen, O King of nature, though I turned my back on you and ran away from you, I forsook and denied your face.

These lines precede Francis Thompson's *Hound of Heaven*. They are in the same vein. He continues:

Ag cé rinneas go minic siúd
Ná cuir druim Do láimhe liom
Mar is leat atáid ag tnúth,
Mo chroidhe, m'anam is mo dhá shúil.

Though I did that frequently, do not turn away from me – for my heart, my soul and my two eyes are longing for you.[31]

He has written twenty-five religious poems – on Christ, Mary, the Holy Spirit, the Eternal Father, the Rosary, the saints and some on spiritual topics. Some of his poems were used as hymns, sung to well-known Irish airs. In his poem on the Rosary he points out that the fruits of prayer should be seen in the avoidance of gluttony, malice, sins of the flesh and other failings. They should spur the one who prays to appreciate the Mass and to practice almsgiving. His final stanza shows his detachment from the world:

Is cuma liom féin cá taobh 'na leagfaidhear
i bpéin nó in aicíd bháis mé
ach go mbeadh duine den chléir ann ghléasfadh m'aibíd
is céir do lasfaidhe ar clár dom.[32]

I care not where I be laid in the pain or sickeness of death, provided there be one of the clergy to dress me in my habit and have candles round my bier.

His hymns were a consolation, joy, source of counsel and spiritual direction for the ordinary people. There is good reason to believe that he died in the cathedral in Waterford while saying his prayers. One cannot help recalling Matt Talbot's conversion and his life thereafter. Both were outstanding because of their simple but very genuine piety supported by their suffering.

Eoghan Rua Ó Súilleabháin (1748-84), who was a character whom one might call typically Irish in a good sense, died at the early age of thirty-six. He was an odd-job man who had a fine gift of poetry. He had his ups and downs with the clergy but that did not bother him or them. His aithrí, *Is mithid dam féin*, is out of the ordinary run:

> *Do chaitheas tréimhse 'em shaoghal go coirtheach, cionntach,*
> *cealgach, creimeach, claonmhar, cleasach, cúrsach,*
> *gangaideach, clé nar ghéill do reacht na n-Úird Chirt*
> *is go maithidh Mac Dé ár mbearta le chéile dúinn.*

I spent a period of my life sinfully and culpably so – deceitful, abusive, perverse, wily, wandering, calumnious, wicked, disobedient to the law of right orders. May the Son of God forgive us all our sins.)

So far this is the traditional *aithrí* in his general listing of faults, but he moves into deeper feelings:

> *Aifreann Dé gan bhréig ba bheag mo dhúil ann,*
> *Is gach annamh nuair a théinn dá éisteacht creididh, chúibh-se*
> *an uair stadaid na h-éisc le géill san sruth dá gcúrsa*
> *in am easbarta an Naomh-Chuirp, is léir gur magadh dúinn-ne.*

In truth, I had no great desire for God's Mass – the few times I went, believe me, that the fish stop on their course in the stream at the time of the offering of the holy Body – it is clear that they put us to shame.

He freely admitted his rakiskness which he enjoyed:

Níorbh annamh mé sealad san tábhairne traochta
idir scata geal-bhéithe le carrbhas óil,
teagasc na n-aithreach n-aitheantach naomhtha
ní thagadh im bhréithre ach magadh is móid,
a nglacainn de rachmus ón tseachtain go céile
do scaipinn gan séanadh idir aicme lucht ceóil
bhíodh meanma ar m'aigne is aiteas dá n-éisteacht
is ní creidim ó aoinne go mbfhearr leigean dóibh.

Not rarely did I find myself in the tavern, exhausted, carousing among a group of nice damsels. The teaching of the holy and wise fathers used not cross my lips but rather tomfoolery and curses. What money I earned from week to week I would scatter, in truth, on the band of musicians. My mind used to lift with joy as I listened to them and I don't believe anyone (who says) that it is better to avoid them.

That is the picture of the generous, gifted, erring rake. But he could raise the hopes of his listeners:

I mainistir naomh beidh céir ar lasadh aca
is eaglais Dé go salmach fós
ag canadh Te Deum *gan bhaoghal gan eagla*
cé do bhéir gur searbh an sceól.
Is gach mangaire méith don tréad so atharruigh
fearta an tsoiscéil le taithneamh don phóit
gan fearann ná féasta gléas nár cleachtadar,
tréith fá léan ag grafadh is ag rómhar.

There will be candles alight in the holy monastery and God's church will be again singing psalms, chanting *Te Deum* without fear or danger, though this is bitter news to the invader. And every fat covetous member of the flock who changed the strength of the gospel through love of drink will be without land or feasting, something they were not accustomed to, but weak and suffering from digging and hoeing.[33]

One notes in the poetry of Tadhg Gaelach and Eoghan Rua the note of hope which was beginning to sound in the hearts of the people in the last quarter of the century, when vague hopes of Emancipation were being mooted and the American War of Independence had brought a certain change in the attitude of the English government towards Ireland.

Notes:

1. *Éigse Éireann* No. 126 mentions a poem by Fr Eoghan Ó Caoimh when John B. Sleyne, Bishop of Cork was banished in 1702.

2. Archives of the Carmelite Order, Rome II Hib. I, *Litterae* 1715-1870.

3. Corish, P. J., *The Catholic Community* (Dublin, 1981) 89. Most towns had their booksellers as the notice 'Tim Nowlan, bookseller and seed-man, Tullow Street, Carlow' clearly indicates.

4. Ó Súilleabháin, P., OFM, 'Clódóireacht Chaitiliceach in Éirinn san ochtú haois deag', *Irishleabhar Mhuighe Nuadhat* (1964) 95-101.

5. Ó Fiannachta, P., 'Seanmóireacht Ghaeilge san Ochtú agus san Naoú hAois Déag, *Irishleabhar Mhá Nuad* (1983) 141-50. Some of Gallagher's sermons were known by heart. *DDU,* 70.

6. *IER* 100 (1963) 240-44.

7. Ó Cuiv, B., 'An Irish Tract on the Stations of the Cross', *Celtica* II (1952-54) 1-29.

8. Ó Súilleabhain, P., art. cit. p100.

9. Ibid. 95-101. I have drawn feely on this valuable article.

10. *v.* n. 5 *supra.*

11. Ó Súilleabhain, P., OFM, 'Leabhair Úrnaithe an ochtú haois déag.' *IER* 103 (1965) 301-2.

12. Pochin Mould, D., *The Irish Dominicans* (Dublin 1957) 158.

13. *Coll. Hib.* V (1962) 9-10.

14. *v.* n. 12 supra 178-9.

15. Brady, J., 'Eighteenth Century Press', *Arch. Hib.* 19 (1956) 225.

16. Fenning, H., OP, *The Undoing of the Friars in Ireland* (Louvain, 1972).

17. O'Dwyer, P., O Carm, *The Irish Carmelites* (Dublin, 1988) 142 ff.

18. Wall, M., 'The Age of the Penal Laws', Moody, T.W. and Martin F.X., OSA, (eds), *The Course of Irish History* (Dublin, 1967) 225-231. Henceforth *CIH.*

19. Donnelly, J. S., 'The Righboy Movement 1785-88', *Stud. Hib.* 17-18 (1977-8) 164.

20. *A Tour of Ireland 1780* ii pt. 2, 35-6. cf also *CIH* chap 14.

21. Dineen, P. S., and O'Donoghue, T., *The Poems of Egan O'Rahilly*, ITS (1909) 1911,116.

22. *Mary* 230-33.

23. Ní Fhaircheallaigh, Ú., 'Dánta a Conndae na Midhe', *Féil-sgríbhinn Eoin Mhic Néill* (Dublin 1940) 97-99. *v.* also Maynooth MS B9, 48-9. cf *As trom do chodla, a Mhuire mhóir*, RIA G vi I, 89. NLI G. 135, 157-8; *Sgiathlúireach na Maighdine Muire*, TCD Ms 1411, 336 ff and *Laoi na mBuadhann*, *DDU* 183.

24. Ó Canainn, P., *Filidheacht na nGaedheal* (Áth Cliath 1940) 250-1.

25. Ó Raibheartaigh, T., *Máighistrí san Fhilidheacht,* (Áth Cliath 1939) 243-262.

26. *Stud. Hib.* 11 (1971) 90-93.

27. n. 25 *supra* 258-9.

28. Tórna (T. Ó Donnchadha, ed.) *Seán na Raithíneach Ó Murchadha* (Áth Cliath, 1954) 136-7. v.also APD 536 with Seán Ó Duinn's art. in *Intercom* (March, 1992) p 6.

> Go mbeannaí Dia dhuit, a Ghobnait naofa,
> Go mbeannaí Muire dhuit, is beannaím féin duit,
> is chughatsa thánag ag gearán mo scéil leat,
> is ag iarraidh mo leighis ar son Mhic Dé ort.

29. Ó Foghlú, R., *Amhráin Phiarais Mhic Gearailt* (Áth Ciath, 1905) 44-5.

30. Ó Foghlú, R., *Tadhg Gaelach* (Áth Cliath 1929) 17.

31. Ibid. 29-30.

32. Ibid. 65

33. n. 25 *supra,* 163-74.

CHAPTER 9

The Nineteenth Century

Is cuaille gan mhaith mé i gcoirnéal fáil
nó is cosmhúil le bád mé a chaill a stiúir,
do brisfídhe isteach a n-aghaidh carraig 'sa bhfráig
's do bheadh dá bháthadh 'sna tonntaibh fuar'.
(I am a useless stake in the corner of a fence like a boat that
has lost its rudder, which would be smashed in against the
rocks of coast and be drowned in the cold waves.)
(*Rafterí*)

The early nineteenth century was an age of rehabilitation for
Irish Catholics. In it much was done to repair the material loses
of the previous centuries. The Catholic community was in general a poor community. The full report of the revenues of the
bishops, parish priests and curates of the different dioceses,
which Dr Troy had been requested to draw up by Castlereagh
and the Irish government, showed that the clergy was extremely
poor. There were four Catholic archbishops, twenty-two bishops, one thousand and twenty-six parish priests and about eight
hundred curates. The average annual income of the bishops was
about £300, though in the diocese of Kilfenora and Kilmacduagh
it fell as low as £100, that of the parish priests was £65 and that of
the curates £10, together with free board and lodging.[1] In the
forty years which preceded the famine, newly-built slated chapels
replaced the low thatched barns of the penal days practically all
over the country. Several cathedrals were begun, parish schools
were started, new monastic houses, charities, diocesan seminaries, secondary schools for boys and girls were built. Continental
seminaries were in a poor state after the French Revolution so
the number of Irish students studying in them was greatly re-
duced. The national seminary in Maynooth grew steadily in im-

portance till by 1850 about half the Irish secular clergy had been educated there and were in sympathetic touch with Irish politics.[2] This strengthened the bonds between the Irish Catholic laity and clergy. Moreover, the clergy were maintained by the voluntary offerings of their parishioners.

In towns and cities, middle-class Catholics were reasonably wealthy and many of them helped generously in the support of the secular clergy and of the religious and the charitable works undertaken by them. Daniel O'Connell had obtained Catholic Emancipation by organising Catholics under the influence and leadership of their clergy. They used constitutional means and gained liberty of religion, the right to enter parliament and other positions. Middle-class Catholics were the main beneficiaries in the material sphere.[3] In 1840 the average was one priest for three thousand parishioners. By 1850 it had become one per two thousand. Regular clergy were still suffering from the novitiate regulation of 1751. The clergy had great influence on the people in all matters. One Maynooth professor laid down that a priest, when dealing with an uneducated congregation, was entitled to tell them, even from the altar, whom to vote for and it was the moral duty of the uneducated man to vote as his priest directed him. Several of his colleagues, however, were more conservative.[4] Gustave de Beaumont, a Frenchman in Ireland in 1839 stated that:

> The Catholic clergy is the most national body in Ireland. It belongs to the very heart of the country. We have seen elsewhere that Ireland, having been attacked at the same time in its religion and its liberties, his creed and his country were mingled in the heart of every Irishman, and became to him one and the same thing ... When the altar is thus national, why should not the priest be so likewise? Hence arises the great power of the Catholic clergy in Ireland. When it attempted to extirpate Catholicism, the English Government could not destroy the creed without overthrowing the clergy. Still in spite of the penal laws, which besides sometimes slumbered, there have always been priests in Ireland ... But now the Catholic faith exists publicly in Ireland; it has built its churches, it has organised its clergy, and it celebrates its

ceremonies in open day … Those in Ireland who do not op-
press the people, are accustomed to despise them. I found the
Catholic clergy were the only persons in Ireland who loved
the lower classes, and spoke of them in terms of esteem and
affection.[5]

One could always find instances of domineering priests. At the
mission in Dingle in 1846, the priest used a whip to keep the
queue for confession in order. While Carleton's picture of the
priest may have some bias in it, it probably has a share of truth
also. He was:

regular but loose and careless in the observances, he could
not be taxed with any positive neglect of pastoral duty. He
held his stations at regular times and places with great exact-
ness; but when the severer duties annexed to them were performed, he relaxed into the boon companion, sang his song,
told his story, laughed his laugh, and occasionally danced his
dance, the very beau-ideal of a shrewd humourous divine …
the priests can, the moment such scenes are ended, pass with
the greatest aptitude of habit into the hard gloomy character
of men who are replete with profound knowledge, exalted
piety, and extraordinary power.[6]

The half century also saw a remarkable development in the
church to meet a very urgent need. It seems that in the more
prosperous areas it had an effective system of parish schools in
the late eighteenth century. But with the rise in population in the
nineteenth century the church did not have sufficient resources.
The school master of the early nineteenth century is a very interesting character, if Amhlaoibh Ó Súilleabhain of Callan, Tomás
Ruadh Ó Súilleabhain of Uibh Ráthach and Bartholomew
Keegan of Bargy, Co Wexford, are average examples.[7]

Institutions dedicated to education and works of charity sprang
up and increased to such an extent that by the closing decades of
the century general education was reasonably catered for, secondary education being almost completely cared for by
Religious. The Irish Christian Brothers, founded by Edmund
Ignatius Rice in 1802, had 43 schools, attended by 7,500 pupils in
1838 and in 1862 they had 181 schools with an attendance of

20,280.[8] The existing Religious Orders were also engaged in educational work and contemplative Orders, such as the Cistercians and Carmelite nuns, did their share. Orders devoted to the education of girls were founded or introduced. In 1816 the Irish Sisters of Charity were founded to increase educational facilities and to nurse the sick and the poor, and by 1879 they had twenty houses.[9] The Loreto Sisters were founded by Mrs Ball in 1822. They devoted themselves completely to educational work, and at the death of Mrs Ball in 1861 they had founded thirty-seven convents, twenty-one of which were outside Ireland and the Province numbered eight hundred sisters.[10] The Irish Sisters of Mercy began in 1827. Being directly under diocesan control, they flourished in an unprecedented manner. By 1881 they had one hundred and seventy convents and were to be found in every diocese. They worked in education, in the visitation of the sick, in nursing, in work-houses, with female prisoners, fallen women etc., so that they were welcomed everywhere.[11] The first native institute, founded by Nano Nagle, dedicated its services to the education of the lower and emigrant classes. They were the Presentation Sisters.[12] About the time that O'Connell was setting himself fully to the Repeal of the Union (1839), a strong Temperance movement against the use of intoxicating liquours was undertaken by the famous Capuchin, Fr Matthew. His efforts were very much strengthened by Fr Spratt O. Carm and other priests in the parishes.[13]

Bishop Cantwell, incidentally a great supporter of O'Connell's Repeal movement, sent a short *relatio* of his diocese (Meath) to Dr Cullen in 1845. In it he says that since 1839 he has succeeded in building a cathedral, at least forty churches, nearly one hundred schools and his seminary is flourishing and he has two new convents of the Sisters of Mercy.[14] More interesting is the account from the diocese of Down and Connor which had been the seat of the heaviest Presbyterian plantations. The bishop, Dr Denvir, had forty parish priests and thirty others on active duty. In Belfast in 1785, he says, there were not more than fifty Catholics. In 1845 there are thirty thousand there. Sixty years ago there was neither chapel nor church in the city. Now there were three in the city and four outside. The Confraternities of

Christian Doctrine and of the Blessed Virgin did great work in educating the poor in the faith.[15] The Primate's diocese was in a very satisfactory state. He had forty-nine parish priests, four administrators and sixty-five curates, 'all of whom I personally examine in our ecclesiastical conferences'. During the previous decade (1836-46) he consecrated seventeen new churches and five more were awaiting consecration, making a total of one hundred and two. Each parish had a school.[16]

It is difficult to give an adequate picture of the Christian life of the people in the period, but some indications may be had from the apostolate of the clergy. In the little town of Castlemartyr, Co Cork the curate, Fr John Forrest, had an average of ten hours confessions in the day (probably on Saturday, the normal day for confession).[17] But thirty miles east of him, Fr Cooke did not find things so satisfactory:

> For many months all have been observing how little there is to do in the confessional … During the evenings of the whole week past, I have heard just two confessions, others not so many … For the first time in Lent for my rememberence there has not been a word of instruction for the people … Dr Daly, the Protestant bishop, common known as Bob Daly, a man perseveringly active against God's reign through his church, has brought a whole host of stranger parsons here, the greatest bigots he could find … by sermons and handbills and printed letters do they work daily and I believe not without success in their unholy mission.[18]

But he was able to paint a much brighter picture four months later. 'The Retreat by the Jesuits has worked wonders. The city (Waterford) and neighbourhood rose to near 13,000 communicants.'[19] Catholic literature was also filling a very useful role in the cities. Dr Doyle of Kildare got the hierarchy's approval for the Catholic Book Society in 1827 and it produced something like five million books in ten years. These were often distributed through the Confraternities. During the following decades men like W.J. Battersby, who launched the *Catholic Penny Magazine* in 1830 – it ceased publication in 1835 – and the *Catholic Directory* in 1836 which has lasted until today, provided very valuable information concerning Christian life for the first half century of its existence. James Duffy and Michael Gill also did a great service to the church in this century.

A notable feature of the second quarter of the century is the disagreement on many important questions by leading members of the hierarchy. Thus on the question of National Education, Dr McHale, Archbishop of Tuam, refused to have any dealings with the government, while most of the bishops accepted the system at least till the Synod of Thurles (1850) if not longer. Nine years later these government schools were still flourishing in the diocese of Kerry and the bishop, Dr Moriarty, writing to Dr Kirby, Cullen's successor in Rome, says:

> I am just after finishing the visitation of half the diocese. As the number of non-confirmed are gradually diminishing I had only about 5,000 to confirm. The children were admirably instructed wherever there were National Schools and where there were not, the people are in ignorance of the catechism. I hope that the Holy See will tread lightly until we succeed in getting something better. The National Schools have been our only protection against Proselytism and Apostasy.[20]

While it is obvious that there is a little exaggeration in some of these letters, it does throw a new light at least on some of the National Schools. On the question of the church's involvement in the Repeal of the Act of Union, there was disagreement. Armagh and Dublin considered it a purely political question while Tuam and Cashel were more affected by its effects on the lives of the people.

Taking a cross-section of the archives of the Irish College, Rome from 1830-60, the progress in the practice of their religion is clear and many of the letters are requests for faculties to bless sacramentals and to enrol people in various religious societies. These are the years in which devotion to the Sacred Heart spread throughout the country and with it the practice of the May devotions and of the Forty Hours. Young enthusiastic Irish priests, educated in Rome, helped to spread these devotions on their return and, when occasion offered, were only too eager to introduce a fuller liturgy and ritual.

But the church was not without its difficulties. The long struggle for emancipation was not without its effects on the country. Members of the Established Church, who had, in general, resisted this concession to Catholics, had begun to adopt a new style of action, which tended to arouse the religious feelings of the people. A Bible Society had been established in 1804. It spread branches into different parts of the country and by means of some schools and popular missions it was determined to save Irish Catholics by inducing them to read the pure word of God. In 1822 Scripture Readers Society was instituted to aid this work. So objectionable were the methods used by the new preachers that most of the Protestant bishops refused them any assistance, and some went so far as to prohibit their clergy from attending their meetings.[21] It cannot be doubted but that this campaign did have results. This was the case in the Archdiocese of Tuam. A letter from the Bishop of Cork, Dr Murphy, to Dr Cullen shows that the practice of invalid marriages was not uncommon in his diocese, due in large degree to the measures offered by other churches.

> We are greatly exposed to invalid marriages, more from the Presbyterian than from the Protestant ministers. In the Protestant church the dispensation in Bann would amount to 3, whereas the Presbyterian ministers marry without banns in their private houses at all hours, by night as well as by day. The emigration to foreign countries is constantly increasing and as whole families emigrate in a body the young folks who are often related 2 x 2 and 2 x 3 whether by affinity or by consanguinity seek marriage at our hands.[22]

During the Famine the seeking of converts by material gain or relief was widespread. The *London Standard* commented:

> The present sufferings of that country have greatly contributed to break down the barriers, which have so long existed, against the entrance of divine truth among the unlightened portions of the people. Men are brought together by common calamity, and the gospel is now, more readily than heretofore, received from hands which have willingly administered relief to their temporal necessities.[23]

In 1847 it was suggested in the House of Commons that if England fed the starving in Ireland it would have to postpone the task of changing their religion.[24]

Certain dioceses suffered from shortage of priests. In Raphoe the bishop had nine curacies vacant in 1840.[25] Similarly, in Down and Connor Dr Blake was obliged to request Dr Cullen to ordain some students as soon as possible as he was in need of assistance.[26] At this time Ireland was predominantly a rural society. 30% of the people lived in towns and only 5% lived in cities with a population of 50,000. It was also the eve of the famine and mortality among the clergy was high in the years 1847-50. Writing from Kinsale, Co Cork, Fr Murphy says that 'mortality among priests is beyond conception. We have buried seven or eight priests since the Bishop's death'.[27]

The Famine years saw a considerable number of defections from the Catholic faith. MacHale could write that the:

> ... spectacle along the western coast exhibited almost an entire population literally and voluntarily renouncing the distinctions of ownership, and like the primitive Christians, putting their little possessions into a common fund for the relief of common misery.[28]

But this was not true of his own archdiocese as a whole and elsewhere where proselytism had made considerable inroads. Nonetheless the clergy did do their best to relieve, selling watches, plate and even clothes to provide what help they could. This must have caused Lord Lieutenant Clarendon to write to MacHale on 5 December 1847:

> I do not hesitate in saying that no clergy in Europe can be compared with the Irish for their zealous, self-sacrificing, faithful performance of their most arduous duties.

This was poor consolation for the young priest sent to Newmarket, Co Cork, just about this time:

> I am just removed to Newmarket in order to oppose a system of proselytism that has been progressing there too successfully for the last year. 190 poor starved Catholics with their miserable families joined the congregation of the Protestant

clergyman and so they continue! This is an awful state of things but what can be done – their children are starving about them and they would go to hell, they say, to relieve them. I am preaching as zealous and as forcefully as I can, and I have succeeded in bringing over three in as many weeks. The Protestant clergyman has funds supplied from the Societies of England and the state of things precludes the possibility of our giving any relief. We are scarcely able to support ourselves.[29]

The half century prior to the famine had helped to deepen the faith of the people. We have indications that Waterford cathedral was providing an adequate religious service from entries in the *Catholic Directory* for 1840. Sunday morning had Masses till noon. Benediction was given three times monthly. There was a sermon on the first Sunday of each month. Lent, Advent and May had devotions each evening. Thackeray remarked on the piety, stern, simple but unaffected of the Waterford people. Their whole soul seemed to be in their prayers, as rich and poor knelt side by side on flags. Thackeray was not always impressed by the Irish scene. Dublin was offering a fine service even earlier than this:

> In each of the parish chapels and friaries there is a regular succession of Masses, generally from 6 a.m. until 11a.m. on Sundays and Holidays; and from 7 a.m. until 11a.m. in the same chapels on every other day. On Sundays and Holidays all these Masses are attended by crowded congregations. In the parish chapels and friaries, sermons are preached on the evenings of every Sunday and Holiday during the Winter season, and immediately after last Mass in the Summer and Autumn months, and generally in the evenings of every day during the penitential times of Lent and Advent. On these occasions the chapels are crowded to excess.[30]

The parish missions were introduced in the 1840s. Athy and Carlow had one in 1843. The numbers for confession were so great that one suspects that previously there had been a goodly number of defaulterers. The Stations of the Cross were common in churches in 1830. Devotion to the Sacred Heart had been introduced in Cork by Bishop Moylan (1787-1815) and in Dublin by Fr Mulcaile SJ, at the close of the eighteenth century.[31] On 10 March 1873 every parish in the country was consecrated to the Sacred Heart.

We have seen that sexual morality was not as carefully observed in the seventeenth century as one had been led to believe earlier. There is, however, a general consensus that in the nineteenth century Irish women valued and preserved their chastity to quite a remarkable degree. Hall's well-known book on Ireland remarks on this and it is the opinion of the English husband rather than of the Irish wife that is recorded. He held the majority of Irish women of all classes were the most faithful and devoted wives and the best mothers, probably equalled nowhere else.[32] This observation is attested to by many others, foreigners among them. The main exception to this took place at wakes when some young men and girls remained in the precincts of the house. Amhlaoibh Ó Súilleabháin, whose diaries are most valuable, was in full agreement with the bishops' ruling that young un-married people should not go to wakes and he, though a wid-ower of fifty-one, did not attend them.[33]

Patterns had also been severely criticised. Dr Bray, Archbishop of Cashel, had suppressed the one held in Dooneskeagh at the turn of the century. In 1829 the bishops decided that pilgrimages to wells be totally abolished and Lough Derg be supervised more closely.

For the greater part of the century, Sunday devotions were limit-ed to towns and cities mainly. But missions did great good, es-pecially in country parts. They drew great numbers and the fre-quentation of the sacraments increased. Though the preaching was not on traditional lines, it created great enthusiasm and also provided a certain amount of diversion. Often at the close of a mission a confraternity was set up which gave a good impetus to the practice of monthly Confession and Holy Communion. The relation between people and priest was closely linked and the people knew their priests. To quote Amhlaoibh again:

> Fr Seamus Henebry was buried to-day. Young and old, big and small, are weeping after him. The little children of the

town are crying over his grave in the chapel, for he was a child-like priest among them. He was generous at his own table and he was lively-spirited company, easily satisfied in regard to money, though it is said that he had plenty of it.[34]

Teachers like Amhlaoibh must have been a great assistance to the clergy in teaching religion and exemplifying it in their own lives. The missioners developed a strong counter-reformation spirituality which already had some base in the towns and cities. By 1830 such devotions as the Novena of Grace, the Three Hours Agony, Exposition of the Blessed Sacrament on First Fridays, the Stations of the Cross, May Devotions and Novenas had taken root.

* * *

The famine in 1845 caused many changes both in political life and in the religious sphere. Though some Catholics grew wealthy in commerce, in professions and in the public service, the tenant farmers became the important class in politics and it was they who also provided most of the priests. The labourer had lost his little potato plot and though he worked and received greater remuneration, he was landless. It is not surprising then that the Fenians did not attract members easily from the countryside in the beginning since they sought political independence while agricultural and social reform was what the average countrypeople needed. It was at this period that the Irish language definitively lost ground. Many of the traditional religious values were to be found in Gaelic culture but they did not necessarily die with the language.

In the third quarter of the nineteenth century, the church was marked by greater centralisation at home and abroad. The Council of Trent became a reality in Ireland and, in addition, Italian devotion coloured urban Irish Catholicism. Paul Cullen, especially in his period as Archbishop of Dublin 1852-78, made a considerable contribution here as did the diocesan and regular clergy who had been educated in Rome or elsewhere on the continent. Centralisation was one of the marks of the synod of Thurles in 1850. Heretofore there had been no national synod for seven centuries and provincial synods carried little obligation on bishops to attend. In addition there was no clear agreement on the binding force of their decrees. At Thurles all had to attend or be represented. The decisions, once ratified by Rome, would then be binding on all.

The question of attending or of taking posts in the Queen's Colleges, established in 1845 was heatedly discussed and a small majority, led by Cullen, opposed them strongly with the backing of Rome, which proposed that a Catholic University should be founded on the model of Louvain. This never really took root, though John Henry Newman was appointed its first Rector.

Pastoral decisions caused little problem. In fact the decrees of the provincial synod held in Dublin in 1831 formed the bulk of the decrees accepted in Thurles. Now they were binding on all bishops and priests. The conferring of the sacrament of baptism was to be transferred from the home to the church. Confessions should be heard in a church and a confessional should be used. These changes were not easily accepted. A difficulty noted in the correspondence with Rome was the divisions between bishops but especially between Paul Cullen and John MacHale of Tuam, who incidently had supported Cullen's appointment. MacHale was a very powerful character in his early years as professor in Maynooth and later in the diocese of Tuam. But by the time of his death (1881) he had outlived his usefulness and was an impediment rather than a blessing to the Irish church, his own archdiocese being in very poor shape.

The diocesan clergy increased in numbers and quality. In 1850 there was roughly one priest per 2,000 people. In 1870 it had become one per 1,250. The pattern for the priest was that he was to consider himself a person apart, be prayerful, studious and maintained by an annual retreat and conferences, dressed in black with a Roman collar. The friars were experiencing a difficult time throughout this century due to penal provisions against them in the Emancipation Act of 1829 which was aimed at their eventual extinction, and also to the opposition of the bishops and diocesan clergy. This resulted in their numbers being quite small until near the close of the century but they did excellent work in Dublin, especially in the confessional, in the pulpit and in church building. Clarendon Street, built in the early years of the century, was the biggest church in the city. After the Synod of Thurles many of their country houses opened secondary schools and provided the best education they could until the Orders specially dedicated to education had grown in numbers and were in a position to take over that duty. They also did considerable good in conducting missions from the middle of the century onwards and were thus an excellent response to proselytism. The Jesuits and the Vincentians were the first in the field. The Passionists arrived in 1848, the Oblates of Mary Immaculate in 1851 and the Redemptorists in 1853. A mission in Athlone in 1853 lasted for a month.

Denominational schools were sought by the different religions and denominational teacher-training came in 1883. As a result of religious instruction, based on the catechism, Catholic practice was becoming more institutionalised and Christian life was seen as obedience to concrete rules. The second big influence on Christian life was the Sunday sermon. The increase in church-building led to an increase in Mass attendance especially in the poorer parts and a gradual relaxation in applying the rule strictly limiting the bination of Masses made attendance at Sunday Mass possible for many more people. From Emancipation onwards, as churches were being more solidly constructed, the Blessed Sacrament was being reserved in them and not as heretofore in the priest's house. The church was becoming a real *teach an phobail* through the transfer of baptism, confession and marriage from the home. Cullen initiated the custom of nuptial Mass which gradually spread through the country, though in some districts the effort to move the sacraments from the home to the church was proving less easy and took quite a while in the country. Devotions to Mary increased and the Family Rosary gradually was incorporated into 'evening devotions' in the church in urban areas.

The Fenians were founded in 1858. Unlike the constitutional methods of O'Connell, they favoured the use of violence to achieve greater freedom for the country. As a secret society they required that their members should take an oath. For Cullen and for many of the clergy, this caused considerable anxieties. Cullen, perhaps somewhat unfairly, classed them with the Carbonari, a secret society which was then attacking the papal States. The ordinary priest was torn by conflicting loyalties. He had an obligation to denounce secret societies as plotters against the Government. He also had the interests and welfare of his parishioners at heart. His own experience told him that these types of movement always ended in greater misery for the people, as had been evident after the abortive rising of 1848. Yet he had sympathy for their aims as he pondered on the sad economic situation of the vast majority of his parishioners.

He had played a vital role there. Now he seemed to be turning against the people. He was blamed as an interferer in politics. Bishop Keane of Cloyne was afraid that the people might desert the priest. Many of the Fenians were also unhappy at the rift. The priest did not lack sympathy for the Fenians nor for their ultimate ideal. Keane felt that there was some justification for the feeling that the priests had let the people down and they had turned to the Fenians. The latter, in their turn, could very tellingly make the point that if it was right for the clergy to encourage enlistment of Irishmen in the papal brigade to fight for the preservation of the papal states under Pius IX, it could hardly be less virtuous to fight for one's own country.

Sometimes where condemnations were loudest, individual priests were most sympathetic. At the Fenian trials, appeals for amnesty were supported by Cullen and other clerics who had been steadfast in their condemnations. Two priests, Canon Sheehan and Fr Peter O'Leary (An tAthair Peadar), both of Cloyne and writers, did much to defuse the whole situation.

While the Synod of Thurles said nothing about wakes and funerals, the Synod of Maynooth in 1875 required that parish priests put an end to the unchristian wakes and this injunction was frequenly repeated. This encouraged the habit of bringing the remains to the church and the funeral Mass being said there and not in the home. Traditional patterns and pilgrimages were also in decline as they often ended in faction fights. But Lough Derg always retained its popularity as an ascetic practice and was supervised carefully by the clergy. The pilgrimage of Our Lady's Island in Wexford was fully revived by 1900. It was the Synod of Maynooth also which declared for a standard catechism, known later as the *Penny Catechism*, which became the main source of instruction for Irish Catholics for practically a century. The second half of the century gave Ireland a new identity which was religious and Catholic rather than political. Its influence extended far and wide through emigration, and through priests taking up missions abroad in England, Scotland, America, Australia and Africa. This is very evident in the list of bishops who attended the first Vatican Council. One tenth of the 700 bishops present were born in Ireland and one fifth were of Irish descent. Dr Cullen, was one of the influential speakers present and, seems to have been the spokesman for the group which formulised the definition of papal infallibility.

At the time of his death, 24 October 1878, the Catholic church in Ireland had taken on the shape which it held up to the Second Vatican Council to a large degree. A dominant Tridentine spirituality had evolved among the urban middle class. A French priest, Adolphe Perraud, visited Ireland in 1860. He belonged to the Oratorians and had been ordained in 1855. He held political views and had a strong social conscience. He was named a member of the *Academie Française* in 1883 and cardinal in 1893. In his book, *Ireland under the English Rule*, published in Dublin in 1894 he was indignant at the servile position of the Irish Catholics but he does pay tribute to the fact that the English government allowed the church manage its own affairs. He remarks on the positive economic improvement after the Famine but he comments on the real poverty existing in many parts of the country. Priests in Donegal confirmed for him that frequently when a person came from Mass, he took off his clothes and gave them another to go to a later Mass. He noted a good deal of Prostestant discrimination against Catholics and the sad effects of the evictions. In the case at Partry, Co Mayo a man of 80 and his wife aged 74 were evicted. The wife in her distress turned to her husband and said, 'Here I am at 74 without a shelter in the world – I, who never wronged anybody and often opened my door to the poor and the unfortunate, what have I done to deserve this? The old man replied, 'Peace, my dear, peace, the Passion and Death of Christ was more than this.'[35]

The disestablishment of the Protestant church in 1879 wounded Protestant feelings but did not make any great difference in the development of the Catholic church. Since the middle of the century more Catholics had entered public life – Daniel O'Connell had been Lord Mayor of Dublin in 1841. Some Catholics were becoming more affluent. From c.1880 the Catholic hierarchy was in sympathy with and supporting the nationalist movement which eventually evolved into the independence movement. They had a very strong influence on their flocks, while bishops became more autocratic in their relations with their priests, who had enjoyed considerable liberty due to the conditions during the penal days.

Denominational schools, which were controlled by the clergy at both primary and secondary levels, received State support. In the purely political and social sphere, priests lent strong support to the land movements since most of them were from the farming class, but as yet the Dublin clergy had not come to grips with the problems of urban poverty. Discipline in seminaries and houses of religious formation became stricter and intellectually narrower. Monastic spirituality was unconsciously being imposed on the diocesan clergy which made them less attentive to social issues. But they did receive good practical formation for the confessional and the pulpit. The Cathechism of the Council of Trent was still the pattern and sometimes the source of the Sunday sermon and of the catechetical instruction in the schools.

This programme had the advantage of achieving its relatively modest aims. It set out a system of belief, based, as belief must be based, on the Creeds of the Church. Catholic theology was then in a defensive mood, and at times it might have suggested, and doubtless at times it did suggest, that the answer was clearer than an informed believer had any right to expect; for the relatively uninformed believer it was clear and it was a system, despite defects, through which much of the central tradition was passed on. As well as presenting a system of truths to be believed, the catechetical tradition presented clearly a set of duties to be carried out. But in practice moral theology was tempted towards an over-categorisation of offences, in turn tempting the less-finely attuned mind to pose the moral question in terms of 'How far can I go?'[36]

General religious practice at the close of the nineteenth century was mainly Tridentine, with the addition of devotions which tended to become duties. While Dr Cullen was mainly responsible for initiating the latter, ease of communication and the centralisation, which received a very strong boost from Vatican I, produced a general pattern among Irish Catholics. Marian devotion, which had always been strong, became more personal and developed very appreciably after the apparition at Lourdes in 1858. This devotion was further developed by the increase in the number of Sodalities of the Children of Mary. In January 1890 the Children's Mass was introduced in Claredon Street church in Dublin. It spread and helped people develop a simpler approach to the Mass.

The fast of Lent was observed very strictly. From c. 1840 Temperance movements had been initiated. As we have seen, Fr Matthew OFM Cap and Fr John Spratt O Carm, developed this apostolate very widely because the vice of drunkenness was endemic throughout the land, especially in the cities. It was the cheap recreation of the poor. The movement grew weak after their deaths but Fr Cullen SJ devoted himself to it in the 1880s by establishing the Pioneer Total Abstinence Association which attracted very large numbers up to the middle of the present century when it began to decline. We get an interesting picture of Ireland from Canon Sheehan's writings which were very widely read and admired, some being translated into other languages. He identifies nationality and Catholicism. In a sermon Luke Delmege says:

> And as the two illusions disappeared – that of Ireland, built from its ruins on purely material and selfish principles, and that of Ireland built without the foundation of security and independence, the young priest woke up suddenly to the vision of his country, developing under new and stable conditions her traditional ideas, and becoming, in the face of a

spurious and unstable civilisation, rocked to its foundation by revolution, a new commonwealth of Christ. The possibility of such an event had been vaguely hinted at by priests, who evidently were struggling to evolve coherent ideas from a mass of sensations and instincts, righteous and just, but yet unformed. It was foreshadowed by the manner in which the people, untrained and illiterate, groped after and grasped the highest principles of Christian civilisation; it was foretold by the energy with which men condemned the mere acquisition of wealth, and felt ashamed of possessing it; it was outlined in the simple, human lives, with all their Spartan severity towards themselves, and all their divine beneficence towards others.[37]

Louis Paul Dubois widens the picture in *Contemporary Ireland*. He was a well-trained observer and historian who had made several visits to Ireland. He did not mince his words in describing Irish problems. 'He wrote of "the mental and moral decadence of the nation", the "general absence of energy and character, of method and discipline" among a "people distracted by denominational struggles, sectarian fanaticism and the first phases of anti-clericalism".'

He noted shrewdly, however, that whereas Protestants were anti-Catholic as well as anti-nationalist, Catholics were anti-English rather than anti-Protestant. Among them no one was more popular than a Protestant who was also a nationalist. The Catholic priest he saw, with some exaggeration, as the only leader in 'an unorganised plebs of destitute peasants'. He judged the growth of the middle class slow even in towns. 'The Irish Catholic,' he said, 'still bears the mark of servitude' and he recalled Beaumont's judgment of seventy years before, that he was 'half a slave'. The priest was in truth the father of his people, and no doubt an authoritative enough father. He had immense power but (Dubois) noted that it had been 'singularly little abused'. Any charge that the Catholic priesthood 'was the direct and exclusive cause of all the ills of Ireland' he dismissed as 'a gross and fanatical theory' but he did note areas where its influence was 'apter to restrain evil than to forward good'.[38]

As had been noted, the notion of faith and fatherland was un-wittingly welded by Cromwell. At this juncture, when nation-hood was gradually becoming a reality, the Catholic religion provided an identity and an inspiration. Despite the difficult re-lationship between the Fenians and the church, the ordinary Fenian, as we have seen, was loyal to his faith. Gradually a glamour grew round 'the bold Fenian men'. Pearse's writings made the ideal of the priest and Fenian almost indistinguish-able. John O'Leary once remarked that the politician should have on his side either the priest or the Fenian. Pearse might have coined a beatitude: 'Blessed indeed would he be who could manage to have both'. Though emigration was particularly heavy in the nineteenth century, Irish Catholics could now talk of 'Ireland's spiritual empire' especially in the English-speaking countries where priests from All Hallows College and from the seminaries in Carlow, Kilkenny, Wexford and Thurles was pro-viding a supply of priests, many of whom became bishops in these countries.

A more concerted effort to meet the needs of the reading public was supplied by the Catholic Truth Society of Ireland which was based on the lines of the similar Society in England. It provided more than two hundred different penny booklets in its first few years. The Jesuit *Irish Messenger* had a circulation of close on 75,000 in its early years. Vocations continued to increase. This 'empire' was considerably enlarged by the end of the century and in the early decades of the present century, when the Holy Ghost Fathers, who had come to Ireland in 1859, the Society of the African Missions and the Irish Missionary Orders of Brothers and Sisters took over missions or opened new ones, es-pecially in Africa and Asia. While it may be a little odious to single out one person, Joseph Shanahan CSSp (1871-1943), who went to Nigeria in 1902, was an outstandingly hard worker and developer of new means of promoting missionary activity there. Much of the same calibre as marked our early missionaries was evident in his life and work but he was a far more active and cre-ative man.

Literature

There seems to have been a falling off in poets of stature writing in Gaelic in the nineteenth century, possibly because the English language was spreading widely through the rural districts. Pádraig Denn, who was born in 1756, came to settle in Cappoquinn, Co Waterford after 1800. He taught there until in died in 1828. He was also clerk of the chapel and had the duty of reading the prayers before Mass. When he died he possessed just 10/-. He translated Bishop Challoner's *Think well on't* into Irish. His poems have often been ascribed to Tadhg Gaelach because they were printed as an appendix to his works. Many of them, like Tadhg's, were written to well-known airs.[39] He had great devotion to Our Lady[40] and also wrote *Araoir is mé ag machtnamh* in which he ponders on the passion, a subject frequently in his thoughts. He also showed that he had a keen appreciation of the fear of death in *Aighneas an pheacaigh leis an mbás* (The sinner's contest with death):

An Peacach:	*Do shaoileas ríamh ná rinneas éinnídh*
	a thuillfeadh píanta síoruídh, céasta;
	ní dheárna goid ná broid ná éigean,
	murdar ná feall aon am dem shaoghal.
An Bás:	*Acht bhís paiseónta, droch-labhartha, bréagach,*
	imeartheach, ólach, cancarach, scléipeach,
	barbardha, galgarnach, ag dearbhadh éithigh,
	is tuig go dtuillid siúd do dhaoradh

The Sinner:	I never though that I had done anything
	which would deserve eternal, crucifying pain.
	I did not steal, oppress nor use force nor did I
	commit murder or treachery ever in my life.
Death:	But you were passionate, ill-spoken, untruthful,
	gambling, drinking, wrangling, ostentatious, cruel,
	argumentative and swearing false oaths.
	Remember these merit you condemnation.)[41]

One poet who achieved great popularity was Antoine Ó Reachtabhra (1779?-1835). He suffered from blindness from the age of nine. Though he learned to play the fiddle he was not a

good player but he had to earn a living. Neither was he considered to be a good poet, though his poems were very popular. He
lived most of his life in Co Galway but he shows his love for his
native Mayo in the poem *Anois teacht an Earraigh*, and he proposes
to return there as spring is coming. The old medieval idea is
found in his *Cholera Morbus*. The disease is an affliction sent by
an angry God.

> *Sé mo thuairm's dubhach liam trácht air*
> *gur uair í seo atá ag iarraidh sásughadh*
> *guidhfimid ar fad ar Mhuire Mháthair*
> *tá fearg ar Dhia 's a sgiúirse tarrainte.*

I believe and I'm sorry to say that now is the time that satisfaction is being sought. We will pray only to Mary our
Mother (since) God is angry and He has His scourge in action.

His *aithrí* is one of his most sincere poems:

> *Ó a Íosa Críost a d'fhulaing an pháis,*
> *a's do h-adhlacadh mar do bhí tú úmhal,*
> *cuirim cuimrighe m'anma ar do sgáth,*
> *a's ar uair mo bháis ná tabhair dom cúl.*

> *A bhainríoghan phárrthais, máthair's maighdean,*
> *sgathán na ngrása, aingeal is naomh,*
> *cuirim cosaint m'anama ar do láimh,*
> *a Mhuire, na diúltuigh mé is beidh mé saor.*

> *Is cuaille gan mhaith mé i gcoirnéal fáil,*
> *nó is cosmhail mé le bád a chaill a stiúir,*
> *do brisfídhe isteach in aghaidh carraig 'sa bhfráigh,*
> *'s do bhéadh dá bháthadh 'sna tonntaibh fuar'.*

O, Jesus Christ, who suffered the Passion and was buried because You were humble, I place my soul's protection in Your
care. At the hour of my death don't turn your back on me.

O queen of paradise, mother and maiden, mirror of graces, of
angels and saints, I place the custody of my soul in your
hands. O Mary don't refuse me and I'll be safe.

I am a useless stake in the corner of a fence. I'm like a boat
that has lost its rudder, which would be smashed in against
the rocks on the coast and be drowned in the cold waves.

He is probably pretty honest in recounting his own transgressions:

> *Nuair a bhí mé óg b'olc iad mo thréithe,*
> *ba mhór mo spéis i scléip 's in achrann,*
> *b'fhearr liom go mór ag imirt 's ag ól*
> *ar maidin Domhnaigh ná triall chum aifrinn.*

> *Níor bhfearr liom suidhe in aice cailín óig*
> *nó le mná pósta ag céilidheacht tamall,*
> *do mhionnaidh móra bhí mé tughta,*
> *agus drúis nó póite níor leig mé tharm.*[42]

When I was young I had bad habits. I was very interested in showing off and in strife. I much preferred sporting and drinking on Sunday morning than going to Mass.

I asked nothing better than to sit near a young girl or to woo a married lady for a while. I was given to using strong oaths and I did not avoid lust nor drink.

Raftery's blindness does not seem to have affected him too severely, as he replied to one of a crowd who asked who was the musician:

> *Mise Rafterí an file*
> *lán dóchais' gus grádh*
> *le súile gan solas*
> *le ciúineas gan crádh.*

> *Dul siar ar m'aistear*
> *le solas mo chroidhe*
> *fann agus tuirseach*
> *go deireadh na slighe.*

> *Féach anois mé*
> *is m'aghaidh ar bhalla*
> *ag seinm ceóil*
> *do phócaibh folamh.*

He faces the reality of his situation with hope and love, with peace and resignation though he is tired of getting little financial recognition for his musical accomplishments.

Mícheál Ó Longáin (c. 1765-1837) straddles the turn of the century. He and his sons Micheál Óg and Pól did very valuable work in the conservation of manuscripts. The older Mícheál wrote quite a number of religious poems as did his contemporary Dáibhí de Barra from Carrigtwohill which were very popular in the area. One of Micheál's poems, *Le croidhe suilbhir suairc seinim-se fáilte*, or one copied by him, is a nativity poem.

> *Aonchnú mhullaigh na cruinne thar mhnáibh sin*
> *do thogh an tAthair mar dhalta seoch cach eóin;*
> *do thogh an Mac le searc mar mháthair,*
> *'s an Spiorad Naomh mar chéile ghrámhar.*[43]

The father chose Mary of all the women in the world as His child, the Son chose her as His mother out of love and the Holy Spirit chose her as spouse.

Tomás Ruadh Ó Súilleabháin (c. 1785-1848) is a poet who is rarely read and yet was very typical of the Irishman of his time. Born at Banard, near Derrynane, Co Kerry, he was educated at the school in Gortnakilla. The people admired his gift of composing simple poems – many of his quatrains were extempore. He became a schoolmaster but, being of a restless disposition, he went from school to school throughout Uíbh Ráthach. Generally he was housed by local families and people gathered in at night to hear his poems and stories. Daniel O'Connell was his hero and contemporary. The Liberator saw his genius and tried to help him get a better education. He sent him to Dublin. But Tomás got homesick and returned on foot as soon as the opportunity offered. A woman in whose house he received shelter said to him one morning, 'You suffered a lot last night.' Tomás replied, 'The Son of God suffered more.' Tomás gradually made his way back to Banard and for the three days of life that remained to him he sang the sacred hymns which he had composed.

In his poem praising his friend Fr O'Sullivan, whose family had once been of the nobility, he says:

> *Sé dochtúir diadhachta na geanmnaidheachta,*
> *is fearr gníomhartha i gcóta;*
> *is feairrde an tír seo ó tháinig inte*
> *an té chuirfeadh suím ina chomhairle.*

Craobh na soilse de chléireach Íosa,
ár saighdiúir gníomhamhail, cródha,
'sé Diarmuid groidhe, geal an prionnsa maoidhim-se,
plúr na dtigheasach bhfóghanta.

He is doctor of holiness and purity. He is an active man in harness. Whoever would seek counsel from him since he came here is much the better for it. Our active brave soldier is the shining servant of Christ. Bright, sturdy Diarmuid is the prince I am praising. He is the gem of generous entertainers.[44]

A sample of his extempore quatrains runs:

An diabhal nuair a bhíonn sé 'na luí go tláth, lag, fann,
is rialta bhíonn 'na chroidhe, ná'n bráthair mall;
an diabhal nuair a bhíonn arís 'na shláinte teann
an diabhal a mbíonn de chuimhne an bráthar ann.[45]

When the devil is lying weak and faint, he is more rightheart-ed than the humble brother. The devil when he has regained his powerful health, 'the divil a bit' does he remember of the brother.

Pádraig Ó Callanáin, writing round the middle of the nineteenth century, is a good representative of the devotion of the West.

Ó, a Íosa Críost, a rígh na reann,
a céasadh ar chrann na hAoine,
tabhair grásta dhúinn mar fuair Magdalen,
a d'éirigh as peaca an tsaoghail seo.

Ár n-anamnacha bochta a cheannaigh Tú
go daor i mbruach an tsléibhe,
ná leig Uait iad, lá an bhreitheamhnais,
le spiorad na láimhe cléithe.[46]

O Jesus Christ, O King of the stars, who was crucified on the Cross on Friday, give us grace as Magdalen received it when she renounced worldly sin. Do not leave our poor souls, which You bought dearly on the side of the mountain, with the spirit of the left hand, on the day of judgement.

Maelseachlainn Ó Máille, another nineteenth-century western poet, was loud in his praises of Seoirse Brún. He describes the happiness in his home especially while Mass is being said:

> *Bíonn guidheadh easbog ann, sagart is bráthar,*
> *'s gach nídh dá áilne d'á bhfacadh súil,*
> *léightear aifreann ann ar hallaí bána,*
> *'s gur geall le párrthas tigh Sheóirse Brún.*

Bishops, priests and brothers pray there where there are the loveliest things that eye has seen. Mass is read there in white halls – George Brown's house would remind you of heaven.[47]

In the collection of poems found in *Dánta Diadha Uladh*, which has been edited by Enrí Ó Muirgheasa, one finds a considerable volume of religious verse stretching back over three centuries. While the majority of the poems are from Ulster, some of them are also found in other areas. Enrí holds that they were widely known and used by the laity. They knew them because they had often heard them.[48] The prayer of the wives as their husbands were on their dangerous labour in the fishing boats is very poignant.

> *Tá siad dár bhfágáil, a réalt na mara*
> *ó sábháil sinn ar dhainséar na mbád,*
> *bídh leo go bhfillidh siad treasna an bharra,*
> *is a óigh, beir buidheachas uainn go bráth.*[49]

They are leaving us, O Star of the sea, guard them from every danger of the boats. Be with them till they return across the bar (sea) – and O Virgin, you will have our eternal gratitude.

He provides us with a very useful grace before meals:

> *Bail na gcúig n-arán is an dá iasc*
> *ar an cúig mhíle do roinn Día;*
> *rath an Rí ar an roinn.*
> *A Thighearna Íosa, ós tú cheannaigh sinn*
> *beannaigh anois ár gcuid 's ár gcuideachta.*[50]

The blessing of the five loaves and the two fishes which God divided among five thousand. May the blessing of the King who did the sharing be on our food and on our sharing. Lord Jesus, since it is You who redeemed us, bless our food and our companions.

Paidreacha Dúchais

These prayers are from various centuries, it is suggested, some from a very early period. Diarmuid Ó Laoghaire SJ is of the opinion that most of the prayers in the collection are at least two centuries in existence.[51] Names of some eighteenth and nineteenth century poets are connected with some of them and one may safely say that the clergy composed some of them. These prayers and pious stories were a force in the devotion of the rural people. Many of them are related to ordinary occasions of prayer, e.g. rising, lighting the fire, putting a child to sleep, work, cockcrow, going to bed, making the bed, grace before and after meals. Others treat of the Mass, the passion, the Blessed Trinity, Mary. Many are pleas for help, temporal and spiritual. A typical example is:

> *A Íosa ar maidin screadaim is glaoim ort,*
> *A Aon Mhic bheannaighthe a cheannaigh go daor sinn,*
> *coimrí m'anma faoi Do chroise naofa*
> *mé a choimeád ó pheaca i gcaitheamh an lae seo.*[52]

> O Jesus, I cry and call to You in the morning; O Blessed Only Son who bought us dearly. I place the care of my soul under the protection of Your Holy Cross that it may keep me from sin throughout this day.

Another prayer which is often used in the liturgy today asks for Christ's constant protection:

> *Ó fhás go haois*
> *is ó aois go bás*
> *Do dhá láimh, a Chríost*
> *anall tharainn.*[53]

> As we pass from growth to age and from age to death may Your two hands, Christ, surround us.

These prayers are often connected with the Passion and God's forgiveness. Special help at the hour of death is commonly sought. I have treated of the frequent appeals for Mary's help.[54] The archangel Michael, who figures regularly in bardic poetry, is called upon to help the soul to heaven:

Go n-osclaí Peadar na flaithis go réidh duit,
is nár ghlac Micheál ar a láimh chlé thú,
Dia agus Muire go dtige id' éileamh
is go mbeirid siad d'anam go cathair na naomh leo.[55]

May Peter open heaven easily to you, may Michael not call
you to his left; may God and Mary come claiming you and
bear your soul with them to the city of the saints.

These prayer-poems are generally simple, easy to memorise and
sometimes in litany-form.

Míle fáilte romhat, a Rí an Domhnaigh
a Mhic na h-Óighe, a rinne an t-aiséirí,
A Mhic Mhuire, fóir orm!
A Íosa Mhic Mhuire, déan trócaire orm.[56]

A thousand welcomes to You, O King of the Sunday, son of
the Virgin who rose from the dead. Son of Mary, help me,
Jesus, Son of Mary have mercy on me.

Bás ola, bás sona, bás sóláis, bás aithreachais, bás gan chrá,
bás gan scáth, bás gan bás, bás gan scannradh, bás gan dólás.[57]

Death with anointing, happy death, comforting death, death
with repentance, death without anxiety, death without
worry, death without (spiritual) death, death without fear,
death without sorrow.

Many of the prayers are marked by a simple, personal devotion
to Jesus and Mary:

Is binn lem' chuimhne D'ainm án
is ait lem' chroí Do dhíograis ghrá
ach mil liom foillsiú D'éadan bhreá
a Thiarna ghrámhar Íosa.
Is Tú ár mian, is Tú ár só
ár gcuid den tsaol thar acmhuinn óir
is Tú ár n-aoibhneas thall go deó
a Phéarl ghléighil Íosa.[58]

Ó Mhuire mháthair, mo mhíle grá thú
mo choimirce chúnta in am gach gá thú.[59]

Sweet to my memory is Your glorious name. Joy to my heart
is the sincerity of Your love. Honey to me is the brightness of
Your fine forehead, o loving Lord Jesus. You are our wealth,
our happiness, our earthly possession which far surpasses
the wealth of gold. You are our bliss forever yonder, o bright
pearl, o Jesus.

O Mary mother, you are my greatest love, my protecting help
at every hour of danger.

One could cite many prayers recalling the Passion, the Trinity,
Our Lady, repentance, the Mass etc. but as these occur regularly
throughout our spiritual literature in prose and verse there is no
need to dwell on them here. But when one remembers the faction fights and similar incidents at patterns in the nineteenth
century it is good to recall the themes of peace and love of neighbour which are frequently found in these prayers even if they
were forgotten at times by the men who participated in these
events.

Síoth Athar an áidh
Síoth Chríosta an pháis
Síoth Spioraid na ngrás
dúinn féin is don ál atá óg.[60]

The peace of the Father of good fortune; the peace of Christ in
His Passion; the peace of the Spirit of graces be on us and on
the young folk.

Nár fhaghaimid anbhás ná gearrbhás ná bás in aon cheann
desna seacht bpeaca marfacha, ach bás le h-ola agus
le h-aithrí, i síothcháin le Dia is le daoine.[61]

May we not have a sudden or quick death or die in any of the
seven deadly sins but rather death with anointing and repentance, at peace with God and man.

This prayer recalls the common entry in the annals 'death after
anointing and penance'.

Irish saints are frequently appealed to for help, notably Patrick,
Brigid and Colum Cille. Gerard Murphy has recorded a touching, simple poem of a woman whose husband and all her children had died:

A Rí ghil na naomh
a's Fuasgalthóir an tsaoil,
a bhainríon na n-aingeal 's a bhanaltra shéimh,
iarraim cabhair an Spioraid Naoimh
is bhúr gcúnamh go léir
chun mo chrosa d'iompar go tuirseach liom féin.[62]

O bright King of the saints and Saviour of the world, O queen
of the angels and gentle nurse, I ask the aid of the Holy Spirit
and help from you all to carry my cross in sadness and all
alone.

It is obvious that there is great variety and richness in these
prayers. One hopes that one day we will be able to get a clearer
idea as to how widely they were used. A manuscript dated 1848
has a poem which springs from a repentant heart:

Deóraidh bocht brónach mé, a Dhé na ndúl
cuir lón liom is treóruigh mé féin chun siubhail',
déan m'fhothragadh le deora ro-ghéara mo shúl
'sna dheóigh sin tabhair cóisir Do Chuirp ghéighil dúinn.

Bí mo chreideamh gan easbaidh, a Mhic Dé na ngrás,
bí mo mhisneach go seasmhach le ré mo lá,
bí dom spreagadh is ná caillim go h-éag Do ghrá,
is cuir im'aigne bheith ag faire go h-éag an bháis.

'Íosa, 'Spiorad Naomh, Athair na sluagh,
bí go síorruidhe dom'dhídean, táim lán de bhuairt,
tabhair smaointiughadh an mo chroídhe-se ar Do pháis gach uair,
is tabhair arís dham a bheith ag síorghol go cráite cruaidh.[63]

O God of the elements, I am a poor sad exile, provide for me
and guide me in my travels; wash me with the very sharp
tears of my eyes and then give me the banquet of Your bright
Body. Be Thou my perfect faith, O Son of God of graces. Be
my strength continuously as long as I live. Arouse me that I
may never lose Your love and remind me to be watchful till
my death. Jesus Holy Spirit, Father of the hosts, be my constant protector as I am very worried. Make me think constantly of Your passion in my heart and grant also that I may
be constantly lamenting with deep sorrow.

A considerable number of sermons are to be found in Gaelic manuscripts written in the nineteenth century. Some have been edited: *Don aithrighe cuirtear ar cairde*[64] (on postponed Repentance) written by Fr Maurice Power of Cloyne (1791-1877); *An raoile agus an t-arbhar i ngort Dé*[65] (The cockle and wheat in God's field); *Sochar mór an Chrábhaidh*[66] (The great benefit of Piety); *Smaointe ar pháis ar Slánathóra*[67] (Thoughts on our Saviour's Passion). All these have been edited by Risteard Ó Foghludha. Fr Pádraig Ó Súilleabháin OFM has provided a list of 'Catholic Sermon Books in Ireland 1700-1850'.[68]

Notes:

1. *Memoirs and Correspondence of Viscount Castlereagh* (London, 1850-3) ed. by his brother. Vol IV, 97-193.

2. Report of Her Majesty's commissioners appointed to inquire into the government and management of the college of Maynooth. Appendix pp 133-159.

3. McDowell, R.B., *Public Opinion and Government Policy in Ireland 1800-1846*, 32.

4. *CIH* 250-55. *v.* also Grogan, G., 'Daniel O'Connell and European Catholic Thought', *Studies* (Spring 1991) 56-64.

5. Carty, J., *Ireland from Grattan's Parliament to the Great Famine*, 108-110.

6. Quoted in *ICE* 160.

7. *ICE* 183.

8. *Edmund Ignatius Rice and the Christian Brothers* (Dublin, 1926) cf. 448-9.

9. *Mary Aikenhead, Her Life, Her Work, Her Friends* (Dublin, 1879) 498-505.

10. William Hutch, *Mrs Ball* (Dublin, 1879) 523.

11. Leaves from Annals of the Sisters of Mercy Vol i, 518-9.

12. Walsh, Rev T.J., *Nano Nagle and her Presentation Sisters* (Dublin, 1959).

13. Ir. Coll. Rome Archives, Cullen Letters No. 723, 18 April 1842, and cf. ibid. No. 725, 25 April 1842, ibid. No 727, 9 May 1842.

14. Ibid. No. 1122, 20 December 1845.

15. Ibid. No. 1123, 20 December 1845.

16. Ibid. No. 1149, 26 January 1846.

17. Ir. Coll. Rome, Kirby Letters No. 604, 5 June 1848.

18. Ibid. No 684, 9 March 1850.

19. Ibid. No. 736, 13 July 1850.

20. Ibid. No. 2408, 1 September 1859.

21. Killen, W. D., *The Ecclesiastical History of Ireland* (London, 1875) Vol II, 418.

22. Ir. Coll. Rome, Cullen Letters No. 270.

23. McNamee O.M.I., B., "The 'Second Reformation' in Ireland", *Irish Theological Quarterly* 33 (1966) 49, 55.

24. Ibid. where he cites Hansard, *Parliamentary Debates* LXXXIX pp 502, 634.

25. Cullen Letters No 593, 12 April 1840.

26. Ibid. No. 1120, 12 December 1845.

27. Ibid. No. 1308, 18 January 1847.

28. O'Reilly, Rev B., *John MacHale Archbishop of Tuam* (New York, 1890) Vol I, 308.

29. Kirby Letters No. 604, 5 June 1848.

30. McGregor, J. J., *New Picture of Dublin 1821* (Dublin, 1821) 148.

31. Ronan, M. V.,*An Apostle of Catholic Dublin* (Dublin, 1944) 126-7.

32. Mr and Mrs S.C. Hall, *Ireland* (London, 1842) II, 314-5.

33. *Cinnlae Amhlaoibh Uí Shúilleabháin*, 24 April 1831.

34. Ibid. 10 January 1834.

35. Perraud, A., *Ireland in 1862* (Dublin 1863) 131.

36. *ICE* 232.

37. *Luke Delmege* (London 1905) 563.

38. *ICE* 237.

39. Ó Foghludha, R., ed., *Dúanta diadha Phádraig Denn* (Dublin, 1941) 1x-1xi.

40. *Mary* 256-7.

41. Ó Ceallaigh, S., *Éigse Éireann* (Dublin, 1942) 267.

42. De hÍde, D., *Abhráin agus Dánta an Reachtabhraigh* (Áth Cliath, 1933) 164-5.

43. RIA 23C20, 170-6.

44. Séamus Dubh, *The Songs of Tomás Ruadh O'Sullivan,* (Dublin, 1914) 5-24.

45. Ibid. 112.

46. Ó Raghallaigh, T., *Filí agus filidheacht Chonnacht* (Áth Cliath, 1938) 510.

47. Ibid. 526.

48. Dublin, 1936 (henceforth *DDU*) 6.

49. *DDU* 258.

50. *DDU* 260.

51. Ó Laoghaire, D., SJ, *Ár bPaidreacha Dúchais* (Áth Cliath, 1975). Henceforth *APD*.

52. *APD* No 17.

53. Ibid. 380.

54. *Mary* 281-4.

55. *APD* 340.

56. Ibid. 60.

57. Ibid. 324.

58. Ibid. 420.

59. Ibid. 440.

60. Ibid. 109.

61. 326.

62. *Éigse* VI (1948-52) 17.

63. McKernan, O., 'A Religious Poem', *Éigse* III (1941) 105-6.

64. *IER* Vol 65 (1945) 21-27.

65. Ibid. 19-31.

66. Ibid. 235-45.

67. Ibid. 103-113. *v.* also *IER* Vol 65, 161-72.

68. Ibid. Vol 99 (1963) 31-36.

Addendum to notes 32 and 33:

The sleeping accommodation, where small houses and large families were concerned, has been the subject of frequent comment by travellers and others. 'Beds for the most part of the common people,' says Dineley, 'are mere straw and that scarce clean, some have ticking stuffed with straw, without sheets, nay they pull off their very shirts so as not to wear them out. These cabins abound with children, which, with the man, maid and wife, sometimes a travelling stranger, or pack-carrier, or pedlar or two; aye nine or ten of them together, naked heads and points'. (*Observations* p. 21) A description of the same custom written in 1841 is so much to the point that I venture to quote it in full: 'The floor is thickly strewn with fresh rushes, and stripping themselves entirely naked, the whole family lie down at once together, covering themselves with blankets if they have them, and, if not, with their day clothing, but they lie down decently and in order, the eldest daughter next to the wall, furthest from the door, then all the sisters according to their ages. Next the mother, father and sons in succession, and then the strangers, whether the travelling pedlar, tailor or beggar. Thus, the strangers are kept aloof from the female part of the family; and if there is an apparent community, there is great propriety of conduct. This was the first time my friend had seen the primitive but not promiscuous mode of sleeping (A.D. 1799). He has, however, often seen it since.' (*McLysaght* 66-7).

CHAPTER 10

The Twentieth Century

Do thugas mo ghnúis
ar an ród so rómham
ar an ngníomh do-chím
's ar an mbás do gheóbhad.
(I set my face on this road before me, on the deed I see and on the death I'll suffer.)
(P.H. Pearse)

At the turn of the century, housing conditions in Dublin were in a wretched state. One third of the families were housed in single rooms. There were some industries, a good deal of casual employment and there were many unemployed. Trade unions came into existence. Dr Peter Coffey, though of farming stock, published a pamphlet, *The Church and the Working Classes*, in 1906. He showed that the Poor Law was degrading and private charity, though highly commendable, were not the answer to poverty. It was not long since Leo XIII, in *Rerum Novarum*, had laid down the obligation of a just family wage. Coffey favoured Christian socialism but the very word inspired fear among the establishment in church and state. Clergy tended to make general recommendation to employers and workers. James Connolly, however, rejected Christian socialism and the notion of Catholic trade unions, though they already existed on the continent and worked with good effect in countries like Belgium. Connolly held that workers should stand by their rights as citizens and fulfil their duties as Catholics, and he predicted that the church would adapt to socialism despite the fact that there were misunderstandings on both sides.

These same years also saw learned, wise Catholics give excellent example and advice to youth. Torna, professor of Irish in University College, Cork expresses this idealism very beautifully:

A dhuine óig,
nár luigh an saoghal cruaidh ort fós,
mo chomhairle duit, is glac uaim í,
bí ullamh don tslí atá romhat.

Seachain an t-olc
is an dream do-ní a áiteamh ort,
ná géill dá mbagairt, ná dá bplás
nó is mairg do chás 's is bocht.

Mar críostuidhe cóir
lean-se lorg an Mháighistir mhóir;
bí dílis d'A reacht abhfus,
's is aoibhinn duit, a dhuine óig.[1]

O youthful one on whom life has not yet lain heavily, (this is) my advice to you and take it. Be ready for the road before you. Avoid evil and those who would persuade you to do it. Yield neither to their threats nor their seduction or your lot will be poor and sad. As a good Christian follow the path of the great Master. Be faithful to his law and you will be a happy youth.

An unknown poet has given similar advice:

Ar maidin duit, a mhacaoimh óig,
iarr teagasc ar an dTrionóid,
ionnail go cáidh. Gaibh go glan
gan sail id' láimh do leabhar.

Ar mhuir mhór an léighinn láin
bí id' loingseóir mhaith, a mhacáin,
más áil leat id' fháidh eagna
i ndáil catha cóimhfhreagra.[2]

In the morning, O young lad, ask the Trinity to teach you. Wash carefully and take your book in your hand. Be a good steersman, o youth, on the great sea of wide learning if you wish to be a wise prophet and a good respondent in keen debate.

The desire to pass on one's acquired experience is evident:

A leinbh atá i dtús do shaoghail,
mo theagasc go cruinn beir leat,
an t-é dá dtáinig a chiall le h-aois
cuir-se gach nidh 'na chead.

Ná sanntaigh ráidhte baois'
ná 'n dream d'á mbid aca,
sula dtiocfaidh an iomad ded' aois
bíodh aithne ar Chríost agat.

Ná caith do shaoghal díomhaoin,
is ná leig an tslighe thar ceal
óir an tslat nuair a chruadhann le h-aois[3]
is deacair í shníomh 'na gad.[4]

O child, who is beginning your life, listen carefully to my instruction; entrust everything to the person to whom the years have given understanding. Do not be given to foolish sayings nor to those who use them. Know Christ before you are advanced (much) in age. Lead not an idle life and don't neglect the (proper) way because it is hard to twist an aged branch into a withe.

If Patrick Pearse's personality is to be judged by his poetry he was endowed with deep faith, tender feelings and a great idealism. Children appealed very strongly to him as is clear from his writings and from the fact that he founded St Enda's school. Though his volume of poetry is small it is very significant. In his *Crónán mná sléibhe* he has these simple but touching lines:

A chinnín óir is a choinneal mo thighe-se,
déanfair solas dá siubhlann an tír seo;
a bhéilín bhig do dheól mo chíocha
Pógfaidh Muire ar a slighe thú.[5]

O little golden head, O light of my house, you will enlighten the people of our country; O little soft mouth which drank from my breasts, Mary will kiss you as she passes by.

Personally I find *Bean tsléibhe ag caoineadh a mic* the most expressive lament in any language.

Brón ar an mbás 'se dhubh mo chroidhe-se,
d'fhuadaigh mo ghrá is d'fhág mé claoidhte

gan caraid, gan compánach fá dhíon mo thigh-se,
ach an léan-sa im'lár 's mé ag caoineadh.

Ag gabháil an tsléibhe dham trathnóna
do labhair an éanlaith liom go brónach,
do labhair an naosg binn 's an crotach glórach
ag faisnéis dom gur éag mor stórach.

Do ghlaoidh mé ort, is do ghlór níor chualas,
do ghlaoidh mé arís 's freagra ní bhfuaireas;
do phóg mé do bhéal 's a Dhia nár bhfuar é!
och is fuar í do leabaidh san gcillín uaigneach.

's a uaigh fhód-ghlas 'na bhfuil mo leanbh,
a uaigh caol bheag, ós tú a leaba,
mo bheannacht ort, 's mo mhíle beannacht'
ar na fódaibh glasa atá ós cionn mo pheata.

Brón ar an mbás, ní féidir a shéanadh
leagann sé úr is críon le céile
's a mhaicín mhánla is é mo chéasadh
do cholainn chaomh bheith ag déanamh creafoíg'.[6]

The sadness of death has blackened my heart. It has snatched my love and left me desolate, without friend or companion under the roof of my house – but this sorrow in my heart and I am keening.

As I went along the mountain this evening the birds spoke sadly to me; the sweet snipe and the noisy curlew making known to me that my dearest was dead.

I called you but I did not hear your voice. I called again and got no answer. I kissed your mouth and, my God, how cold it was! Ah, cold is your bed in that lonely cell.

O green-sodded grave where lies my child, O small narrow grave, since your are his bed, my blessing on you and a thousand blessings on the green sods which are covering my pet.

The sadness of death – it cannot be denied; it strikes both young and old and O gentle, little son it is my crucifixion that your beautiful body is turning to dust.

Pearse reveals his inmost thoughts about happiness and sadness in his own life in *The Wayfarer*, which is his last poem treating his philosophy of life:

The beauty of the world hath made me sad,
this beauty that will pass,
Sometimes my heart hath shaken with great joy
to see a leaping squirrel in a tree,
or a red ladybird on a stalk,
or little rabbits in a field at evening
lit by the slanting sun,
or some green hill where shadows drifted by,
some quiet hill where mountainy man hath sown
and soon would reap; near to the gate of heaven;
or children with bare feet upon the sands
of some ebbed beach, or playing on the streets
of little towns in Connacht,
things young and happy.
And then my heart has told me:
these will pass,
will pass and change, will die and be no more,
things bright and green, things young and happy;
and I have gone upon my way
sorrowful.[7]

During Christmas 1915 his thoughts were already set:

O King that was born
to set bondsmen free,
in the coming battle
help the Gael.[8]

He expresses it even more clearly:

Do thugas mo ghnúis ar an ród so rómham
ar an ngímh do-chím 's ar an mbás do-ghóbhad.[9]

I set my face on this road ahead of me, on the deed I see and
on the death I shall suffer.

On the political level, it was not easy for the ordinary Catholic to
judge what was the right course to take. The Rising in 1916 was
considered foolhardy by most of the clergy and laity though
they sympathised with the ideals and ambitions which inspired
men like Pearse. Just before it he expressed his mother's feelings:

I do not grudge them; Lord I do not grudge
my two strong sons that I have seen go out
to break their strength and die, they and a few,
in bloody protest for a glorious thing.
They shall be spoken of among their people,
the generations shall remember them
and call them blessed.
But I will speak their names to my own heart
in the long nights
the little names that were familiar once
round my dead hearth.
Lord, Thou art hard on mothers:
we suffer in their coming and in their going;
and though I grudge them not, I weary, weary
of the long sorrow – and yet I have my joy:
my sons were faithful and they fought.[10]

A touching mark of his devotion to Mary comes from his period in gaol before his execution. His mother had made one last request 'I'm thinking,' she whispered tearfully, 'that – if you go – there will be one to write something for me – as your father used to do … . Do you think you could write something for me – if you get time.' 'Yes,' he promised her, 'I will write something for you if I get time.' Just as the last hours came he wrote:

Dear Mary, thou did'st see they First-born Son
go forth to die amidst the scorn of men
for whom He died;
receive my first-born son into thy arms,
who also hath gone out to die for men,
and keep him by thee till I come to him;
Dear Mary, I have shared thy sorrow,
and soon shall share thy joy.[11]

Fr Aloysius OFM Cap, who ministered to the sentenced men in Kilmainham, was able to report to Pearse on the morning of the executions

'You will be glad to know that I gave Holy Communion to James Connolly this morning.' 'Thank God,' Pearse replied, 'it is the only thing I was anxious about.' Pearse assured me that he was not in the least worried or afraid; that he did not know how he deserved the privilege of dying for his country .... Then he made his confession. After that I gave Holy Communion to him.[12]

Pearse had that admirable approach to this moment

Do ghlanas mo chroidhe anocht
amhail mhnaoi do ghlanfadh a teach
roimh teacht d'a leannán d'á fios
a leannáin, is áluinn do theacht.
Do leathas doras mo chroidhe
amhail fear do-ghéanadh fleadh
ar theacht i gcéin d'a mhac,
a mhic, is áluinn do theacht.[13]

I cleansed my house to night as a woman would clean her house for her loved one's visit, O loved one, delightful is your coming. I opened the door of my heart as would a man making a feast for his son coming home from afar. O son delightful is your coming.

Nationalist Ireland from 1923 onwards assumed a certain Catholic ethos and the government maintained the traditional values. Legislation to exclude undesirable literature and films was introduced in 1923 and again in 1929. People as a whole accepted this as the feeling was that prevention is easier than cure. But its choices and its application hurt quite a number of people unnecessarily. The State and the hierarchy failed to give proper appreciation to good critical writers. The Catholic conservative ethos was strong and gave security. The Eucharistic Congress of 1932 was a combination of Catholic faith and national pride. De Valera shared the hierarchy's views on many points but when he differed he went his own way. His ideal for the Irish people, expressed in 1943, was 'a people who were satisfied with frugal comfort and devoted their leisure to things of the spirit'. The Constitution which he wrote and which was promulgated in 1937 was liberal and democratic with a number of Catholic emphases grounded in a Catholic world.

On September 7 1921 the Legion of Mary was founded in Dublin

by Frank Duff and a number of people interested in the lay apostolate and devotion to Mary. It was Ireland's response to the call
of the church for the involvement of the laity in the apostolate
which was to be voiced so strongly a little later by Pius XI. In
addition to a simple and regular prayer-life, members of the Legion
began visiting the poor in the South Dublin Union Hospital. Their
guiding principle in this matter was that their apostolate should
be performed in a spirit of faith and in union with Mary, in such
a way that the person of Our Lord is seen and served by Mary,
his Mother. The Legion spread quickly, first to the cities and
then throughout the country. In a relatively short time it had
been established on the five continents. Referring to the extraordinary success which it had in its early days in China, when the
church, and in particular the clergy, were being persecuted,
Antonio Riberi, the representative of the Vatican there said: 'It is
one of the best things for the church in our times .... I would
venture to call it a miracle of the modern world.'[14] Its splendid
idealism, the devotion of its members, its practical approach to
the problems in the poorer areas, its great regularity in its meetings and its inculcation of the meaning of the spiritual life and of
Mary's part in the development of its members, had a deep influence on a large section of youth in the country for half a century. Though Drs Byrne and McQuaid, both Archbishops of
Dublin, were a little anxious about certain facets of it, the clergy
as a whole gave it any assistance it needed. Seán Ó Leocháin
catches the atmosphere of the weekly meeting in his poem.

Ní raibh ann ach bláthanna feóite
le tabhairt don mhaighdean
ag fanacht i lár an bhúird
i ndiaidh an phaidrín ligeadh
meánfach. Léadh smut
do leabhar, a dúirt
gur daoine sinn, agus ní putóga innill.[15]

There were only a few withered flowers to give to the Virgin
in the middle of the table, waiting (between candles). After
the Rosary somebody yawned. A little bit was read from a
book which told us that we were human beings not cogs in a
machine.

The Legion continues its demanding apostolate, especially in its *peregrinatio* aspect, but it does not attract the same membership which it did thirty or forty years ago. That was the period of first fervour and of the corresponding enthusiasm which one hopes may revive with the present spirit of renewal.

In 1931, Fr John Hayes, a Tipperary priest, founded Muintir na Tíre, a rural organisation which benefitted rural areas in particular, while Dr John Charles McQuaid, who had become Archbishop of Dublin in 1940, organised centres to provide meals for the poor of Dublin during the war, and its excellent work still flourishes. Dr John Dignan, Bishop of Clonfert, was appointed by the government in 1936 to help devise a national insurance scheme, while Dr Browne of Galway was involved in the establishment of vocational education in 1944.

J.H. White, in his book *Church and State in Modern Ireland*, states that the number of statutes enacted by the Dáil from 1923 till 1965 was roughly 1800. In the case of sixteen of these, the members of the hierarchy were consulted or made representations. His concluding words are interesting:

> The extent of the hierarchy's influence in politics is by no means easy to define. The theocratic model on the one hand, and the church-as-just-another-interest-group model on the other, can both be ruled out as over simplified, but it is by no means easy to present a satisfactory intermediate between these two. The difficulty is that the hierarchy exerts influence not on a *tabula rasa* but on a society in which all sorts of other influences are also at work. Party traditions can affect the bishops' power; so can the nature of the issues on which they are seeking to exert pressure. The best answer to the question 'how much influence does the hierarchy possess in Irish politics?' is that no simple answer is possible; it depends on the circumstances. This may seem an answer disappointingly lacking in precision, but it corresponds to the reality of things; any more definite answer would do violence to the evidence.[16]

Modern Gaelic Poetry

> *A innsint féin ar fhlaithius Dé*
> *ag sin oileán gach éinne,*
> *an Críost atá 'n-A fhuil ag scéith*
> *an casadh atá 'na bhréithre.*
> *Is macsamhail do oileán*
> *Oileán seo Bharra Naofa*
> *an Críost do bhí 'n-A fhuil ag scéith*
> *an phúcaoicht ait ngeagaibh.*

A personal perception of God's heaven,
that is each one's island, one's retreat;
the Christ that in his blood is bleeding
gives shape and purpose to his speech.
The island where lived the sainted Barra
is an image of each man's island soul,
the Christ that in his blood was bleeding
is the hauntings in the branches we behold.[17]

With these stanzas, Seán Ó Ríordáin (1977) concludes his poem *Oileán Bharra Naofa* (Finbarr's Holy Island). Obviously he had great love and deep spiritual insight which moved him to make such comparisons. In his poem, *Cnoc Mellerí*, he voices his own confusion about the role of the church and his own spiritual experience in that monastery through his confession and his presence at the choral Office. The final stanza would be echoed by quite a number of people today:

> *Sranntarnach na storime i Mellerí aréir*
> *is laetheanta an pheaca bhoig mar bhreoiteacht ar mo chuimhne*
> *is na laetheanta a leanfaidh iad fá cheilt i ndorn Dé*
> *ach greim fhir bháite ar Mhellerí an súgán seo filíochta.*

The storm that was growing loudly last night round Melleray
Within was sin languid and leprous sprawled across my memory,
The future lies in God's clenched hands, I know
But desperately I cling to Melleray by this, my wisp of poem.[18]

Máire mhac an tSaoi, in a short poem, gives a freshness to the old Christmas-night theme:

> Le coinnle na n-aingeal tá an spéir amuich breactha
> tá fiacail an tseaca sa ghaoith ón gcnoc
> adaig an tine is téir chun na leapan
> luighfidh Mac Dé sa tigh seo anocht.

> With candles of angels the sky is now dappled
> the frost on the wind from the hills has a bite
> kindle the fire and go to your slumber
> Jesus will lie in this household tonight.[19]

In a lighter vein, Seán Ó Sullivan concludes his account of Oscar Wilde's death after a life of earthly pleasure:

> Dá aoibhne bealach an pheacaigh
> is mairg bhíos gan beannacht,
> mo ghraídhn thú, a Oscair,
> bhí sé agat gach bealach.

> No matter how pleasant the way of the sinner,
> sad is death without a blessing;
> Bravo to you, Oscar,
> you had it both ways.[20]

In a different vein, Pádraig MacFhearghusa queries what heaven is like and fears that he may be disappointed if it is not in the nature of a continuous *fleadh cheóil*. But opinions vary:

> Sé adeir daoine eile
> nach eol dúinn roimhré
> cad a chífidh súil ann,
> nó cad a bhraithfidh croí.
> Ach, cogar chúm, a Dhia,
> an mbeidh caifé ar fáil ar maidin
> nó piúnt leanna istoiche ann
> is na h-aingil an bhfuilid baineann?

> Other people say that we know not beforehand what eye will see there or what heart will feel. But give us hint, God, will there be coffee in the morning or a pint of beer at night; and the angels – are they female?[21]

Pádraig Ó Fiannachta has made a very great contribution to our spiritual poetry over the years in *An Sagart, Léachtaí Cholm Cille* and his many books of poems. In his poem, *An Aidbhint*, written in 1969, he opens with the remark that we are all waiting for Christ ever since we left our mother's womb. Our mothers taught us the Rosary to prepare for his coming. In *Ave na Stáisiún* he asks Mary, the mother, nurse and protector of her family to gather everyone to the celebration of the Cross and the feast of the Son of Man. He asks her to unite us all in his Passion, to make us a clean offering, to crush us like the wheat of the saints to be offered up to Christ.[22] His poem, *Moladh do Mhuire*, is a fine expression of theological and personal devotion to her

> In his thought from all eternity was Mary, conceived without sin, like the image of holy wisdom, the virgin, who was mother of Christ.
>
> She was never under the power of sin because of the Redemption to come. She was freed from all eternity through her Son, who got shelter under her cloak.
>
> Mary it was who nourished the Son of God – who first knew who he was, who revealed him to the world in a stable and Cana of the saints. She has a true share with Jesus in his life and death; she helped him at the high offering of the sacrifice of the Cross.
>
> When the earthly crowds threaten and our salvation is in danger, let us remember that she dearly earned our liberation from every need. Glory to God who sent this jewel of pleasing face; she is our way, our guide, our star, our friend in court. Our mother, our friend and our victory has been raised up to the heavens; no need for us to be fearsome or sad since Mary and her Lamb are our protection.[23]

On Whit Sunday he wrote:

> *Nach agam a bhí an misneach*
> *agus seasamh ós bhúr gcomhair*
> *ar fhéile seo an Naoimh Spioraid,*
> *a phobal Dé, a chomharsain.*
>
> *Ach is chughaibhse féin a thagann Sé*
> *le cuireadh is iarradh an dtacaidse*

tá fios a bhéasa ag an dTeachtaire
a sheól an Tiarna chun a eaglaise
le fios is léas is carthannacht
is cúram uile a h-anma.[24]

Hadn't I the nerve to stand before you on this feast of the Holy Spirit, O people of God, my neighbours! But it is to you He comes inviting you, imploring you to come. This Messenger whom the Lord has sent to his church knows his manners. (He comes) with knowledge, light and charity and the whole care of her soul.

Pádraig shows his sense of understanding and empathy clearly in the following lines:

Peggy and Judy
carry the loaves
and earnestly offer
their heart and their soul.

By the lilt of their voices
the heavens are stormed
without creaking of hinges
all doors were ajar.

By my priestly stutter
we realised the mystery
but the bridal encounter
of Jesus and ourselves
was sealed by their music
on the feast of Mary assumed.

Both were nuns and Peggy returned to secular life after seven years. He writes:

May the Lord direct you
when you move out among us
as he did direct you
to convent-shelter of bell and chant.
Blessed be your going out
to the winter of our loveless life
just as blessed was your coming in
to the comfort-company of Christ within.[25]

Elsewhere he reveals the joy of his own calling:

Géilsine a thugas
Géilsine a rinneas
deich mbliana geala fichead ó shoin.
Do chuing na seirbhíse chromas
barróg na h-íobairte d'ías
póg na geanmnaíochta bhlaiseas
Libhilé na bochtaine ghlacas.[26]

I promised service, I made commitment, I promised obedience 30 happy years ago. I submitted to the yoke of service, I donned the sackcloth of sacrifice, I tasted the kiss of chastity and took the levelling (sacrifice) of poverty.

Micheál Ó Huanacháin emphasises the materialism of our times:

Smeid sé orm, bhuail sé bleid, ar sé
'feicim na tithe, na monarchana
banc na mbancaerí, siopa
na siopadóirí
teampall na ndia bréige
ach ní fheicim an spiorad
an t-anam
an miotas ilchasta
an bob uafar é?
Tá sé ann, tá ainm na tíre slán,
sa tsreang aibhléise
sa bhád aeir, sa tseic,
sa nóta púnt:
leictreóin agus adamh
ár mbrú 's ar gcoipeadh.[27]

He beckons to me, accosted me and said: 'I see the houses, the factories, the banks of the bankers, the shops of the traders, the temple of the false gods but I do not see the spirit, the soul, the tortuous fragmentation. Is it a dreadful fraud? It is there, the name of the country is sound – in the electric wire, in the airship, in the cheque, in the pound note – electrons and atoms which are crushing us and driving us crazy.

TOWARDS A HISTORY OF IRISH SPIRITUALITY

Notes:

1. Seán Ó Ceallaigh, *Éigse Éireann* (Dublin, 1942) Introduction.
2. Ibid. 293.
3. I have emended the text.
4. Ibid. 294.
5. *The Complete Works of Padraig H. Pearse (Scríbhinní)* (Dublin, 1919) 201.
6. Ibid. 202.
7. Pearse, P. H., *Plays, Stories, Poems* (Dublin, 1950) 341.
8. Ibid. 340.
9. n. 5 *supra*, 212.
10. n. 7 *supra*, 333.
11. Pearse, Mary Brigid, *The Home Life of Patrick Pearse* (Dublin 1934) 51.
12. Dudley Edwards, Ruth, *Patrick Pearse: Triumph of Failure* (Dublin, 1977) 320-1.
13. n. 5 *supra*, 212.
14. *Mary*, 300:1.
15. *An Dara Cloch* (Áth Cliath, 1945) 165, Poem 24.
16. J. H. Whyte, *Church and State in Modern Ireland* (Dublin, 1971) 376.
17. Declan Kiberd & Gabriel Fitzmaurice, *An Crann faoi Bhláth (The Flowering Tree)* (Dublin, 1991) 26-7.
18. Ibid. 34-5. Translation by Muiris Ó Ríordáin.
19. Ibid. 96-7. Translation by Gabriel Fitzmaurice.
20. Ibid. 102-3.
21. Ibid. 196-7.
22. *Ponc* (Áth Cliath, 1970) 49; 25-6.
23. *Irisleabhar Mhuighe Nuadhat* (1954) 38.
24. Rúin (Má Núad, 1972) 59.
25. Ibid. 18-20.
26. *Léachtaí Cholm Cille* VIII (1972) 70.
27. Ó Huanacháin, Mícheál, *Go dTaga Léas* (Dublin, 1971) 65-66.

Epilogue

It is not easy to grasp the Christian character of an age. It expresses itself in manifold forms of piety and charity, in the willingness of people to make sacrifices for ecclesiastical and charitable purposes, in art and literature, and through the participation of the people in the important duties of the community. But spirituality is not measured according to the visible achievements of an epoch, but rather by the quality, depth and degree in which Christ's life is imitated. The vitality of monastic life and the degree of striving towards an ideal are always the most reliable guages for the genuineness of the religious life of a period.

The deepening of the knowledge and of the practice of the faith was greatly helped by the Catholic education so ably supplied, considering the times, by the diocesan and regular clergy and particularly by the new Orders of Sisters and Brothers founded for or directed towards this apostolate. A special place must be accorded to the valuable work done by teachers like Amhlaoibh O'Sullivan and his counterparts. One naturally will note today many deficiencies in this work, but it would be criminal to overlook or to underrate the contribution which these sets of people have made to Irish spirituality from the Reformation to the present day.

Speaking of the future of Ireland in 1922, Michael Collins noted:

> In the ancient days of Gaelic civilisation the people were prosperous and they were not materialists. They were one of the most spiritual and one of the most intellectual peoples in Europe. When Ireland was swept by destitution and famine, the spirit of the Irish people came most nearly to extinction. It was with the improved economic conditions of the last twenty

269

years or more that it has awakened. The insistent needs of the body more adequately satisfied, the people regained the desire once more to reach out to the higher things in which the spirit finds its satisfaction.

What we hope for in the new Ireland is to have such material welfare as will give the Irish the spirit of freedom .... The uses of wealth are to provide good health, comfort, moderate luxury, and to give the freedom which comes from the possession of these things.

Our object in building up the country economically must not be lost sight of. The object is not to be able to boast of enormous wealth or of a great volume of trade, for their own sake. It is not to see our country covered with smoking chimneys and factories. It is not to show a great national balance sheet, not to point to a people producing wealth with the self-obliteration of a hive of bees.

The real riches of the Irish nation will be the men and women of the Irish nation, the extent to which they are rich in mind, body and character.[1]

One often hears the question to-day: What is Irish spirituality?

It is not easy to define it as a distinct entity from other spiritualities. All Christian spirituality has the evangelical basis. In Ireland we do not have great spiritual classics till we come to men like Edward Leen CSSp, or perhaps Canon Sheehan or Robert Nash SJ. Undoubtedly men like John MacHale and Cardinal Cullen had a certain influence in their pastorals and other writings, but it was neither deep nor widespread. As I understand Irish spirituality it would include these points specially: the closeness of the relationship between this world and the next; the deep harmony between nature and the Godhead as experienced in visits to places like Glendalough, Clonmacnoise, Gougane Barra and Lough Key etc.; the natural religious spirit in the ordinary people, obvious in programmes like *Donncha's Sunday* and in quite a number of programmes in *Radio na Gaeltachta*; faith is firmly rooted in the gospels, psalms, poems and prayers; throughout the centuries there is a combination of fear, awe and a great love and devotion to the person of Christ, especially in the Passion, Mass and Eucharist. One notes a great devotion of trust, without any sense of fear, in Mary as Mother of God and of mankind, sometimes unbalanced, sometimes verging on superstition. The angels and saints, especially the local saints, are very dear to them. There is also a certain fear of and familiarity with the devil. The quality of *muintearas* (intimacy) is seen in their prayers and prayer-poems and consequent generosity with the neighbour in sharing themselves and their goods. The church (*teach a' phobail*) was the place to meet God and also to hear the local news, as is well portrayed in the television serial *Glenroe*. Hospitality and charity are the living expression of the gospel – the guest or the poor person is none other than Christ. The spirit of pilgrimage is seen in its deepest form in the separation from kith and kin, which is the missionary spirit, or in its milder form of prayer and mortification in Lough Derg and even milder form in journeys to Lourdes, Lisieux, Rome or the Holy Land etc., where a little relaxation is also combined; the deep sense of unity with one's dead, marked with a sense of gratitude to them and with a spirit of continuity with the spirit of their forbears.

It would be very unrealistic if we did not look at Irish Catholicism to-day and try to see where its future lies. Sunday Mass is well-attended. Weekday Mass attendance is also good, especially during Lent. But one has to ask the question, what is the motivation underlying the attendance at Sunday Mass? Very probably it varies from a deep appreciation of the Mass to the fact that there is the obligation to attend. One notes a greater incidence of non-attendance in the group aged between 18 and 35. This is more the case among men, often third level students, the majority of whom live in cities. What is the cause of the decline in vocations to the priesthood and in the very large fall-out in vocations to brotherhoods and sisterhoods and in the missionary movement? What should both clergy and laity be doing for the people who are marginalised? Why is it that quite a section of Irish youth have no interest in religion or church?

An uneasy gap has grown up between many of the clergy and intellectuals, artists, people in the media, many of whom are creative people. Writing on this impasse in 1947, Seán Ó Faoláin remarked:

> In Ireland today priests and laity rest at ease – with one qual-
> ification. Only one group is held at arm's length, the writers
> or intellectuals .... The priest and the writer ought to be fight-
> ing side by side, if for nothing else than the rebuttal of the
> vulgarity that is pouring daily into the vacuum left in the
> popular mind by the dying out of the old traditional way of
> life.[2]

Violence, robbery and permissiveness have become widespread, mainly through poverty, ignorance or selfishness among people who are nominally Catholic. The breach between political and commercial life on the one hand, and the gospel standards on the other, is very evident. To remedy this involves not just a fundamental change in economic and social policies but also in our set of values and ways of thinking as Irish men and women. It would also be both interesting and profitable to try to investi-gate why practically all Catholic marriages worked up to thirty years ago and why many of the more recent marriages en-counter the problem of break-up. There is also a certain weaken-ing of genuine faith, based on the gospel and church teaching, often among the more highly educated. What may have been ig-norance three centuries ago is now lack of instruction or study or the desire to bend the rules of Christian morality to one's per-sonal needs or wishes.

Many people in Ireland, young and old, hunger for reasons for living. This is a difficult situation for them. It is up to us to do our best to make them want to follow Christ. As members of the church, our lives must be identifiable with the gospel which gives joy and love. The needs of the people must have top prior-ity on the church's agenda. True, it is the church's duty to correct harmful teaching, but the church should never appear as pre-dominantly negative. The church affirms peace, justice and charity but these sentiments rarely make the headlines, even though much of her time is spent in pursuing these goals. Much time is spent today in mobilising pressure-groups and, unfortu-nately, these are opposing something most of the time. We need 'pro' groups which promote life, employment, culture and good entertainment, in addition to the good use of money and the gifts of nature. It is abundantly clear that on-going education is needed by all. The art of critical reflection needs to be developed so that it may have positive results. As members of the church we must learn to recognise that it is composed of a structural, a critical and a mystical element if we are to function fully as we should. All three must be permanently present.

Our age is dominated and manipulated by organised advertising and by peer influence. All television is educational in the sense that is teaches values, role models and world views. When people begin to reflect intelligently on themselves, their responsibilities and their role in the community, gradually they will see themselves and their society from their own perspective and become aware of their own potentialities. Apathy or helplessness is replaced by hope. If real genuine values were being promoted by the national newspapers, rather than the sensational or shocking, Ireland would be a much better country. Perhaps the newspapers' revenues might fall but the contributors might feel happier that they were doing a better service, as undoubtedly most of the provincial weeklies do, and thereby help to promote greater happiness among the people. On the whole, national radio and television give a poor service to Irish Christians. They do not provide much in the way of spiritual or mental uplift. Even the daily *Just a thought* is so much inferior to what BBC 4 provides. Local radio has great potential and is often a very cohesive force for enriching people morally and culturally and providing many items of local interest.

The future of the faith in Ireland depends on our ability to appreciate the present dangers as clearly as possible. This involves the admission that older responses and forms are not sufficient. The unique situation that still exists as regards the practice of the faith here is not unbelief but shallow belief. Religion is no longer the dominant value in our society. Economics has gradually replaced it – not that economics has created a mentality hostile to Christianity but one cannot fail to notice how greed, dishonesty and envy have been quietly developed in attractive forms in some sections of our society. There is a real danger that religion will become a convention retained on the margins of life but having little effect on our values.

On the other hand, there is the fidelity to Sunday Mass which gives Ireland a uniqueness by contrast with western Europe and America. This is a consolation and a ground of hope for the future, provided that we pay attention to a growing absenteeism and to the malnutrition of those who attend. This Sunday practice needs support and development to nourish a mature religious faith.

Probably the third millennium will see a higher number of atheists, marginal believers, liberal Catholics and of people unhappy with church authority. The problems now are how can one develop the potential for Christian maturity in the majority and at the same time understand and meet the needs of minorities who are drifting from practice and faith. The level of conviction and maturity must be raised. Cardinal Cahal Daly has said that 'many Irish men and women seem to go through life with the childish concepts of God and religion which they learned years ago.' Irish Catholics seem to be over-sacramentalised and under-evangelised. Attendance seems to become a matter of obedience or duty rather than an occasion for a special meeting with Our Lord, for nourishment and for celebration. The knowledge of scripture, even of the gospels, is a good deal lower than we think it is. Cahal Daly adds that 'these movements of renewal can be more effective in a society of high religious practice, such as Ireland, than in one which has been massively secularised. I believe that conciliar renewal can be more efficacious as a preventive of de-Christianisation than a remedy for it'.

Michael P. Gallagher SJ suggests a triple renewal could be the solution for Ireland. This would embrace spiritual renewal, small support groups and social commitment. He would describe the three forms of decline as apathy, alienation and anger. Apathy is largely passive and stems from a new environment in the country dominated by money and its unfortunate effect of inducing a dull indifference to the spiritual values in life. It also means that, though there is church attendance, the religious spirit is largely dead and God seems to a certain extent unreal in daily life. Real prayer is non-existent. It is drifting with the secular environment that is uninterested in faith. Watching television for hours each evening produces apathy quite easily on all fronts. To yield to the consumerist way of life, leads ultimately to casual inner abandoning of faith. The cure for apathy lies in various forms of spiritual renewal, which can bring back faith from the margins of life to its centre. A good proportion of young people have some form of daily prayer. But prayer seems to be a subject that is rarely treated in the Sunday homily. There seems to be a spiritual hunger that is not being answered by any adequate initiation into prayer either in school or in church. A reawakening and deepening of prayer-life is a sure antidote to apathy, since a person who learns genuine prayer will not only be less deceived by the consumerist drift of his or her surroundings, but will discover a hidden treasure, a way of realising that one is loved by God, which banishes apathy.

For the alienated the religious question is far from dead, but forms of worship and preaching are found to be boring, irrelevant, annoying, more a nuisance than help. It is disillusionment with the church rather than unbelief. Some young people consider the church as a sterile institution. Such alienation can perhaps best be met by various forms of small group renewal. There is an urgent need for small cells, larger than the family but smaller than the parish. Parish activities need to be supplemented with forms exposing people to the real life of the church through prayer, witness and service.

Anger is very different from apathy. It is much more active, chosen, conscious and ideological. Apathy is a danger for a large number of people. Alienation affects mainly the more searching and the more educated, an increasing proportion in Irish society. Anger applies as yet to a small but important fringe. It subdivides into at least two major forms of vocal and even vehement rejection not only of the church but of the Christian faith itself. On the one hand, there are various kinds of intellectual rejection of faith. On the other there is the more socio-political anger with a religion of mere piety and obligation. There is a real danger of not hearing the truth behind this anger and of dismissing it as unfounded and irresponsible. Paul VI spoke of such atheists as 'sometimes people of great breadth of mind, impatient with mediocrity and self-seeking'. In Ireland a lot of anger is caused by the gap between the content of the gospel and the lifestyle of priests, religious and influential lay people. Religious congregations, in particular, can give a lead in actually sharing the life of the deprived and then, with the authority of the lived experience, they can awaken more effectively the life of the church. In many respects the cultural tide has turned and will no longer offer the same support for religious faith. There will be less reliance on authority and much more on interiorisation and commitment. If Irish priests and religious can read the strengths and dangers of the present situation of the faith, and can give courageous priority to the new pastoral needs, then a certain guarded optimism about the future is well justified. Innovation has often been the special contribution of Irish missionaries throughout the ages. It is a question of the same missionary zeal and adventure and penetration being brought to bear on the local situation. The causes of lessening practice and belief lie in two directions – in the secularism of our age and in our human failures as witnesses of the gospel. Many large forces in our western world erode our freedom as 'fishers of men' but we may be more free than we realise.

On the occasion of Pope John Paul's visit to Ireland he said:

> The degree of religious practice in Ireland is high. For this we must be constantly thanking God. But will this high level of religious practice continue? Will the next generation of young Irish men and women be still as faithful as their parents were? After my two days in Ireland, after my meeting with Ireland's youth in Galway, I am confident that they will but this will require both unremitting work and untiring prayer on your part.[3]

In spite of the troughs and the crest in our people's spiritual life, in spite of the ironic combination of the drab and the magnificent that marks our religious history, the impression which we get from a glance at the past is one of a people who, although not always devoutly religious, were always real believers, who very frequently practised those virtues that helped to bring light, meaning and happiness into people's lives. The ideals that kept successive generations of believers from getting lost in the by-ways or detours in their journey to God must surely have some

inspiration to offer us as we search for fresh directions on our
journey of faith.

It is abundantly clear that all members of the church must play
their full part. The laity is the largest and most important influence in the church. To-day it must come into its full apostolic
role, through the family, through various ministries in the
parish, through its influence in work and leisure, through its respect, sympathy and aid for the unemployed and marginalised,
but especially through its prayerlife and through its self-denial
as a sign of its will to conquer materialism and make Christ the
model of its life. Groups to stimulate and encourage one another
to these ends could grow with a little effort. That does not mean
that the clergy and religious stand idly by. Firstly, their prayer
and their spiritual life is their greatest contribution. Their apostolic effort in carefully prepared sermons and in their adminis-
tration of the sacraments, their availability to and empathy with
those who most need their help, will have a profound effect on
the people of God. After this, their function will be to encourage,
aid and lead, when necessary, the work of re-evangelisation
which will become more and more the role of the laity.

Quite a number of years ago, Fr Donncha Ó Floinn said that it
was the clergy's duty to bring the young men and women of
Ireland to believe in their destiny – to tell them what their destiny is and show them how to set about achieving it, and this is
the most urgent work of apostleship in Ireland to-day. It must be
fifty years since he said these words, but the prophetic note is
clear and has been re-echoed by the Pope and is the way forward for the Ireland of the future.

Notes

1. *The Path to Freedom* (Dublin, 1922) 127-8.
2. *The Irish* (Dublin, 1949) 150-2.
3. *The Pope in Ireland* (Dublin, 1979) 70.

Selected Index of Persons

Selected Index of Places